THE LIBERTY OF STRANGERS ◈

THE LIBERTY OF STRANGERS

MAKING THE AMERICAN NATION

DESMOND KING

OXFORD
UNIVERSITY PRESS
2005

OXFORD
UNIVERSITY PRESS

Oxford   New York
Auckland   Bangkok   Buenos Aires   Cape Town   Chennai
Dar es Salaam   Delhi   Hong Kong   Istanbul   Karachi   Kolkata
Kuala Lumpur   Madrid   Melbourne   Mexico City   Mumbai   Nairobi
São Paulo   Shanghai   Taipei   Tokyo   Toronto

Published by Oxford University Press, Inc.
198 Madison Avenue, New York, New York 10016

www.oup.com

Oxford is a registered trademark of Oxford University Press

Library of Congress Cataloging-in-Publication Data
King, Desmond S.
The liberty of strangers : making the American nation / by Desmond King.
   p. cm.
ISBN 0-19-514638-7
1. Pluralism (Social sciences)—United States.   2. Multiculturalism—United States.
3. Nationalism—United States.   4. National characteristics, American.   5. Group identity—
United States.   6. United States—Ethnic relations.   7. Immigrants—United States.
8. Assimilation (Sociology)   9. United States—Emigration and immigration.   10. United States—
Foreign relations—20th century.   I. Title.
E184.A1K46 2004
305.8'00973—dc22   2004007153

9 8 7 6 5 4 3 2 1

Printed in the United States of America
on acid-free paper

For Malcolm Anderson,

Friend and scholar,

and in memory of Michael Comber (1944–2004),

Classicist

Acknowledgments

For encouragement throughout the book's composition, responses to presentations at annual meetings of the American Political Science Association and at seminars in Oxford, Austin, New York, Paris, and Dallas, comments on draft material, provision of references or suggestions about additional sources, I wish to thank Malcolm Anderson, Tim Barton, Nigel Bowles, Alan Brinkley, Lisa Budreau, Michael Burleigh, Dominic Byatt, Steven Casey, the late Michael Comber, Carolyn M. Cowey, Gareth Davies, Harvey Feigenbaum, Michael Freeden, Francisco E. González, Robert Goodin, Randall Hansen, Victoria Hattam, Sudhir Hazareesingh, Jennifer Hochschild, James Hollifield, John Holmwood, David Hollinger, Bonnie Honig, Ira Katznelson, Daniel Kryder, Melvyn Leffler, Patrick Le Galès, Robert Lieberman, Paul Martin, Ross McKibbin, Lois McNay, Julian Murphet, Amrita Narlikar, Catherine Nash, Melissa Nobles, David Plotke, Gretchen Ritter, Rogers M. Smith, Sven Steinmo, Anders Stephanson, Margaret Weir, Laurence Whitehead, Mark Wickham-Jones, and Aristide Zolberg. None bears responsibility for the remaining errors.

At Oxford University Press in New York, Dedi Felman has been a superb editor, bringing an intellectually demanding and analytically rigorous set of standards to the project's development, and I have been fortunate to work with her. With her comments on earlier drafts and ambitions about what intellectual scholarship and argument can achieve

Dedi has helped improve the manuscript in numerous ways for which I warmly thank her. Dedi's colleagues Niko Pfund and Tim Bartlett have been consistently encouraging of the project for which I am enormously grateful.

For financial support to research and write the book I should like to express my gratitude to the British Academy and to Nuffield and St John's Colleges, Oxford. I have made extensive use of libraries and archives during the writing of this interpretive work, and for their assistance I should like especially to thank staff at the Vere Harmsworth Library in Oxford University's Rothermere American Institute and at the National Archives in Washington, D.C.

Contents

THE LIBERTY OF STRANGERS ◆

1 ◈

"One People" Nationalism

In June 1965, President Lyndon Baines Johnson received an honorary doctorate from Howard University, America's most prominent black university. He took the opportunity to outline his views of America's racial history. In his commencement speech, the president tackled the issue of merging two hitherto separate peoples into an inclusive democracy. Johnson declared, "[I]n far too many ways American Negroes have been *another nation*: deprived of freedom, crippled by hatred, the doors of opportunity closed to hope." Echoing Malcolm X, Johnson conceded that "the great majority of Negroes" experience the United States as if it were a foreign state, an accusation made by America's international allies and enemies alike.

Yet even as he acknowledged historic injustices toward a definable group of Americans, Johnson strategically tied his reforming agenda to an individualistic conception of American nationhood: "American justice is a very special thing. . . . [A]ll of every station and origin . . . would be touched equally in obligation and in liberty." The president proclaimed that the moment of democratization had arrived: "[I]t is the glorious opportunity of this generation to end the *one huge wrong* of the American Nation and, in so doing, to find America for ourselves, with the same immense thrill of discovery which gripped those who first began to realize that here, at last, was a home for freedom."[1]

The integration of groups, the central theme of Johnson's speech, has been a recurring motif of the American nation. Around the world, the principal experience of nationalism in the nineteenth and twentieth centuries has been of one group defining itself as a nation and pursuing national self-determination for its members. In the nineteenth century, the United States expanded geographically across the North American continent, winning huge areas from Mexico, displacing Native Americans from their land, claiming it for the new nation, and acquiring other portions of territory by treaty, contract, or conquest. A political vision and intellectual myth was built around the very idea of a "frontier." But, by 1900, that frontier had reached its limits and a solution to the problem of integrating the nation's diverse groups was urgently required. Fashioning the idea of "one nation" or "one people" became the response of American nation-builders.

The formation and revision of the "one people" ideology in the twentieth century is the story of American nationalism. And the marked way in which this has been an *internal* process, rather than one of national self-determination against rival nations, makes the American experience unique. Today, in twenty-first-century America, the physical boundaries of nationhood have been largely settled but, as Johnson's quotation suggests, the terms of inclusion have changed radically over time. To remedy past injustices and to satisfy new demands, what can be called the internal borders of membership have, of necessity, been fluid.[2] The persistence of group identities (arising from race, ethnicity, and national background) and the intensity of feelings that they arouse defied the expectation, held by Johnson among others, that individualism would supplant group loyalties in the fabric of the U.S. state. Instead, group divisions continue to loom large in American nationhood.

Nationhood typically refers to a set of shared cultural values and political beliefs, based in historical memories, which bind the members of a polity together.[3] It rests on a combination of formal stipulations (such as how the criteria for naturalization are defined in law) and symbolic rituals (such as how major events, like a nation's founding, are commemorated).[4] These formal and informal arrangements are sustained by an ideology of nationalism. Nationalism commonly has cultural, linguistic, and economic dimensions as well as a political content.

Achieving nationhood is difficult and subtle. The presidents, reformers, and law makers building the American nation had to pursue an ideology, often against stringent opposition, that was capable of balancing individualism and group identity. Fostering congruity between the nation and the government[5] has entailed drawing, and redrawing, the boundaries of nationhood, sometimes broadening the concept of nation to include previously excluded groups, sometimes tightening the boundaries of membership to enforce new divisions, and always negotiating them in the face of countervailing pressures, including powerful international influences. Membership has both formal or legal aspects, bundled together into the rights of citizenship, and a set of complementary informal or cultural attributes, which enable Americans to feel that they belong in their nation.

Since the Civil War (1861–1865), one rhetorical feature of American nationalism has been a constant: that the United States is composed of "one people" sutured by shared loyalty to the polity.[6] This ideology invites people of all backgrounds to be made socially, culturally, and politically American. Throughout American history, the one-people ideology, together with its concomitant melting-pot metaphor, has played a powerful role in American political debate.

But ideology and experience often clash. This rhetoric of one-people nationhood ran into obvious obstacles as its narrowness was exposed in respect to groups based in race, ethnicity, and national background: for many groups, the pot failed to melt.[7] "Who are the people?" has not been answered primordially in America but defined in documents and laws, and each such source has been contested at key moments in American history by groups demanding inclusion and challenging groups already included.

The political upshot is that American nationalism is, in fact, built on a community of groups, more than individuals, despite the national ideology to the contrary.[8] Paradoxically, in a nation many define by its exceptional individualism, it is this community of groups in which the basis for a genuinely inclusive nationalism lies.[9]

Nationhood and Inclusion

The demand for democratic inclusion confronts many countries.[10] In liberal democracies the process of nation-building is no longer simply about forcing minority groups into a dominant ethos of nationhood,[11] which can be termed *assimilationist democracy*, but requires demonstrating a capacity to respect and include group identities and rights in order to build what can be called *democratic nationalism*. This distinction captures the problem of nation-building as one shaped by the terms of political inclusion within a state. Assimilationist democrats defend a majority culture or group and make assimilation to that standard a condition of membership. They value the nation above democratic inclusion; that is, ensuring the integrity of the political system is deemed more important than guaranteeing equality of rights. By contrast, builders of democratic nationalism work to avoid creating "other nations" (groups of citizens whose membership is in some way unequal) within the polity while tolerating strong group identities, including transnational ties. Democratic nationalists want nationhood to be a correlate of political equality and inclusiveness.[12]

These two models provide competing ways of combining or reconciling individualism and group identities, ways rooted in how the demands of fostering nationalist loyalty and establishing democratic inclusion are prioritized. Ironically both visions of nationalism evoke individualism (the rights, such as equality of opportunity or equality before the law, accruing to each citizen separately from any group identity) as a core value, and advocates of each vision draw upon a recognizably Hartzian liberal individualism to advance their interests.[13] But the relationship of individualism and group identity differs significantly: in an assimilationist democratic vision, group identity is a danger to patriotic fervor and political stability, while in addressing and accommodating group sources of exclusion, a democratic nationalist vision of nationhood allows group identity to complement individualism, without displacing either.

My emphasis upon group identities differs from many existing accounts of American nationalism. Most scholarly and popular writing on American nationalism assumes the progressive elimination over time of group distinctions.[14] In this view, the United States has gradually shifted from a condition of imperfect individualism to one in which equal rights of citizenship prevail—an ideal held out as graspable in the Declaration of Independence and other founding documents. The nation has moved from a period in which individuals incurred discrimination because of their identity with certain groups, to one of formal equality of individual rights.[15] On this trajectory, individualism absorbs and displaces group distinctions, a view mirrored in the U.S. Constitution's emphasis on the rights of individuals and hostility to group-based claims.[16] The historian David Hollinger describes the "national narrative" in such individualistic terms as "the notion of *a national solidarity committed—but often failing—to incorporate individuals from a great variety of communities of descent, on equal but not homogeneous terms, into a society with democratic aspirations inherited largely from England.*"[17] Elsewhere, Hollinger sketches out a "'postethnic," cosmopolitan, individualistic vision for American nationhood.[18] The authenticity of this individualistic perspective has many supporters. Observing that "our nation grows ever more diverse," President Bill Clinton added, "Today there is no majority racial or ethnic group in Hawaii or California or Houston or New York City. In a little more than 50 years, there will be no majority race in America." For Clinton, the United States' individual diversity is "the promise of America."[19] His conclusion echoes the arguments of cultural pluralists in the 1920s and 1930s and of Nathan Glazer and Daniel Patrick Moynihan's account of the melting pot in the 1960s.[20] All presume the triumph of individualism and the erosion of groups.

Such conventional narratives of American nationhood's transformation have important flaws. Their proponents underestimate the endurance of group-based distinctions in American nationhood: these divisions did not disappear in a melting pot but continue to shape American politics, often strengthened with new group divisions. They neglect how divisions once considered settled recur as political issues: historical grievances, such as American Indians' land claims or demands for reparations for historic injustices can win fresh political salience.[21] Understanding the firmness of these group divisions is a necessary step to explaining how the ideology of American nationalism performs. Scholars writing about nationalism, in a variety of settings, commonly anticipate a future point in a nation's development when conflicts about nationality and membership will be resolved and assimilation secured.[22] But this expectation elides the dynamic character of nationalism, that is, how the politics of inclusion generate fresh demands in liberal democracies and how meeting these demands changes the very content of assimilation as a nationalist ideology.

Presuming an end point for the U.S. nation underestimates the relentless importance of group divisions to the drawing and redrawing of the boundaries of the polity, that is, who is included and who is excluded. It overlooks the rhetorical lure, for politicians and parties, to promote competing conceptions of nationhood with distinctive group appeals. As is the case in respect to most nations' values and beliefs, there is no definable end point to the ideology of American nationalism and always the potential for group eruptions in America. The equality and group tolerance fostered by democratic inclusion rests on a battery of political, cultural, and legal norms and rights always open to revision. Dramatic events such as war, acts of terrorism, or grassroots protests commonly prompt changes in the boundaries of political membership. Such events modify prevailing views about who belongs, throw suspicion on some groups, and exempt others from charges of disloyalty to the nation.[23] Anticipating an end point in nationalist sentiment introduces an artificial single-country emphasis too. In practice, no nation-state or nationalist ideology can be understood in isolation from international influences because these often galvanize or deflate nationhood sentiment.

President Johnson's sobriquet, "another nation," certainly applies to groups other than African Americans in the United States. Johnson was speaking a mere twenty years after the freeing of Japanese Americans interned during the Second World War (an event by then erased from the public memory) and only four years after the U.S. Senate learned that American Indians endured a "separateness" of status inconsistent with legal equality.[24] Johnson's own Texas background meant he appreciated the distinct problems of Mexican Americans as a group in America.

Race, ethnicity, and national background are the principal bases of group distinction because each relates to nationhood in a way which has conflicted historically with assimilationism. They crystallize the differences between assimilationist democratic and democratic nationalist models of one-people nationhood. Constructing a nation is commonly a narrowing process requiring a polity's members to shed group identities. Its architects also make decisions about who should be included and who left out. Building a democracy is usually an inclusive activity, intended to confer equal rights.[25] Politically and historically,

this conferment implies accepting the coexistence of one-nation sentiment and group identities in America.

Politicians and political parties use intellectual and cultural markers
of people's differences in terms of race, ethnicity, or national background
in appeals to group interests, both in a minimal sense of appealing to the
majority against the demands of minority groups and by purposefully
targeting groups of voters who share an identity based in race, ethnicity,
or national background.[26] Since the founding of the republic, coexisting
doctrines have permitted both surges of support for or opposition to either tolerant or intolerant views about "different" members.[27] For example, Manifest Destiny provided, in the late nineteenth and early
twentieth centuries, a political language to privilege the territorial expansionism of nation-building rooted in the interests of white Americans.[28]
The ideology of "racial uplift," articulated by leading African Americans
during the era of segregation, exposed inequalities in the social order and
set out an agenda for Black Americans to transcend discrimination.[29] In
the first part of the twentieth century, ethnological and eugenic values
and beliefs about hierarchical differences among peoples shaped public
opinion and government policy. These ideas were articulated through
school curricula, citizenship and patriotic ceremonies, newspapers and
journals, photography, and mass entertainment. Such values and measures are dynamic and changing, but their content at particular points in
time influences prevailing opinion. These beliefs and values about differences among peoples established a group hierarchical language of
American nationhood.

Many individuals have experienced race, ethnicity, or national background as sources of exclusion from membership in the nation. Indeed,
these group divisions compete with Americans' own understanding of
their society's individualism, an individualism expressed both in political rhetoric and in rights.[30] For instance, Democratic president Harry
Truman exclaimed, "[O]urs is a nation of many different groups, of
different races, different national origins. . . . The American principle
. . . that all men shall have equal rights before the law . . . is always under
attack. Some people are always trying to . . . block the progress of racial
or national groups different from their own."[31] In its importance for
U.S. politics, this group dimension of the American nation rivals the
history of assimilation.

Lyndon Johnson's speech at Howard University marked a key moment in the ideology of America's nationalism, enlarging the population of those able to exercise individual rights of citizenship, challenging group hierarchies, and opening up the possibility of a democratic nationalism in which members of politically excluded and marginalized groups could gain equal status. But the American nation was not rendered free of group divisions by Johnson's or later initiatives; rather, it was modified to recognize and accommodate group distinctions in American society. Even in advancing the integration of African Americans, Johnson had to use political language which presumed these group-based distinctions.[32] This tendency remains. Individual citizens who experience discrimination (and fail to win redress) frequently conclude that such treatment arises because of their association with a particular group, an inference encouraging solidarity with other group members in order to win an equal presence in the American nation.

The Boundaries of "One People" Nationalism

The formation of American nationalism must be understood through the experience of groups. Groups are here defined by race, ethnicity, or national background. Their members have encountered discrimination and exclusion from the core of American nationhood, whether at home or abroad or both. The approach of this book does not presume the erosion of group-based conflicts. Rather, it will show how groups have been distinguished by politicians, parties, and reformers for reasons of political calculations and ideological hatreds and how, despite political espousals of individual rights and equality of opportunity, the U.S. government has to address the problems posed to nation-building by group-based inequalities.[33] A group-centered approach provides a means of understanding the differences among America's competing views of nationhood. It will demonstrate too a paradox of one-people nationalism: groups are now a necessary condition of American nationhood and constitute the basis for the sense of community necessary to its renewal.

Two terms bear highlighting as a guide to this argument about how American political leaders historically and at present balance the contested claims of individualism and group politics: membership and international influences.

MEMBERSHIP

Americans have disagreed historically about how wide or restrictive membership in the nation should be. Boundaries specifying who may be or who may not be a member of the polity are not intractable. It is members who exercise rights of citizenship: though these rights may be extended to resident aliens, their exercise of them is more tenuous. Legislators' response to the question "who belongs?" has changed over time. Answers concern not just legal status as a citizen but a more general sense of belonging, a sentiment which can be broad and generous or narrow and prejudiced. For both those who would restrict membership in the nation and those who would enlarge it, group divisions have served as defining criteria, that is, in some periods a certain ethnic or racial identity has meant exclusion from membership. These criteria have practical consequences, as in legal rights. And they influence how membership is conceived in the public's consciousness.

How the Civil War was remembered in both the North and the South is a good starting point to illustrate how membership helps to define the content of American nationhood.[34] From the conclusion of the Civil War and with the enactment of the Thirteenth, Fourteenth, and Fifteenth amendments, the United States was clearly a nation with a federal government and was no longer a mere confederacy. In this political context, the victorious North wanted to integrate the disaffected white South.[35] Decades elapsed before southerners abandoned Confederate Memorial Day and joined in commemorating Memorial Day.[36] To forge national integration, monuments concentrated on the common ethnicity and whiteness of fighters in the North and South and ignored other aspects of the war.[37] The monuments served a specific political function for American nationhood. The role of the African-American soldiers was outside the collective memory and their service on the battlefield ignored.[38] Today, in contrast, the new African-American Civil War Memorial in Washington, D.C.,[39] deliberately commemorates black soldiers in the Union army. The boundaries of who are members of the American nation, both as citizens and culturally, thus look quite different at the end of the twentieth century compared with the close of the nineteenth.

To advance political unity in the hundred years after the Civil War, national office holders encouraged assimilation and reproached Americans' retention of group attachments. The United States' openness to immigrants, its displacement of Native Americans and conquest of their lands, and its support until the 1960s of racial segregation—all pressured nation-builders to advocate assimilation and a common ideal of nationhood: the construction of this bond trumped claims about democratic inclusion and was cited to excuse unequal treatment of certain groups. But the expectation of assimilation by newcomers paradoxically necessitated a government policy centered on group classifications, stipulated in terms of race, ethnicity, or national background. The selection of these criteria mirrored their use in popular and intellectual discourse and their measurability: they provided a means of assessing how "American" the population had become. But this very government policy, distinguishing among citizens by group, amplified the political and social salience of these categories, and individual experiences of discrimination ensured the political relevance of group divisions.

Examples of government-made distinctions include naturalization law (which excluded many groups until the 1940s), the targeting of ethnic immigrant groups (through Americanization programs), the wartime treatment of Japanese Americans (who were interned), and racial profiling (used by some city police forces). The racial classifications employed both historically and at present in the U.S. Census show the federal government grappling with, and perpetuating, distinctions that harden group identities and differences: the federal government needs such information to make decisions about policies such as affirmative action or minority-majority voting districts. Immigration policy epitomizes the way in which myth and practice about membership combine in American nationalism. The rhetoric of openness is touted in political debate, and the centrality of immigrants' values to the nation is celebrated in countless political speeches and histories.[40] Yet often in practice rigorous selection prevails. Until 1965, potential immigrants were assessed for their racial or ethnic compatibility with American nationhood, classifications which fed into domestic politics by reinforcing extant group divisions. Tens of millions of immigrants have settled in the United States since 1965. They are discussed in popular discourse and in official classifications less as individuals than as "new immigrants," principally of Latino or Asian origin, and their significance is assessed for existing group divisions. New immigrants reinvigorate and revise the group divisions in American nationhood, for instance, through linguistic distinctness and transnational ties. Underlying such group-drawn distinctions is disagreement about who is a member.

Expressions of the primacy of groups within a purportedly individualistic culture are subtle.[41] For instance, individual Native American soldiers' acts of heroism during the Second World War drew plaudits because they were taken as symbolic of a group. But recognition of such gallantry ironically detracts from the celebrated individual and, when someone is singled out as a representative of a group, it reinforces the distinctness of that group's identity in society.

Contested memories of membership continue. Consider the Confederate flag. South Carolina and Georgia recently removed it from state buildings while Mississippi's residents voted to retain it;[42] supporters cited resentment at "outside interference" as a reason. These variations illustrate the group differences sustaining rather than eroding America's divisions: what does the Confederate flag symbolize if not a defiant group identity? Through such countervailing pressures, American nationhood is continually remade.

National memories alter as boundaries of membership change. The African-American Civil War Memorial is an example noted above. Another example is how Thanksgiving, an occasion designated in 1863 after the battle at Gettysburg, is celebrated. Early events commemorated a single dominant group memory of the European settlers. The Plymouth tercentenary festival in 1920 reflected the views of assimilationists like Theodore Roosevelt and Woodrow Wilson, as one organizer explained: "[T]he celebration is to be 100 per cent American."[43] But the conception of "100 percent American" was in fact quite restricted.[44] An envoy to the tercentenary festival from Plymouth, England, could confidently expect his hosts to share his approval of the "majestic onward march of the Anglo-Saxon race" represented by the United States.[45] The tercentenary ignored the carnage inflicted upon American Indians, for whom the Pilgrims' arrival was hardly a cause for thanksgiving.[46] This omission was challenged in 1970 when a descendant of the Wampanoag tribe marked Thanksgiving Day in Plymouth as the first National Day of Mourning, to honor the Native American ancestors and their survivors. (His invitation to speak at the official ceremony was withdrawn because of the content of his address.) Attendees threw a Pilgrim dummy into the water from a replica of the *Mayflower*.[47] Thanksgiving Day is no longer simply an expression of an undifferentiated American nationalism. Its celebration affirms the multiple senses of American identity arising from its group bases. As a consequence, Native Americans won a fuller role in the 1976 commission on the bicentennial celebration. By this date, Native Americans' rights were salient internationally, and it is such international influences which are the second concept employed in this book to understand the ideology of American nationhood.

INTERNATIONAL INFLUENCES

Although all nations and all ideologies of nationhood are shaped in part by international pressures, such influences are far more profound on the United States' ideology of nationhood than that of many other nations because of America's disproportionate power globally, its international leadership roles, and its repeated absorption of millions of foreigners as immigrants who self-identify with a preexisting group or, more commonly, find themselves so classified by those already there. Each of these aspects of the United States' international engagements has affected directly the way in which debates about political inclusion within American nationhood have developed. Being a global leader of liberal democracy and a defender of individual freedoms opens the United States to foreign influences and, more important, to external scrutiny of how its image of nationhood presented abroad matches its own policies at home. And receiving immigrants on the scale of the 1900s or 1990s, for instance, makes the United States central to other countries' experiences in a unique way. Americans whose ancestors were violently kidnapped and taken to the United States involuntarily have also looked periodically to forge links with their countries of origin, a connection described in the phrase *black Atlantic*.

While the shaping of American nationhood has been driven by the demands of reconciling conflicts about membership and inclusion within the polity, an internal process of nation-building, these accommodations have been inextricably shaped by the United States' exposure to and engagement with international influences. But these influences have operated in complex ways.

Judging the significance of international factors in the formation of American nationhood presents two tasks pursued in later chapters. First, these influences need to be unpacked historically and in the present day. Second, this discussion needs to be done in terms of a central puzzle about American nationalism as a domestic ideology. Neither America's projection of assimilationist nationalism as an ideal of liberal democracy (as, for example, in Woodrow Wilson's Fourteen Point Plan) nor the United States' exposure to international influences mirroring this assimilationism has resulted in the erosion of group divisions at home. Examining this international setting reveals how the United States has diverged from the liberal democratic expectation that American nationhood would develop into a one-people melted pot with an observable decline in group identities. Most liberal democratic states have converged on an assimilationist membership whereas the United States is much more locked into the multicultural trajectory inherited from how Americans have, over the past century, confronted, sometimes relinquished, but mostly retained group identities. The way in which historical group injustices have been addressed to reduce inequalities and hierarchies has not eroded these group cleavages but instead refashioned them.[48] The internal dynamic of group conflicts in nation-building is primary.

International influences occur in a number of ways, but the main force of such factors has been to subject America's domestic policies to foreign scrutiny. Outsiders form an image, whether favorable or critical, of the United States' nationalist ideology from what they observe and learn about America's military power, economic reach, political influence, and cultural representations. Often the exercise of American power, as during the two world wars, impresses as an expression of the United States' commitment to democracy. The U.S. representatives who helped to plan the United Nations reflected this spirit. The United Nations' Universal Declaration of Human Rights, issued in 1948 (and complemented by UNESCO's statement rejecting race as a biological category),[49] imparted rights to individuals as individuals and displaced the notion that only states enjoyed rights in the international world (and indeed states signing the declaration were surprised to find themselves eligible for reproach under the new regime). The United States was closely involved in the projection of this new postwar standard for individual treatment; its adversaries used this projection as a rod with which to excoriate American policies toward so-called minority groups. These criticisms helped the process of civil rights in America.

During periods of global ideological tension, such as the Cold War, or military conflict, such as the Second World War, the United States' efforts to present and defend a version of Western liberal democratic values and institutions create an international expectation about Americans' own practices. For instance the United States' support for anticolonialism as an aim of the Second World War set up an external image to which subsequent independence movements looked for support (often with disappointment). It concurrently permitted reformers for civil rights at home to draw comparisons between the position of colonial peoples and groups discriminated against within the United States for reasons of race, ethnicity, or national background.

The capacity of the United States to mobilize its population around a one-people ideology in foreign engagements seems at first glance to affirm an international image of American nationhood as that of an assimilated nation. This quality has featured in propaganda measures. For instance, the official guidebook to the U.S. exhibit at the world fair in Brussels in 1958 included a map of America entitled *The Land and the People*. This map depicted a homogeneous United States enjoying racial and ethnic harmony.[50] Its authors painted an American nationalism which had transcended divisions common in other countries, a misjudgment given the conflicts looming in the 1960s. Furthermore, many aspects of U.S. foreign policy derive from group divisions in American society, a connection missed if discussion of American nationalism presumes it is solely an expression of individualism.[51]

The United States' exceptional history of immigration imbues American nationhood with a relevance and empathy for many of those remaining in the emigrant-exporting countries, who are keen to learn about the country to which their relatives have migrated and who are confident in the authenticity of experience and knowledge they feel themselves to have acquired through first- or second-generation reports. Many immigrants become joined, formally or casually, to groups (such as Cuban Americans or Irish Americans) that lobby for U.S. foreign policy to follow specific policies in respect to their countries of origin. The sense of connectedness between emigrant-exporting countries and the United States was conveyed in President John F. Kennedy's four-day visit to Ireland in June 1963. He exploited the sentiment of being owned by the Irish people and their sense, through him and millions of other Irish emigrants, of being part of the United States. America was a country, the president and his audience seemed to believe, in which Irish immigrants could prosper, remain Irish, and be American. Polish people and Polish Americans could offer a similar vision as can, more recently, Mexicans and Mexican Americans. Many descendants of those brought involuntarily and violently to the United States have looked to their countries of origin, principally in Africa, as potential homelands, which inverts but does not remove this relationship of connectedness.

These engagements with international influences have weighed upon American nation-builders throughout the twentieth century but especially since the Second World War. They have created the opportunity for foreign scrutiny of American domestic policy, a scrutiny to which its nation-builders are highly sensitive. During the Second World War and especially during the Cold War years, American leaders responded to criticisms of how groups such as African Americans or American Indians were treated at home.[52] Were members of these groups enjoying the rights associated with liberal democracy of the sort consistent with America's international image? Often they were not treated equally, and reforms to establish such rights appeared to coincide with these external pressures.

By aiding the reform of group-based injustices and discrimination in a way consistent with liberal democracy, such international influences seemed to push America further on the road toward one-people nationalism, of the sort celebrated in the standard narratives of American political development encountered earlier. In fact, such influences did not reduce the central way in which group-based divisions set and shape the parameters of American nationhood. These external pressures helped to refashion some of the sources of group injustice, but group divisions themselves were not eliminated.

This constancy of group divisions despite international pressures is ironic because of the way in which America's external image projected the nation abroad as a liberal democracy based on an assimilationist ideology. Liberal individualism was consistent with the sort of membership implied by the nationalist mantra of self-determination, which presumed an assimilated people fighting for its nationhood. From the end of the nineteenth century until 1945, this doctrine of self-determination gave nation-building around the world an implicit and often explicit logic that members of a given society should assimilate to a common standard of national identity, a principle which shaped America's restriction of immigration in the 1920s. President Woodrow Wilson's Fourteen Points manifesto, issued in 1917, placed the United States at the center of this movement by validating the rights of "a people" to self-determination. Such an image dominated external perceptions during the Second World War and the Cold War, which ended in 1989, and in many ways it still shapes the post–Cold War values which the United States continues to promote and to present abroad. This projection of liberal democracy abroad did help make the United States more liberal and just at home, as later chapters will show, but significantly it was not the case that America became more liberal through the assimilationist democracy it sold to others. Rather, America became more inclusive and less discriminatory as it made peace with historically based group divisions and excised the main sources of discrimination, consistent with democratic inclusion. As President Johnson's speech, with which the chapter commenced, testifies, American nationhood has been altered to forge better strategies for tackling group-based distinctions and injustices, strategies which aim to end hierarchical orderings. But American nationhood has not become any less calibrated by group divisions and loyalties as sources of identity. Even with the international influences encouraging a shift to assimilationist democracy, the group strains, which are pivotal to the U.S. nation, did not disappear. Such enduring group cleavages preclude the United States' embracing of postethnic cosmopolitanism.

This contradiction between the rhetoric of one-people nationalism and the practice of group politics can better be appreciated by bringing the international dimension into any account of American nationhood. Considered historically, the international expression of American nationhood always overemphasizes or inflates America's assimilationist side at the expense of camouflaging its group diversity, a diversity that, despite the presumptions of one-nation historians, will always remain. An international perspective sharpens appreciation of the extent to which nation-building in America has been a process overwhelmingly internal to the polity. This remains the case.

Government policy expresses both shifting conceptions of member-ship and international influences in the making of American na-tionhood. Through their speeches and decisions, politicians, reform-ers, intellectuals, and law makers have the opportunity especially during periods of crisis to link public attitudes with government policy and to fashion the symbols of American nationalism. They are the country's nation-builders.

To emphasize the need for integration or the need to transcend the failure to respect some citizens' rights because of their (mostly invol-untary) group membership, these nation-builders celebrate individual freedoms rather than group membership as fundamental to American nationalism. Lyndon Johnson couched his remedy for the costs of "an-other nation" in individualistic terms. Another rehearsal of the in-dividualistic image of American nationalism comes from Ronald Reagan's presidency (1981–1988). Reagan tied his record in office with the country's political origins to underline the centrality of individuals and liberal individualistic values, such as freedom.[53] Stressing how the U.S. nation was built by individuals, Reagan's narrative whitewashed the role of group politics in its unfolding. Most presidents have adopted a similar rhetorical style. But the divisions in American society arising from group-based distinctions are too strong in policy and ideology to ever dissolve. These fissures are part of the fabric of American nation-hood. Despite the individualistic rhetoric of the Reagan era, for example, group-based distinctions not only remained powerful political forces during the 1980s but they also fueled the tremendous growth of multi-cultural politics.

It was precisely these group strains and demands which informed President Johnson's epochal speech at Howard University in 1965 in which he acknowledged the United States' record in fostering "other nations," whose members were as integral to American nationhood as were the descendants of European settlers; they retained strong identities despite decades of intense Americanization. Johnson's admission meant that the ideology of American nationalism could not be construed simply as individualistic but, to be an authentic expression of America's diversity, had to prove able to balance individualism with group divisions. Johnson's actions did not end the pressure for liberal individualism but did make this agenda harder to achieve. The failure of radical restrictionists from the 1990s to establish a nativist agenda that was hostile to immigrants reflected in large part the political difficulty of prescribing too narrowly who makes up the "one people" articulated in American nationhood.[54]

The story of American nationhood is not over. Political leaders face new demands about inclusion and membership, and there are continuing international pressures on the United States, the responses to which are bound to alter afresh the ideology of American nationalism.[55] But before engaging such novelties, we need to return to the task of nation-building as it appeared in 1900.

PART I ◈

B y the First World War, *nationalism* referred to self-determination for a people.[1] A group of people who defined themselves as a nation mostly did so in order to declare independence from a larger political unit or a colonial power or to secede
within a polity. These struggles dominated post–World War I
Europe, as small states asserted themselves and a frenzy of nation-
building began.

The United States faced different nation-building challenges. At
home and in its annexed territories, the principal task was to unify a
diverse population. From 1898, its physical boundaries were mostly
fixed (with the independence of the Philippines and the consensual
integration of Hawaii and Alaska being the major subsequent
changes). But internal membership within those boundaries was
unsettled. This fluidity about who did or did not belong to the nation
coincided with a view of the world's peoples that ranked them
hierarchically according to their proximity to or distance from white
Western civilization. The political task of nation-building relied on
these "scientific" rankings.

Distinguishing the American (white) "race," a term widely and
imprecisely employed then as now, from other peoples was politically useful to nation-builders. That this group achieved political
dominance gave the logic to the pursuit of assimilationist nation-

hood and provided a standard for Americanization. American law makers, intellectuals, and politicians contemplated how to "Americanize" Native Americans,[2] how to absorb millions of immigrants, how to retain racial homogeneity, and above all how to build a demographic future governed by the ability to control who entered and became members of the nation, who were excluded, and who among those present were marginalized. Looking abroad, politicians and intellectual leaders wondered how best to modify the ideological boundaries of the American nation to incorporate peoples in territorial acquisitions.

Victory in the Spanish-American War of 1898 also marked the United States decisively as an international force, and this international context began to influence, in novel ways, domestic struggles over membership in the nation. For instance, the process of Americanization assumed relevance not just for new immigrants but for annexed peoples too. African-American veterans found that U.S. foreign policy was as racist as the policies at home. And in 1917, the United States' entry into World War I was defended by Woodrow Wilson as a special mission to "save democracy."

These nation-building challenges invited different categories of membership. Broadly, American voters, politicians, and law makers defined *membership* through two stipulations. First, only certain groups (for instance, people of European ethnic background) could achieve full membership and a complete sense of belonging in the one-people framework. Second, to achieve that belonging would require, for many of them, intense acculturation in the ways and content of American nationhood. These criteria resulted in two categories of membership according to race, ethnicity, and national background: new but assimilated members, such as Eastern and Southern Europeans, and the excluded, such as Chinese or Japanese Americans. Individuals and groups in the second category, that is, those effectively left out of membership, began to develop a consciousness and to devise strategies to counter their exclusion. Inclusion would mean making democracy-building a correlate of nationalism, an achievement helped by harnessing international influences to support domestic political struggles. This did not take effect until well into the twentieth century.

Exclusion was conveyed in the ideology of membership and in the rituals and symbols of nationhood. Rituals and symbols shaped education policy for new members and defined immigration policy toward aspiring members. These policies institutionalized the intellectual hierarchy through which Americans' popular consciousness was shaped and distinctions between groups legitimated. They are the subject of the next four chapters.

2 ◈

How to Become an American

In the first half of the twentieth century, educators and Americanizers designed school curricula to instill a sense of shared national identity. But access to and quality of education varied according to different groups' eligibility for membership in the polity. Indeed, access was a barometer of a group's suitability for membership and citizenship. For some groups, the expectation was that education would provide a smooth route to assimilation, while for others the opposite was intended. European immigrants and American Indians fell into the first category (though practice fell well short of design for the latter), African Americans into the second. Another group, annexed peoples, found themselves in an intermediary position, exposed to a half-hearted regime of Americanizing education.

The discussion in this chapter shows how assimilationist democracy unavoidably attached the most importance to building a singular sense of nation among its members and rode roughshod over democratic rights. This meant establishing a standard of assimilation toward which those deemed unassimilated had to strive. If this assimilationist model was applied independently of judgments about groups' eligibility to be members of the nation, then it need not have become an instrument of exclusion. But by its reproduction of group hierarchies, education became in practice a forum to express who belonged in America's "one people."

This expression was linked, naturally, to a further confusion about membership in the polity. Defined as members of "insular" states by the U.S. Supreme Court in 1901, Puerto Ricans and Filipinos enjoyed education intended to assimilate them.[1] Yet neither population could hope, in the short term, to be full members of the United States. This judicial ruling placed a colonial contradiction at the core of America's national institutions.

Assimilated Education

The killing of Sioux men, women, and children at Wounded Knee in 1890 was a direct imposition of U.S. physical might on American Indians.[2] After this bloody incident, instead of brute force, American Indians were subjected to Americanization.[3]

American Indian boarding schools exposed Indian children to the habits of American life and to the English language.[4] Initiated at the Carlisle School by Captain Richard Pratt,[5] the schools took Indian children from their immediate environment to Americanize them.[6] Asked to advise the adoptive mother of the sole Lakota survivor of Wounded Knee, Lost Bird, Pratt characteristically counseled against permitting the child any contact with her Native American roots. Pratt recommended that Lost Bird be "put as far as possible away from contact with Indians of any sort," saying, "I am very sorry you had her 'tribal rights' established, and for her sake also I am sorry you call her your adopted Indian daughter. It was such a splendid chance to . . . treat her . . . as your own child."[7] Such acculturation, through education, was the necessary condition for membership in the American nation.

Thomas Jefferson Morgan, commissioner of Indian affairs between 1889 and 1893, personified Americanization. Like Pratt, he aimed to build a one-nation American identity to which Native Americans would subscribe in common with other Americans.[8] How would this be achieved? Writing for the secretary of the Interior,[9] Morgan set out his program for Native American education, which included compulsory education, a standardized routine for both day and boarding schools, a curriculum similar to that in the rest of the public school system, English-only instruction, placing Native American children with white families during vacations, and finally Christianizing the children.[10] By 1900, 10 percent of Native American children were placed in 307 schools modeled on Carlisle and spread across the country.[11] More pupils went to day than boarding schools, but the boarding-school ethos to remove children from their families and communities pervaded both.

Commissioner Morgan's outline was endorsed by some Native American educators, such as Henry Roe Cloud. More commonly, Native Americans rejected the acculturation drive. The Creek Alexander Posey,[12] author of the "Heartless Bird" satires on the Bureau of Indian Affairs, condemned boarding schools for cutting off Native Americans from their heritage.[13] The writer Morning Dove resented being forbidden to speak her own language at a Catholic mission school. In his memoir, *The Middle Way,* the Omaha Francis La Flesche describes how Native American children were "given English names" and proscribed from using their own languages.[14] The ethic of Native American kinship, based on extended families and physical proximity, clashed with the individualism promoted in Americanization. Because the curriculum was based in teaching American history as a story of progress and advancing civilization, the traditions and values of Native Americans were ignored or, worse, rejected as backward.

Teachers in some boarding schools were cruel to their charges.[15] Many children ran away. Too many schools had poor records of achievement: attendance was irregular, schools opened and closed rapidly, the turnover of teachers was high, and Indian parents feared for the health of their children at agency schools. Measles, tuberculosis, influenza, and other epidemics took terrible tolls on American Indian children.[16]

Schooling was of general importance to nation-building. It was meant to socialize all groups into a one-people sense of shared nationhood. Country schools taught patriotism to farmers' children. In cities, new immigrants were socialized by public elementary schools, attendance at which continued until age fourteen.[17] At least in theory, education transformed Americans from members of ethnic groups into individuals holding a common national identity.[18] This process meant acquiring competence in the English language and discarding ethnic associations which made immigrants stand out from "ordinary" Americans. Professional educators were prominent advocates of Americanization.

The National Education Association wanted compulsory education extended and all instruction conducted in English.

Elementary schools were the universal experience. Conditions were often rudimentary, and overcrowding was common. In New York City alone, the elementary school enrollment numbers jumped from a quarter of a million in 1881 to 793,000 in 1914.[19] Often two or three children shared a single seat in a class numbering sixty students. But it was differing levels of competence in English which mattered most. Children lacking proficiency in English were placed in the lowest grades regardless of their ages, a procedure bound to humiliate some. A system of "steamer" classes provided brief but complete immersion in the English language for immigrant children before they were transferred to regular classes.[20] But provision of these classes did not meet the demand.

Such was the importance of education to nation-building that schools were mobilized for adult Americanization. Working with the Bureau of Naturalization and financed with fees from those naturalizing, public schools set up programs to educate adult foreigners.[21] Men and women of all ages and all nationalities participated. They acquired literacy sufficient to naturalize and in the process were "transformed into loyal, patriotic Americans,"[22] in the words of Bureau of Citizenship director Raymond Crist. So intense was Crist's belief in the redemptive power of Americanization that he spoke of "this work of reclaiming these human souls, minds, and bodies." American citizenship was the "greatest privilege which can be conferred upon any living human being,"[23] rhetoric that conveys a sense of the mild hysteria which pervaded Americanization, which itself could be alternatively benign or sinister.

Advocating an Americanization bill to the U.S. Senate in 1919, Secretary of the Interior Franklin Lane reported on how widespread teaching in foreign languages was: "[W]e found that hundreds of schools in some of our States were teaching Lincoln's Gettysburg address, if they were teaching it at all, in a foreign language."[24] A quarter of the 1.6 million men enlisted for World War I did not understand English. To Lane, this failure clashed with the United States' international image as a liberal democracy: "[W]e spent millions of dollars in educating grown men in the meaning of the words, 'forward,' 'halt,' and 'march.' And this was in a country . . . that held itself up apparently as the foremost democracy of the world."[25] More practically, it seemed to weaken the basis for ensuring a strong nation.

At the Ford Motor Company in Michigan, the Sociological Department presented immigrant workers with an ideal of American nationhood because, in Henry Ford's words, "[T]hese men of many nations must be taught the American way, the English language, and the right way to live."[26] The men were of European ethnic origin. The department interviewed workers' families to ensure they met specified standards, and they were urged to naturalize. The company's English Department devised short pedagogical pamphlets about home life, consumerism, and the workplace usages of English in an American setting.[27] Participation in these classes was mandatory for employees, and a profit scheme rewarded success. Between 1915 and 1920, more than 16,000 workers graduated from the Ford English school.[28] The graduating ceremony itself was a feast of one-nation symbolism designed to be in line with wider efforts to orchestrate a shared national identity. Graduates entered the hall to see their teachers stirring a colossal melting pot, eight feet high and of about fifteen feet circumference. The graduates descended into the pot, set against a mural of an immigrants' ship, wearing the national costume of their country of origin; they then emerged, after the teachers stirred the concoction, wearing "American" clothes and waving the Stars and Stripes.[29]

In its emphasis on learning English and encouraging naturalization, Ford's schemes complemented nation-building efforts to transcend ethnic differences. The company set a pattern for other industrial plants. These schemes, as with the plans for elementary schools and Native Americans' boarding schools, were designed to foster inclusion in the nation through learning English and acculturation. But proficiency in English did not confer full membership on all groups, as the next section shows.

Schools brought immigrant children under the purview of American national identity. Many groups' children were assimilated in the process. Ethnicity, as a strongly held identity expressed in language and customs, was weakened but only in the short term and often only at a superficial level. Later generations showed much interest in reviving and enjoying the values and traditions of their parents' or grandparents' nationality, thereby broadening the meaning of membership in the one-nation ideology. Immigrants who came from Italy, Germany, Poland, or Russia, for instance, experienced Americanization as a program designed to ensure their acquisition of English and their naturalization. Their children gained both attributes automatically through schooling and birthright citizenship. But a long-term response to immersion in American values was the stirring, in later generations, of an interest in their ethnic origins, which ultimately altered the balance of individualism and group identity in American nationalism.

Separate Education

The writer Chester Himes recollected that "our mother was horrified by the elementary schools for blacks in Mississippi, and she taught Joe and me herself, in our living room, year in and year out, until we finished the seventh grade."[30] When he and his brother did enroll in school, they were placed in a grade two years ahead of their age. Himes's experience illustrates the most egregious gap in the Americanization drive of elementary and high schools: the policy for African Americans. Segregation of Black Americans maintained the Founding Fathers' judgment of who were Americans. Consigned to inferior schools under the 1896 "separate but equal" ruling, the vast majority of Black Americans were educationally disadvantaged in the ensuing six or seven decades.

This educational deficit was known. A federal review of education, published in 1931,[31] included a minority report whose signatories decried the low standard of schools providing education for African-American children.[32] In addition to that in the South, segregated education was common throughout the North until the late 1940s and 1950s, when state legislatures at last began to remove segregation laws from their statute books. The report's authors blamed the federal government for failing to monitor or reproach local providers.

Why was white America—including the law makers and leaders in Washington—so blind to this discrimination against African-American citizens? The only plausible answer is that most white Americans did not see Black Americans as part of the same nation to which they belonged. They were physically within the nation but outside metaphorically and ideologically: as the immigration system of national origins, enacted into law in 1924, expressed it, the American nation was white and of European extraction. The "individualistic" American nation actually had a clear hierarchy of groups at its core.

In practice, a similar attitude faced Latinos. They experienced racial prejudice from the middle of the nineteenth century, as many Americans judged them to be inferior, and the 1848 Treaty of Guadalupe Hidalgo's guarantee of citizenship rights was ignored.[33] Debates, convened in the 1840s at constitutional conventions in both Texas and California on the suffrage rights and "whiteness" (a term employed explicitly) of Mexicans and Mexican Americans, anticipated racist language used in respect to the Chinese in the 1880s and to Southern and Eastern Europeans in the 1910s and 1920s.[34] The California debate defined Mexicans as nonwhites whose inclusion in the suffrage was a limited exception to a general policy.

A half century later, in the early 1900s, attitudes in California had changed at least in the short term. Americanization dovetailed with the needs of industrialists, who wanted immigrant workers to learn English and to Americanize. In California, employers welcomed state efforts to Americanize Mexican immigrants. California established a home teacher program.[35] Teachers visited Mexican immigrants in their homes to urge Americanization and to explain how to achieve cleanliness, a good diet, and health.

But the enthusiasm for Americanizing Mexicans ended abruptly in 1929 as economic recession reduced the demand for migrant labor: Mexican immigrants found themselves characterized as unfit for citizenship and unassimilable in a climate of economic austerity.[36] Even some Mexican-American citizens were abruptly expelled from Los Angeles.

As in African-American communities, Americanization strengthened the sense of distinctive Mexican-American identity among its targets: just as the barrios had developed in the post-1848 decades to defend Mexican customs and traditions in the Southwest, so in the 1910s and 1920s Mexican Americans sustained their values through an enhanced ethnic solidarity.[37] For African Americans, the deficiencies imposed by separate education became a cause célèbre and a rallying point for the civil rights campaign mobilized from the 1930s: the key decision by the

U.S. Supreme Court, in 1954, which found segregation unconstitutional arose from a case about education in the state of Kansas.

Separate education violated the logic of assimilationist nationalism, sharpening instead of eroding group identity. This emphasis on group distinctions created particular conditions for the way in which American nationhood developed. Separate education had similar effects in the annexed territories, to which we now turn.

Education Abroad

Annexation of both Puerto Rico and the Philippines presumed the need to Americanize their respective populations to prepare them for membership in the nation. In the words of one American administrator of Puerto Rico, Brigadier General Guy V. Henry, Puerto Ricans were "still children."[38] Americans mostly equated Filipinos with Native Americans or African Americans, doubting their capacity or competence for citizenship. But it was the general philosophy to "benevolently assimilate" with which President William McKinley and other nation-builders justified their actions.[39] Education was a key medium for Americanizing both Filipinos and Puerto Ricans.

The pressure upon Puerto Ricans to Americanize intensified following the introduction of civil administration, which was instituted via the Foraker Act in 1900. Initially Congress granted bilingual—Spanish and English—status to the island's population. In practice, the governor and his public school teachers and administrators made English the primary language. But for most Puerto Ricans, Spanish remained their first language. Satisfying a proficiency test in English was made a condition of high school graduation, though few children reached this stage. Eleven high schools were in place by 1920 and the University of Puerto Rico was founded in 1925. The university became a significant source of national aspiration and cultural self-realization in later years, in ways not anticipated by its American founders.

In school, children began the day by joining with their classmates in saluting the American flag, proclaiming the Pledge of Allegiance, and singing the U.S. national anthem. In some cases, the school teachers themselves performed these tasks with incomplete English.

A brief return to Spanish in the 1930s was overruled by President Franklin D. Roosevelt, who declared, "[I]t is an indispensable part of American policy that the coming generation of American citizens in Puerto Rico grow up with complete facility in the English tongue . . . the official language of our country."[40] Roosevelt's proclamation had been prompted by a critical review of rural education in Puerto Rico undertaken by U.S. senator William King of Utah, who found widespread ignorance of English among schoolchildren. In 1949, the English-only language policy was reversed; Spanish was made the country's official language, though English dominated in schools until 1965.

Benevolent assimilation was also on offer in the Philippines, but resistance to the U.S. presence and Filipino commitment to winning independence were deeper. Politically, such a tenacity was surely inevitable given the status of Filipinos under U.S. control: they were ineligible for U.S. citizenship and their citizenship of the Philippines was an oxymoron since this entity lacked sovereignty under the insular case rulings. This judicial status sharpened Filipinos' group-based difference, an effect underlined by Moorfield Storey, a future secretary of the National Association for the Advancement of Colored People (NAACP). He observed: "[T]he policy . . . creates a new race problem because [it] rests entirely upon the assumption that the Filipinos, being unfit to govern themselves, should be governed by a race of superior people."[41] Policy makers forgot how the demand for self-government had powered the Filipinos' rebellion against Spain.

The Americans introduced an education system which used English as the language of instruction. Public primary schools were set up in every town and, in theory, there was at least one secondary school per province. A thousand American teachers, who were known as "Thomasites" after the ship, the *Thomas*, upon which many of them arrived, were dispatched to the Philippines. The majority were Protestants, although the education system they administered was secular, ending three centuries of religious control of schools.

Fred Atkinson, the first superintendent of education, believed English instruction was the primary instrument of reform and would prepare Filipinos for membership in the nation. A high school teacher from Springfield, Massachusetts,[42] Atkinson soon realized that American textbooks were of limited relevance: "[S]uch words as 'strawberry,' 'Jack

Frost,' and 'fairy' possess little significance for the children of the Philippines."[43] But he failed to replace them because such textbooks promoted Americanization, the aim of government policy.

Atkinson favored an "industrial education" approach,[44] and he copied the one developed by Booker T. Washington at the Tuskegee Institute for African Americans. The institute imparted skills suitable for industrial work. Much of the training consisted of basic motor skills (such as making a kite or box) with some vocational instruction. Atkinson drew intentionally upon Booker T. Washington's model and wrote to Washington, "[E]ducation in the Philippines must be along industrial lines and any and all suggestions from you and your work will be invaluable."[45] He visited both Tuskegee and the Hampton Institute, the two main centers of African-American education, before embarking for Manila.[46] Just as white Americans endorsed the vocationally dominated instruction offered at Tuskegee as appropriate to the level of "inferior" African Americans, so the appeal of such measures in respect to Filipinos was almost instant.[47] And for both groups, it institutionalized their unequal membership in the nation.[48]

The rapid loss of interest that Americans displayed toward the Philippines, after their initial euphoria about the islands' capture, ensured that Americanization policy was far less forceful in the islands than that administered to immigrants' children at home. The educational reforms were poorly conceived and changed haphazardly as directors of the Bureau of Public Instruction succeeded each other. Policies were often contradictory. Neither basic education for citizenship nor industrially oriented instruction had great success. The number of American teachers and bureaucrats fell from 2,600 in 1913 to 614 in 1921. A policy of Filipinization—to appoint Filipinos where possible and to devolve authority to them—increasingly marked American policy.[49]

Filipino reaction to English instruction was mixed. Administrators reported enthusiasm for the language, but visitors often encountered hostility to its use. English was resisted in the courts and later in the assembly, in both of which Spanish prevailed. English was the language of the annexing power and as such associated with an American nationhood which gave second-class rights to Filipinos. The economist Henry Parker Wills, who visited the Philippines for Moorfield Storey in 1904, concluded after several months traveling the islands, "[T]he fact is that the enthusiasm of the natives in learning English is largely a myth," and "the proportion of the population which comprehends as much as a few simple words is extremely small."[50] Nine years later, another academic, Henry Jones Ford, challenged official statistics about the dissemination of English since in his experience, "everywhere Spanish is the speech of business and social intercourse."[51]

A few educated Filipinos did annually pass civil service examinations, which required competence in English. And from 1903, the colonial government selected a group of Filipino high school graduates and sent them, under the *pensionado* program, to study in the United States—a form of cooptation and incorporation of local elites. By 1912, 209 Filipinos had graduated from American universities under the scheme, most from well-heeled families in Manila.[52] But such measures did not displace the desire for independence.

Americanization through education is often identified as one of the great successes of U.S. nation-building. Millions of immigrants' children from Eastern, Central, and Northern Europe found their footing and assimilated.[53] But this is not the whole story. Americanization often accentuated rather than diluted a group's identity, setting future nation-building challenges.

Among Native Americans, such institutions most commonly reinforced, rather than diminished, a sense of belonging to a distinctive group.[54] Federal policy strengthened group identities and loyalties under the umbrella of American nationhood. As even a government report conceded, boarding schools were "alienating" and fermented a "factional split between young and old" generations of Native Americans.[55] This aspect of assimilationist nation-building left unfinished business for future generations.

In the Philippines and to a lesser extent in Puerto Rico, Americanization failed to foster a sense of belonging in the American nation. For Filipinos, this failure fueled a nationalist movement to demand independence. From President McKinley onward, many Americans evinced a lack of imaginative understanding toward Filipinos and misjudged the capacity and determination of this people to achieve self-determination and to resist Americanization. McKinley, like many of his successors, never accepted the notion of a Filipino nation—seeing only the chaotic "tribes" linked by geographical proximity on the Philippine archipelago, a perspective assumed by ethnologists. As early as 1903, Moorfield Storey spelled out the limits of viewing the Filipinos as uncivilized. Many were Christians and many had impressed some visitors as capable of self-government, with such institutions as courts, newspapers, schools, and literature already flourishing. Storey commented: "[L]anguage is not education. It is a tool by which men get education. Knowing nothing of their tool, we insist that they shall abandon it." He continued: "We in our ignorance are trying to make Filipinos into Americans instead of trying to make them better Filipinos."[56]

Americanization heightened Filipinos' sense of national identity. This outcome suggests an irony about the United States' intervention: contrary to Storey's concerns, Americanization efforts did make them "better Filipinos" by intensifying their sense of distinctive nationhood. But this was an accident, not intentional. It suggests one reason that American imperialism was short-lived—it contained the seeds for encouraging liberation and functioned in terms of hierarchical distinctions among peoples that was unsustainable over the long run. This hierarchy is the subject of the next chapter.

3 ◆

Why Not All Groups Are Equal

Nation-building is in significant part an exercise in circumscription. In America, this process of differentiating between those in and those outside the nation occurred amid a startling explosion in the country's demography. Intellectual, and then popular, comprehension of this expansion drew upon images of difference rooted in hierarchies of ethnicity, race, and nationality or some combination of these markers. This world view helped to address the immediate political pressures to build an integrated national identity in the midst of demographic growth. It obviously clashed with the statement of American values as ones of individualism based in equality of opportunity and rights. Over the long run, this contradiction could not be ignored. Because membership was defined differently across groups, the establishment of equal membership would require a rejection of group-based differences in a later period. At the beginning of the twentieth century, however, identifiable limits determined who belonged and who did not.

This chapter begins with a discussion of the media through which hierarchical assumptions spread before turning to the way in which these assumptions infected attitudes from the end of the nineteenth century. An examination of the myriad ways in which government policy and judicial decisions differentiated among groups concludes the chapter.

Ordering Presumptions

The four-year U.S. Exploring Expedition (1838–1842), guided by ethnologists Horatio Hale and Charles Pickering, assembled a vast collection of artifacts pertaining to the customs, manners, religions, lifestyles, and physical characteristics, including Fijian skulls, from "savage" peoples in the Pacific; its loot was displayed in the National Gallery's Great Hall in Washington, D.C., from 1843 and visited by thousands.[1] A 1600-page, five-volume account of the expedition was widely discussed upon its publication in 1845.[2] The expedition signaled American achievement in the hitherto European-dominated world of scientific exploration. More significantly, it showed how ethnologists understood "different" peoples.[3] The expedition's report was aligned with theories in which humanity fell into different "races," which occupied distinct levels of civilization and savagery. What impressed both the general public visiting the National Gallery and the scientists were the unbridgeable chasms separating different "races."[4]

This was the background to Americans' interest in territories beyond the United States sparked by the Spanish-American War in 1898. Geography was already central to school curricula, and geographic publications became staples of mass consumption.[5] Rand McNally's *Pictorial Atlas of the World* (1898) included a sixfold racial typology set out in evolutionary and hierarchical terms (Orang-outang, Malayan, Ethiopian, Indian, Mongolian, and Caucasian).[6] Such categorizations were widespread in popular and scholarly publications.[7] By printing images of "backward" or "exotic" people of color, they contributed to cultural attitudes about group differences. As a fount of information about the world available to Americans, the *National Geographic*[8] was unrivaled and probably as influential in its time as movies later became: together, these media shaped the dominant images of other countries in American culture. They helped Americans, or at least those white Americans who felt themselves to be full members of the polity, to develop their sense of national identity and their distinctness from other peoples.

Historical narrative was expressed in racial categories. People could only be understood as members of a particular race, and each race had a place on a hierarchy which determined its relative superiority and inferiority.[9] Experts and academics, who were often Progressives, as well as politicians like Theodore Roosevelt embraced and propagated theories of eugenic differences and racial types, which permitted racist ideology.[10] University lecturers in political science or sociology, at this period, did not challenge their students to think other than in categories of racial superiority and inferiority. For the San Diego World Exposition, in 1915–1916, the principal organizer made his central theme "a synopsis of man's evolution," which illustrated the "progress and possibilities of the human race."[11] The Smithsonian physical anthropologist Ales Hrdlicka commissioned busts of "racial types" and undertook field research to gather illustrative material. Hrdlicka's exhibition at the exposition was soaked in evolutionary theory illustrating the three main categories in the American nation: "the 'thoroughbred' white American (for at least three generations in this continent on each parental side), the Indian, and the full-blooded American negro."[12]

World fairs expressed America's self-conception and Americans' idea of the United States' place in the world.[13] The fairs—eleven were held between 1876 and 1916, attended by 100 million people[14]—illustrated how the United States measured itself relative to other nations and how it distinguished among the groups constituting its own citizenry.[15] The fairs evoked a great deal of popular excitement. Scientists' presence at fairs legitimated the group hierarchies on display.[16] The intractability of certain groups' and peoples' backwardness was a key theme in the presentations. "Childlike" was a description deployed at home and abroad to demarcate those beyond assimilation.

Photographs gave American readers access to images and places which few of them would ever directly encounter.[17] In 1898, the United States' first picture news agency was founded, supplying photographic images to newspapers and magazines.[18] Dignitaries such as presidents, visiting statesmen, or military heroes were not just read about but pictured on the page as were images of domestic contentment and overseas adventures. Photographic images presented encounters with foreign peoples and portrayed annexed territories as extensions, if incongruous ones, of the American nation. One example was the use of before and after photographs taken of children, such as American Indians, to record the experience of assimilation in an Americanizing school and to signal the potential for such amelioration.

Why Not All Groups Are Equal   39

Photographs of "backward" peoples at world fairs and expositions or in newspapers and magazines demonstrated the hierarchy of the races, for instance, the widely circulated image of a Negrito man entitled *The Missing Link* (in evolution), which was taken at the St. Louis World Fair. At the Atlanta and Nashville fairs, the Department of State exhibit was a giant globe conveying an image of American strength, which was embroidered with artifacts hierarchically depicting the peoples of the world.

The fairs and expositions reported prevailing values and beliefs about differences among peoples based on race, ethnicity, or national background but did not create those values. However, in giving racial and evolutionary theories scientific authority and linking them to American nationhood, the expositions contributed decisively to defining that nationhood's ideology of membership as a hierarchical one.

Ethnologists used the presence at fairs of Native Americans, who were portrayed as backward and savage, to shape Americans' intellectual understanding of the world's peoples.[19] Native Americans were placed on "reservations" to equate them with other peoples exhibited from the non-Western world. This status reflected the asymmetrical power relationship between Americans and Native Americans, an imbalance enforced by the exhibitors' selection of what clothing and "native" symbols were displayed. At both the Columbian Exposition in Chicago (1893) and the fair in St. Louis (1904) the "civilizing" influence of federal policy was demonstrated to the American public. In Chicago, a Native American man dressed in a traditional blanket was placed next to a child dressed in Western clothes. The effect underscored Native American distance from civilization but held out the prospect for inclusion through assimilation.[20] Only one administrator ever dissented from presenting Native Americans as uncivilized or backward.[21] Americans were not of course the only nation to organize public displays of popular codes of racial hierarchy. Even in the early 1930s, the French were organizing colonial exhibitions in which members of African tribes were on view.

Visitors to art galleries were presented with images of American nation-building as the control of inferior groups. Nineteenth-century landscape paintings set out huge, apparently uninhabited lands which Americans had conquered—overlooking Native Americans' presence and rights. Frederic Remington's paintings *Fight for the Waterhole* (1903) and *Defending the Stockade* (1905) depicted small groups of American soldiers defending American institutions and themselves (or succumbing) against the onslaught of overwhelming numbers of "savage" Native Americans. Remington's images idealized a "winning of the West" narrative—images which film directors such as John Ford and Howard Hawks later conveyed cinematically. As the editor declares in Ford's *The Man Who Shot Liberty Valance*, "print the legend"—it is more real than the complex historical story.

The U.S. exhibits at international fairs carried images of America's group divisions to international audiences. At the Paris Exposition in 1900, a series of photographs represented the "Contemporary American Negro Life." The photographs, taken by Frances Benjamin Johnston,[22] included a series of before and after portraits of African-American children and young people, showing the positive benefits of education at the segregated Hampton Institute and how these benefits could be maintained across generations. The photographs implied the need to deal in a remedial way with so-called inferior groups, whose level of development was beneath that appropriate for full membership in the nation.[23]

During World War I, maps from the National Geographic Society were used in the government's Committee on Public Information's school bulletin, the *National School Service.* These and colonial images, for instance, photographs from America's annexed territories and from Africa, Asia, and Latin America, lacked context other than the photographers' judgment about what would interest the magazine's readers. The photographers' and audience's views about what was and what was not of interest and what contrasted with their everyday experiences probably overlapped. But difference could be found even among groups that might have been expected to be accepted in the nation. The popular descriptions of Eastern and Southern European immigrants illustrates this tendency: their whiteness was no guarantee of their acceptance.[24]

The dominant images helped to define American nationalism as an imagined vision and practice which had at a minimum to accommodate other groups, in many ways by getting them to lose their identities: securing the nation overshadowed debate about the terms for democratic inclusion. This process of including some groups while excluding others in nation-building was the dominant logic of post-Reconstruction federal policy. As the price of forging national unity and a coherent rhetoric of one-people nationalism, America's nation-builders were content to exclude African Americans from this "one people." To justify this end, nation-builders could employ the hierarchical images of different peoples since these provided an allegedly objective measure supporting choices about membership in the nation. These choices presumed a white nation. It was this presumption which determined how commemoration of the Civil War was made to converge with the goal of American nation-builders to promote American nationhood as that of one people.

White Patriots

Collective memory of the Civil War was dominated by white memories in the North and South. A massive equestrian memorial statue of Robert E. Lee, *Lee Circle*, completed by the French sculptor Antonin Mercie, was unveiled on Monument Avenue in Richmond, Virginia, in May 1890. The sculpture, put in place by black workers, conveyed the southern white tradition or, as one of the workers declared, "[T]he Southern white folks is on top, the Southern white folks is on top."[25] Annual celebration of Lee's birthday became a pilgrimage for crowds that sometimes numbered more than 100,000.[26] In the North, the wish to solidify the union resulted in a greater openness to white southerners, and this helped to determine who did and who did not belong to the one-people nation.

Tolerance of southern memories of the Civil War coincided with a more general nationalistic turn. The Spanish-American War in 1898 gave nation-builders such as Theodore Roosevelt an opportunity to stir up patriotism and to further quell the old Civil War divisions.[27] The surge in immigration to the United States provided an additional motive for strengthening nationalist ideology. But the Civil War was the principal reference point for jingoistic patriotism.

Led by the forerunner of the American Legion, the Grand Army of the Republic (GAR),[28] and by the Women's Relief Corps (WRC), veterans' organizations commemorated the Civil War as a way of strengthening the nation. This strategy bore fruit by 1900. Partial reconciliation of North and South and of old and new immigrants was accomplished by suppressing the group complexity of the United States' population and by privileging its white majority. It was a fatal rapprochement for marginalized groups, including people of color, who discovered that despite their participation in defending American values, the group lines of national membership made them second-class members. The huge two-day Grand Review march in Washington, D.C., in May 1865, held to celebrate the lives lost in the Civil War, sent a direct message: no Black American Union regiments were included; worse still, those few black soldiers included were there as a comedy act.[29] This was a step in shaping the national consciousness of the Civil War as a conflict waged not to end slavery and for Emancipation but as one solely to maintain the integrity of the union. The place of African Americans either as participants or as the object of Emancipation left the collective memory of the Civil War.[30]

These veteran and militaristic tendencies dovetailed with the introduction of patriotic Americanism into public schools through such measures as the Pledge of Allegiance. The schoolhouse flag movement wanted a Stars and Stripes flag displayed over every public school, its advocates believing it would unite all Americans. Shared faith in the flag would integrate the diverse peoples comprising the one people.[31] This scheme was adopted.

But all of this patriotic language was group bounded.[32] Efforts to have the Democrat-controlled Congress establish a commemorative Emancipation Day foundered—and what is *not* commemorated is as important to a nation's identity as those events memorialized collectively.[33] Local GAR organizations instituted a color line despite efforts by the national organization to limit segregation.[34] Celebration of the "Lost Cause" grew, and celebrants became more unabashed.

The combined effect of these activities was an American nationalism embroidered with a partial memory of the purposes and effects of the Civil War. By the 1900s, when history teaching was mandatory in close to twenty-five states, most textbooks had removed any reference to Black Americans among the Union soldiers.[35] Almost a century elapsed before this was modified to restore their rightful role in textbook narratives.

This restoration had broader significance. It is only since the 1960s that the full placement of African Americans in the nation's collective memory has begun. As we will see in later chapters, revising this bias is a continuing process.

Dividing Up the Nation

Recalling his trepidation on leaving home in 1915 for Rutgers University (where he was to be one of only two black students), Paul Robeson reflected on the segregated status pushed on African Americans in the nation: "[A]s I went out into life, one thing loomed above all else: I was my father's son, a Negro in America. That was the challenge."[36] This challenge derived from the segregation and discriminatory racism to which African Americans were routinely subject until the 1960s.

Government policy enforced group-based distinctions.[37] Census compilers, bureaucrats, and politicians made "race" and other classifications an instrument of public policy in the nineteenth and twentieth centuries. They assessed exactly how much blood some Americans had of a particular race.[38] By the 1920s, the one-drop rule (that is, one drop of black blood made a person black) was widely accepted as a guideline for policy.[39] This rule and other measurements established a person's approximation to whiteness. They not only helped to normalize the concept of race but made plain who topped the hierarchy.[40] Despite disagreements about the precise categorization of individuals, enforcing and maintaining a system of racial classification bonded lawyers, judges, law makers, juries, and "scientific" experts together until at least the 1940s. A comparable deployment of experts joined in legal decisions about naturalization and citizenship claims.[41] These efforts complemented the United States' segregation laws.

In the nineteenth and early twentieth centuries, Bureau of the Census officials wrestled with racial classifications. They issued detailed instructions about how field counters ought to classify those they were counting. Their assiduity helped to construct and consolidate national identity in terms of groups, some included fully in the one nation, others only partially included. Modifications were commonly made in response to the arguments of scientific experts. The term *mulatto* was included in the 1850 Census at the behest of demographer Josiah Nott.[42] In 1890, Census enumerators included the categories *quadroon* and *octoroon* (which indicated measurements of parentage).[43] The commissioner of Labor, Carroll D. Wright, told the Senate that such information was vital to determine the demographic trajectory of African Americans.[44] The Census Board employed an "expert special agent" (Dr. John Billings) to advise on racial classification and to increase the comprehensiveness of vital statistics compiled for "colored people." For Billings, the results of the 1890 Census showed African Americans moving toward extinction,[45] an idea made meaningful by the parallel assumption held for Native Americans. But the data collected about octoroons and quadroons were considered unreliable by experts, and from 1910 the single category of mulatto was used. By 1930, however, the Census board was again engaged in wrangling about the classification of "mixed" groups, including Native Americans and Mexicans; but its instruction to enumerators for "Negroes" cemented the "one drop of blood" principle, that is, if a person had a single drop of black blood that made her black legally.[46]

In 1896, the U.S. Supreme Court issued its decision in *Plessy v. Ferguson*, establishing segregation of African Americans under the separate-but-equal doctrine. The decision, a culmination of the collapse of Reconstruction, closed any prospect of equal rights for African Americans until the middle of the twentieth century. Many states passed laws segregating Black Americans from public facilities and removing their voting rights. In the *Plessy* decision, the U.S. Supreme Court stamped its approval on this group conception of American nationhood. This judicial ruling (in place until 1954) secured group distinctions—in this case, racial—in American nationhood at home and abroad (as military expeditions overseas were also segregated). Only one Supreme Court justice dissented from the decision.

Racism intensified in the years after World War I. The often oppressive response of whites in northern cities, the revival of the Ku Klux Klan in the 1920s, the downplaying of black veterans' war contributions, and the government's indifference to African Americans' circumstances fueled resentment about the inadequacies of American democracy. These themes were caught by W. E. B. Du Bois in his book *Darkwater* when he wrote: "[I]nstead of standing as a great example of the success of democracy and the possibility of human brotherhood America has taken her place as an awful example of its pitfalls and failures, so far as black and brown and yellow peoples are concerned."[47]

That the United States had just fought in a European war to uphold the democratic principle of self-determination was not lost on African Americans as they experienced the biases of U.S. democracy. What was the value of being a strong nation for democracy abroad if that strength were simply used to exclude and discriminate against part of its citizenry at home?

The importance of allegedly scientific knowledge about hierarchical distinctions among peoples in shaping popular views is plain. The presentations in popular magazines and photographs and in the exhibits at world fairs offered uncritical reportage from the cutting edge of scientific knowledge about different races and physical types as explained by ethnologists, anthropologists, eugenicists, and sundry others, many part of the reforming Progressive movement. This information had the stamp of scientific validity because of the way in which the material was collected, for instance, from expeditions or from Native American sites, and by whom it was collected, that is, respected and respectable scientists. The relationship between the authenticity of the materials displayed and the attendant beliefs is complex. To some extent, we can speculate, by the time of the world fairs in the 1910s and 1920s, such exhibits simply presented or bolstered what was already presumed (and was increasingly expressed in other forums, like silent films).[48] But their widespread influence is not in doubt.

The idea of group hierarchies complemented and reinforced those distinctions employed to determine suitability or unsuitability for membership in the polity. How could political membership be distributed equally across groups that existed on some measurable hierarchical scale? This was a fundamental contradiction. Thus, when during the First World War, President Woodrow Wilson directed that Americans abandon their group loyalties, he was ignoring the very hierarchical codes through which popular consciousness structured how Americans viewed the world's peoples. Wilson told new citizens, "[Y]ou can not become thorough Americans if you think of yourselves in groups.

America does not consist of groups. A man who thinks of himself as belonging to a particular national group in America has not yet become an American."[49] This attack on groups based on ethnicity or national background proved historically unsustainable. The conflicting pressures unleashed by the wartime role of patriotism, which pitched some groups against others, could not be ignored. Underlying this tension was the profound inequalities among groups in the American nation. Wilson's idealistic individualism would founder on the rocks of America's political realities.

Although hierarchical codes were part of an international intellectual framework shared by Western countries, such doctrines were more fateful in the United States. Because America's political leaders made these codes central referents in nation-building, they obstructed the promise of an egalitarian nationhood. Furthermore, the United States helped to solidify this international framework through its policies in the annexed Philippines and Puerto Rico.[50] Its first international ventures were thus tainted by racism.

American soldiers were segregated in the Philippines. As one member of the Twenty-Fourth Infantry wrote home: "[T]he whites have begun to establish their diabolical race hatred in all its home rancor . . . even endeavoring to propagate the phobia among the Spaniards and Filipinos so as to be sure of the foundation of their supremacy when the civil rule is established."[51] Six thousand Black American soldiers served in the U.S. infantry fighting Filipino nationalists. The expedition to the Philippines challenged black soldiers' political convictions, despite their support for the party of Lincoln and their patriotism. Some sent letters to newspapers deploring the treatment of Filipinos and their society.[52] Many black troops realized that serving the United States in the Philippines implicated them in a system of racial oppression, extending overseas the prejudice of white, one-nation America without any erosion of prejudice at home. As one recruit wrote, "[E]very time we get a paper from [the United States] we read where some poor Negro is lynched for supposed rape."[53] Racism overseas paralleled that at home. Writer James Le Roy concluded that the only way Americans seemed to know how to behave in their dealings with Filipinos was to mimic their treatment of African Americans.[54] African-American troops drew links between the justice of the Filipino cause and the domestic struggle for political and civil rights in the United States, one writing of the Filipinos, "[T]hese people are right and *we* are wrong and terribly wrong."[55] Others were in a quandary to explain to Filipinos why American democracy, so obviously color exclusive, was worth defending.

African Americans at home also wondered about the United States' mission to "civilize" Puerto Ricans and Filipinos. The stubborn unwillingness to employ federal policy in the protection of African Americans' rights made the claim to "benevolent" expansion suspect, as one African-American editor, T. Thomas Fortune, made clear in the *New York Age*: "[T]he people of the United States . . . have as much as they can manage at home."[56] How could a U.S. mission of Americanization employ African-American soldiers whose status in American society and the American nation was widely judged to be that of unassimilability because they were not white? *Assimilability* was the buzz-word of the new immigration policy established in the 1920s, which is the subject of the next chapter.

4 ◈

Choosing New Members
The Rise of Immigration Restriction

The enactment of a restrictive immigration regime is one of the clearest expressions of who constitutes members of the American nation under an assimilationist vision. America's policy of restriction was gradual: numerous restrictionist bills were vetoed by successive presidents. But the political pressure to be selective was powerful, and by 1930 the United States had put in place a discriminatory system which made clear who could be considered, from the outside, potential members of the nation and who lay outside membership.

Immigration restriction had a further domestic significance. It not only set criteria for migrants from overseas but clarified the marginal and second-class position of those already residing in the United States whose racial, ethnic, or national background made them victims of nation-building by excluding them from those eligible under the new law.

The obverse of immigration restriction is choosing to exit from a polity. Throughout the nineteenth century and into the opening decades of the twentieth, the experience of segregation and discrimination made some African Americans conceive of a life beyond the United States, as we will see later in the chapter.

Initiating Restriction

The drive to restrict immigration began, from the 1870s, with Chinese laborers. The Maine senator, Republican James G. Blaine, a leading advocate of exclusion, expressed the prevailing sense of hostility to some groups in a letter printed in the *New York Times*. His language was stark: "[I]f as a nation we have the right to keep out infectious diseases . . . we surely have the right to exclude that immigration which reeks with impurity. . . . I am opposed to the Chinese coming here; I am opposed to making them citizens."[1] Blaine's comments were not merely those of an opportunist seeking national advancement by stigmatizing weak members of society. His views were a harbinger of American opinion already shared by the majority of his congressional colleagues, despite their holding a variety of ideological convictions.

In 1854, the California Supreme Court ruled that Chinese people were not eligible for equal protection under the law and excluded Chinese witnesses from testifying in that state's courtrooms.[2] Chinese people lacked the right to naturalize. Hostile views of Chinese people filtered into schools. Of thirty-six geographers producing textbooks by midcentury, seven expressed ambivalent views while the majority, twenty-one authors, were critical of the Chinese.[3] Thus the education curriculum, which had been devised to build a one-people nationhood, contained group markers about those outside its rubric.

The acceptability of singling out Chinese migrants for abuse was made national when President Rutherford Hayes declared, in 1879, "[O]ur experience in dealing with the weaker races—the Negroes and Indians, for example—is not encouraging. . . . I would consider with favor any suitable measures to discourage the Chinese from coming to our shores."[4] "Weaker races" was part of the language of group hierarchy.

The failure of immigration restrictions, enacted in the states of California, Oregon, and Washington, to win U.S. Supreme Court endorsement stirred pressure for federal legislation. This demand culminated with passage by Congress of the first Chinese Exclusion Law in 1882.

Before 1882, about a quarter of a million Chinese entered the United States, generally to work at low-paid manual jobs. Often indentured or bond servants, they had to work off the cost of their passage.[5] Such Chinese immigrants—like the Japanese later—were viewed as unassimilable with Americans because somehow they were "different."[6] In California, both Chinese and Japanese immigrants were poorly treated.[7] Supported by organized labor, politicians and populists exploited racism to whip up opposition to Chinese workers in ways which emphasized their differences from the existing population and their economic threat to American workers. This was not an exclusively West Coast hostility.[8] California's Aaron Sargent chaired the U.S. Senate committee which issued a damning report, in February 1877, about the Chinese in America.[9] It itemized numerous criticisms and concluded that they created "a continual menace" and evinced neither "knowledge of [nor] appreciation for our institutions."[10] In a period of intense political party competition, when presidential elections were resolved with tiny margins, both Democrats and Republicans saw in Chinese exclusion a winning issue. American workers who initially opposed contracted Chinese laborers rather than voluntary Chinese immigrants soon lost interest in that distinction and supported a general ban.

Weak enforcement in the 1880s prompted a toughening of the exclusionary principle by Congress in 1892, to make permanent both the ban on Chinese laborer immigration and the proscription upon Chinese people naturalizing.[11] The law exempted Chinese immigrants from the right of habeas corpus and empowered judges to deport Chinese laborers alleged to be illegal aliens. In protest, China declined to send a commissioner to the World's Columbia Exposition in Chicago.

The anti-Chinese propensity legitimated in 1882 bolstered the hierarchical racist turn in American society which informed nation-building at that time. This contribution to defining membership is a major aspect of its significance. To recall the historical period, Reconstruction had collapsed just over a decade earlier, and both the legal segregation of African Americans established in *Plessy* (1896) and the Native American allotment policy of the Dawes Act (1887) lay in the future. Together, such measures placed group parameters upon membership in the American nation. Exclusion strengthened the willingness of well-heeled Americans to think about certain groups as problematic members of their nation. Of Chinese restriction one Minnesota congressman remarked that the measure revealed among Americans "a general idea, unhappily too prevalent, that we need not deal with the Chinese upon the same footing of equal binding force and obligation . . . that we deal with other people."[12] In the Senate, only Massachusetts Democrat George Hoar retained his traditional opposition to exclusion because its specificity signaled a rupture in the New World's promise of racial equality and civil rights.

The exclusion laws were held to be constitutional by the U.S. Supreme Court in 1889.[13] The justices accepted that race or national origin were appropriate criteria for making choices about admission to the United States. Indeed, in *Plessy*, Justice John Marshall Harlan, the sole dissenter against the separate-but-equal precept, pointed out the peculiarity, as he saw it, of applying this racist system to African Americans and not to Chinese people, "a race so different from our own that we do not permit those belonging to it to become citizens of the United States."[14] So, even opponents of a constricted membership employed the prevailing language of group hierarchy.

Extending Restriction

Not only did the Chinese exclusion show how group-based discrimination could be implemented, but it also shaped the values carried by the United States in its overseas adventures. Congress extended the restrictions on Chinese laborers to those in Hawaii, despite stringent objections by the Chinese representative in the United States. The Chinese Exclusion laws were applied in the Philippines too. Similar restrictive pressures were directed toward Japanese immigrants (whose numbers were limited in the "Gentleman's Agreement," signed by the United States and Japan in 1907) and Japanese people already present in the United States. State governments in the West introduced their own restrictive laws (for instance, California's Alien Land Act, 1913, which made ownership of land conditional upon eligibility for citizenship), and the assimilability problem was a theme of national politics in the 1900s and, more intensely, in the 1910s. In 1905, the school board in San Francisco segregated the education of Japanese children into a separate Asian school. Whether aliens or citizens, Chinese and Japanese immigrants were barred from numerous occupations on the West Coast. A Hearst-commissioned study of attitudes toward "the Japanese problem," undertaken by Cornelius Vanderbilt, Jr., in 1921, concluded,

"[A]bsolute exclusion of all Orientals will be the only solution of the problem."[15] The "problem" was unassimilability. It was a conclusion which converged exactly with the influence of eugenic arguments on the legislators enacting immigration restriction in 1921 and 1924.[16] Both Chinese and Japanese became "American Orientals," who were looked upon as outside the nation despite residing in it.[17] This status epitomizes the most common problem of political membership in the development of American nationhood.

African Americans observed these restrictions with alarm,[18] aware that the use of such explicit racial criteria made the assimilated one nation white. Indeed, from the White House, President Woodrow Wilson made this equation explicit: "I stand for the national policy of exclusion. The whole question is one of assimilation of diverse races. We cannot make a homogeneous population of a people who do not blend with the Caucasian race. . . . Oriental cooleeism will give us another race problem to solve and surely we have had our lesson."[19]

This characterization of African Americans and "Orientals" as "race problems" by one of the United States' greatest presidents would surprise most people today. Not only does it suggest that this statesman was aware of domestic race discrimination when proposing his liberal world order but also that he perceived it as a problem resolvable by tightening rather than enlarging the parameters of American individualism. Consolidating the one-people nation set clear limits upon the scope of democratic inclusion.

Chinese representatives in the United States attempted to counter these negative characterizations. The Chinese consul general in San Francisco maintained that the law reinforced stereotypes about Chinese people in the United States—their alleged unassimilability and willingness to work for cheap wages in order to remit those earnings to China— and damaged U.S. interests. The perception of unassimilability arose from the marginal political status of Chinese people, which yielded a chicken-and-egg circularity: "[W]e are not citizens and voters. . . . The evil and loss to which the United States has been subjected in its relations with China would all have been avoided had the Chinese been treated the same way as other aliens in the matter of naturalization."[20] American voices for a gentler approach had no influence. Lack of voting rights placed Chinese residents beyond the interest of those political parties mobilizing groups of ethnic Americans. By the St. Louis World Fair in 1904, it seemed appropriate to have among the exhibit's photographs one or two Chinese children in traditional silk costumes, casually entitled *Little Chinks.*[21]

The legacy of exclusion was formidable.[22] The language used was intemperate and racist, contributing to a view of Chinese and Japanese as "unfit" for membership in the American nation. This view continued in the 1920s and 1930s and conditioned Americans' attitudes in the Pacific.[23] Based on 400 life histories and interviews, the University of Chicago's Survey of Race Relations, which was conducted in the 1920s among Chinese and Japanese in California, cemented, more subtly perhaps and with a veneer of scientific expertise, a view of "Oriental" difference and unassimilability in the ideology of American nationalism: certain groups were outside.[24] This notion of the "American Oriental"—a domestic source of exoticism—endured until the last quarter of the twentieth century. It is a telling example of how group divisions were made integral to American nationhood beneath the rhetoric of one people.

African Americans and Exit

For African Americans, negotiating the assumptions of inferiority and hostility imposed by a white-biased American nationalism was a compelling and immediate task. Some contemplated leaving America. Inquiring about migration to Liberia in the 1890s, one African-American man in Georgia wrote, "[W]e . . . are anxious to get home. We are quite sure that the U.S. of America is not the place for the colored man."[25] "Home" was an imagined community and place of origin in Africa.

Back-to-Africa movements, which predated the American Civil War, were first promoted by whites as part of a white one-nation ideology. It was later adopted as a strategy by some African Americans, with rekindled enthusiasms in the 1890s and 1920s, the latter period under the leadership of Marcus Garvey's Universal Negro Improvement Association (UNIA). Such initiatives signaled in part the parameters and possibilities of black Atlanticism, that is, the close ties between African Americans and black communities in other countries.[26] For example,

Harvard-educated physician and black nationalist Martin Delany supported the idea of African Americans leaving the United States to build a black state.[27]

The idea of emigration to a more politically and racially tolerant country interested some African Americans whereas colonization was a part of the white American agenda. Founded in 1816 by, among others, Francis Scott Key, author of "The Star-Spangled Banner," the whites-only American Colonization Society worked to send free blacks to African settlements, with the intention that freed slaves would also move there. Some supporters, such as Daniel Webster, envisaged applying a model of white colonization to African Americans and to American Indians in the United States, thereby creating, he conjectured, a horizontal equality of groups. But for congressional supporters of colonization, building the nation meant expelling African Americans as a correlate of Emancipation. The U.S. government bought land on the Grain Coast of Africa, later called Liberia, permitting the establishment of settlements populated with Black Americans.[28] The scheme had limited popularity.[29] Of the total 12,790 African Americans who had moved to Liberia by 1867, 11,703 were from the South (the majority compelled to migrate as a condition of manumission) and 1,087 were from the North.[30] The scheme had some African-American supporters, such as Alexander Crummell, though these people had different reasons than the white backers.[31]

In the closing decade of the nineteenth century, as the tenebrous cloud of segregation descended upon post-Reconstruction America, the appeal of leaving the United States revived and "Liberia fever" peaked. The numbers seeking assistance to emigrate rose. Commentaries about the inevitability of racial hierarchies and the doomed future of such groups as Native Americans and African Americans[32] (that is, the expectation that they faced demographic decline and probably extinction) heightened the United States' inhospitability to people of color and the appeal of emigration. Violence against Black Americans soared.[33] Contemporary versions of American nationalism of the sort propounded by Theodore Roosevelt, hero of the Spanish-American War and a critic of those Americans displaying ethnic identities, portrayed America as a white nation with rigid criteria about membership.[34] New organizations sprang up advocating emigration.

Black emigration was debated in Congress in the 1890s. South Carolina senator Matthew Butler introduced a bill to fund moving African Americans to Africa, conditional on their becoming citizens of their new countries and giving up U.S. citizenship.[35] Debate on the Butler bill brought forth predictably hostile views toward African Americans and calculations about the electoral benefits of the proposed displacement. The senator himself supported only voluntary emigration, a restriction his southern colleagues ignored in their eagerness to transplant Black Americans to Africa. Massachusetts senator George Hoar, a Republican, attacked Butler's bill for proposing emigration before African Americans had gained complete rights of citizenship in the United States. African-American opinion rejected the Butler "repatriation" initiative, and the *Kansas City American Citizen* editorialized, "[Senator Butler's] ancestors had a much easier task in stealing from their humble homes and bringing to these shores our ancestors than he and his posterity will have to remove them."[36] The bill was plainly a Democratic one and had slim prospects in a Republican-controlled Senate. It did not come to a vote. That it was introduced and debated does, however, deepen understanding of how some white members of Congress looked upon their fellow African-American citizens: they were not welcomed as members of the nation.

Colonization clubs and independent orders were formed throughout the United States in the 1890s.[37] These organizations received thousands of letters from African Americans wishing to migrate to Liberia but lacking the means. Victims of racial violence often petitioned one of the emigrant organizations to inquire about such passage. Many African Americans moved to the unassigned lands in Indian Territory and the Oklahoma Territory after they were opened to settlement by non–Native Americans.[38] Others, the "exodusters," moved to Kansas, where the first all-black communities were established. But by 1910, this wave of pro-emigration sentiment had evaporated and integrationist strategies prevailed, whether of the Booker T. Washington or the W. E. B. Du Bois forms. The largest secular African-American organization, Marcus Garvey's initiative in the 1920s, failed to give migration a popular appeal, though as an expression of organized black nationalism, the UNIA was immensely influential.

The failure to find acceptance in American society and bitterness at the daily routine of segregationist racism encouraged individual African Americans to leave either permanently or temporarily.[39] This trend stretches from the nineteenth century. Traveling to Europe in the 1880s, Du Bois experienced a sense of freedom of a sort he never felt in the United States; it increased his anger at the conditions facing African Americans at home.[40] Journeying before Du Bois, Frederick Douglass imbibed influences from German philosophy and English politics and integrated them into his political writings and agitation for racial equality.

Many African Americans, of course, chose a confrontational road to establish civil rights, uninterested in the option of leaving. Through their creativity and direct action, writers such as Ralph Ellison, activists such as A. Philip Randolph, Ida B. Wells-Barnett, and the Reverend Martin Luther King, Jr., jazz musicians such as Max Roach and Charles Mingus, and politicians such as Adam Clayton Powell forced civil rights to the center of U.S. politics. But some opted for exile.

Beginning in the 1920s, when African Americans, including writers such as Zora Neale Hurston, Claude McKay, and Langston Hughes and musicians such as Louis Armstrong and Bessie Smith, were feted as part of the Harlem Renaissance, black artists and intellectuals found a hospitable (and affordable) environment in France. In the fall of 1925, a musical show starring Josephine Baker, entitled *La Revue Negre*, began a run in Paris at the Theatre Champs-Elysees. Jazz musician Sidney Bechet was the orchestra's featured soloist.[41] In the music and sets, the emphasis was upon jazz music and dancing, both presented as distinctively Black American. The show was an example of the enduring rapport between Josephine Baker and France, which Baker exploited in her campaigning for civil rights. Arriving in Paris in 1929, the poet Claude McKay remarked that "the cream of Harlem" was in residence,[42] including African-American Eugene Bullard, who had won a Croix de Guerre for his bravery as an enlistee in the Great War; the musicals *Porgy and Bess* and *Blackbirds* flourished.

Openness to foreign artists was hardly confined to African Americans as émigrés from all over the world found billets in Paris in the interwar decades. However, for African Americans, the experience had a singularity in that Parisian society's openness to and interest in their work communicated the possibility of what a society liberated from group hierarchies would consist in. It was a thrilling encounter for many and deepened their anger toward racism in the United States. The writer Chester Himes, who settled permanently in France, remarked of his reasons for leaving the United States, "I am black and I was born and raised and lived in America, and the fact that race prejudice was one of my reasons for leaving it is inescapable."[43] Himes met Richard Wright, who was also permanently settled in Paris, a residence chosen by James Baldwin too.

The group hierarchy of American society made "passing" as a white person an option for some African Americans.[44] This form of internal exile was a path reluctantly traveled and a rather different journey from the familiar American story of personal reinvention undertaken by Fitzgerald's protagonist in *The Great Gatsby*, for instance, because the consequences of exposure were profound.[45] Charles Chesnutt's novel *The House Behind the Cedars* (1900), whose title hints at the second-class citizenship offered to African Americans, describes the tragic consequences when two light-skinned children's attempts to live in white society are eventually unmasked. Because white values and white people were dominant in American society, whiteness implied greater personal autonomy. Chesnutt's novel *The Quarry*, completed in 1928, addressed a similar theme. His publishers considered it too daring to print at the time, and it didn't appear until several decades later. The book's hero, Donald Glover, is adopted at birth, first by a rich white couple, who then give him up (reluctantly) when the hospital discovers he has African-American parents. But this proves to be an error, and in fact Glover's birth parents are white. However, Glover has been brought up by African-American parents, succeeds as a philosopher, and generally makes his way in the world rejecting the opportunity to pass. When confronted with his parents' racial identity, he declines to revert to a white identity. Set during New York's Harlem Renaissance, *The Quarry* challenges the privileging of white over African-American identity in American nationhood, while demonstrating just how much such identities are themselves culturally and politically shaped.[46]

Thus, while tens of thousands of emigrants poured into the United States at the turn of the century eager to become full members of the American nation, a significant proportion of those already present were denied the opportunity of unequivocal membership and in response created ways of coping and transforming this circumstance. One mechanism was various forms of exile or exit. An unknowable number of African Americans passed as whites for parts of their lives, a strategy which usually meant breaking completely with their pasts and paying heavy emotional and political costs as Nella Larsen's novel *Passing* (1929) depicts so well. Others chose an exit strategy which removed them completely from the American nation, opting to live abroad in permanent exile.

These internal and external exit options only make sense as reactions to the way in which the parameters and boundaries of membership in the American nation were specified by its nation-builders at the time. Such options contrasted dramatically with the experience most frequently coupled with accounts of American nation-building—the narrative of emigrants arriving and building the country. For African Americans, this narrative was meaningless. Their ancestors had been violently captured and transported illegally to the American colonies or later to the United States, and they were given no sense of membership in the ideology of the nation constructed there from the middle of the nineteenth century. Indeed, most aspects of nation-building in the century after the Civil War conveyed precisely the obverse message: they were not equal members of the nation, and many of their fellow citizens wanted to make this status quo intractable. The narrative of an individualized melting pot could not be further from African-American experience.

But even among those arriving as white immigrants, important demarcations were introduced with which to measure, classify, and judge immigrants' suitability for membership. It is this system of national origin categorization which is discussed in the next section.

National Origins

While Charles Chesnutt struggled between 1928 and his death in 1932 to persuade publishers to take *The Quarry*, U.S. legislators were finalizing further restriction to American immigration policy. In 1924, Congress had passed the Johnson-Reed Act, establishing a regime of "national origins" quotas. Countries received a fixed quota of immigrant slots based on their place in the national origins of the United States' population as measured in the 1920 Census. This Census base meant large quotas for the countries of Northern Europe and small quotas for Southern and Eastern European countries, where interest in migrating to the United States was greatest. It further restricted Asian immigration. The result was a distribution of about 70 percent of the annual quota of approximately 158,000 to three countries: the United Kingdom, Ireland, and Germany.

The calculation of the United States' national origins enshrined in the law excluded descendants of involuntary immigrants, that is, principally African Americans (but also native Hawaiians), and of "displaced" peoples, such as Native Americans. These stunning omissions defined the group-based ideology of American national identity.

Political leaders envisaged national origins as a way of building a demographic future which would include acceptable groups and exclude certain defined groups, ruled to be beyond the pale of assimilation because of their ethnicity, race, or national background.[47] The architects of the national origins system believed that immigration would dissolve a "genuine" American identity. To stall this scenario, they defended a narrow membership of the American nation.[48]

The immigration law's significance in formalizing the group basis of American nationhood was remarkable. For Americans of white European national background, the law disentangled race and ethnicity. While hierarchies of European ethnicity could be easily detected (suspicion of Italian Americans, for instance), all such Americans were part of a general ethnic group treated favorably for the most part in the American polity. For Americans whose parents or grandparents came from countries in Asia, the national origins system sealed a second-class identity, already established in judicial rulings about who could naturalize.[49]

Not mentioned explicitly in the 1924 restrictive immigration legislation, many Mexicans and Mexican Americans (including some U.S. citizens) nonetheless found themselves summarily deported within a decade. The economic strictures of the Great Depression in the 1930s resulted in more than a half million such expulsions. In Los Angeles alone, close to one-third of the Mexican-American community left and returned to Mexico in this decade, reaffirming their Mexican identity; those remaining often held an ambivalent attachment to the United States.[50] California's Alien Labor Act (1931) prohibited firms from hiring foreign workers for any publicly funded construction.

The 1924 national origins law made Mexicans a "racial" group whose entry to the United States became regularized under existing administration policy. It illustrates how the group divisions of the American nation were created and established in the government's nation-building policy. Rendering Mexican Americans as foreigners created a distance between them and other Americans, a distinction reinforced by the 1942 wartime *braceros* program, which brought in close to 100,000 Mexicans annually as seasonal workers; it also fed into the subsequent identification of illegal immigrants as primarily Mexicans. In the 1920s, the United States took a liberal view toward Latin America, claiming a "special relationship"; nonetheless, from the late 1920s, with the implementation of the national origins system, American consulates in Mexico tightened the administration of immigration rules such as the ban on contract labor, the literacy test, and the exclusion of those in danger of becoming public charges. The number of Mexicans deported on these grounds grew. The tougher policy toward Mexican immigrants, from the 1920s, opened a gulf between them and Mexican Americans as the latter had to focus on securing their place in the United States.

The clash between the national origins quota system and the presumption of individualism was plain. The national origins law of 1924 affirmed and indeed promoted a conception of American national identity as white.[51] As Harry Truman later remarked, such a quota system was "always based upon assumptions at variance with our American ideals," the ideal of individualism and the one-nation ideology. It institutionalized beliefs and values which were "insulting to large numbers of our finest citizens, irritating to our allies abroad, and foreign to our purposes and ideals."[52] Truman's remarks came in the year that Congress passed, over his veto, the Immigration and Nationality (McCarran-Walter) Act (1952), which upheld national origins quotas. Given the United States' global commitments at this time, the McCarran-Walter law's reaffirmation of group quotas ensured a future reckoning with this policy.

The definition of membership enshrined in immigration law during these decades would haunt American nationalism abroad as well as at home. Appearing before a House committee in 1964, Secretary of State Dean Rusk underlined the conflict between a genuine one-people nationalism and the national origins system: "[A]nything which makes it appear that we, ourselves, are discriminating in principle against particular national origins, suggests that we think less well of our citizens of those national origins, than of other citizens."[53] Reform of this system was inevitable, but the legacy of national origins as a policy that strengthened group divisions was less easily reversed, because this policy had become so fully integrated into the ideology of American nationhood.

5 ◈

The Drive for Authentic Americans
World War I Nationalism

A combination of hierarchical beliefs about relative groups' worth and a commitment to assimilation drove the content of American nationhood from the 1890s until the Second World War. This model had consequences for groups at all levels of American society. The effect was severest for groups considered inferior and outside or, at best, marginal to the nation, though which groups fitted these categories changed over time. The experience of ethnic Americans during World War I illustrates this dynamic.

Members of marginalized groups established routines to shield themselves against and eventually to challenge their inferior status. The world of African-American communities offered the resources for autonomous and strong identities to form, though always within the group boundaries set by a popular consciousness wedded to hierarchy.[1] Churches were important resources within segregated America. In addition, hierarchical codes had to be engaged politically and intellectually. Challenging hierarchy was essential politically as a step to reforming and revising the content of one-people nationalism. However, as this chapter explains, a first tentative step in this direction—to establish a racial equality clause in the League of Nations' constitution—failed in large part because of America's opposition. But the issue would return.

Hyphenated or Authentic Americans?

Theodore Roosevelt's description of hyphenated identity was unambiguous: "an American citizen [who] is really doing everything to subordinate the interests and duty of the United States to the interests of a foreign land."[2] Shared by other politicians, this view made being authentically American a challenge in the first half of the twentieth century. It promoted such a dichotomy in popular discourse.

Groups in the United States strive to assert their identity in the symbols, rituals, and myths through which the American nation is celebrated and remembered. Such symbolic inclusion permits not only a greater sense of membership but fortifies ethnic pride and distinctness. From the end of the nineteenth century, many ethnic groups asserted their authenticity as Americans and devised rituals to support this claim. In cities such as New York, San Francisco, St. Louis, Boston, New Orleans, and Philadelphia, annual *festa di Colombo* were organized by Italian Americans, to secure both the memory of Christopher Columbus among Americans and a positive place for Italian Americans in the United States' popular cultural consciousness and limited memory.[3] This second aim was important because of the harsh stereotypes about Southern and Eastern European immigrants common in American politics.[4] When President Benjamin Harrison made October 12, 1892, a public holiday (though it did not become a federal holiday until 1968), Italian Americans organized events to project an image of their ethnic community as integral to the United States' historical narrative and to remind themselves that they had a shared identity.

Modifying popular cultural perceptions and attitudes proved harder for German Americans. The Census conducted in 1910 counted 8 million people with German backgrounds, some 8.7 percent of the population; of these, almost 2.5 million had been born in Germany. German Americans' sense of community was cultivated through a host of organizations and activities. Festivals in Milwaukee, the United States' most German city, in the forty years up to 1910 were instrumental in forging bonds between newly arrived Germans in America and German Americans. The massive parade in 1871 that celebrated Germany's victory over France in the Franco-Prussian War was attended by 100,000 participants stretching in a six-mile procession of wagons and bands.[5] German

Americans' unity helped to preserve use of the German language and to build their self-confidence as an ethnic group in the United States entitled to its own identity and political influence. These aims were achieved. Huge crowds turned out to welcome the visiting brother of Emperor William II in March 1902. The National German-American Alliance, granted a federal charter in 1907, defended use of the German language and encouraged German Americans to be loyal U.S. citizens.

During the First World War, German Americans were suspected of supporting Germany. The National German-American Alliance's support for U.S. neutrality in 1914 and its intense German nationalism (a position shared in many German-American newspapers)[6] drew other Americans' wrath. What was promoted by the alliance as an argument for good German-U.S. relations could appear as unlimited support for the kaiser's regime. A conference of German Americans held in Washington, D.C., in January 1915 to support those in Congress advocating a neutral embargo policy was denounced in the *New York Times*: "[N]ever since the foundation of the Republic has a body of men assembled here who were so completely subservient to a foreign power and to foreign influence and none ever proclaimed the un-American spirit so openly."[7] Fingered by her neighbors, one German American found herself in a workhouse for six months for failing to display the American flag from her apartment window.[8]

The sinking of the *Lusitania*, a British transatlantic liner, by a German submarine provided the first opportunity for open expressions of simmering hostility, despite German-American condemnation of the attack. It was a poignant moment in American history for both German Americans and their fellow Americans. German Americans had certainly retained strong ethnic traditions and most held dual loyalties to both the United States and Germany, but their entrenchment in American society was incontrovertible. To find themselves subject to opprobrium was a shock. For other Americans, the claim to tolerance as a defining aspect of American nationhood was tested and, on occasion, discarded in their attitude toward German Americans.

Particularly after U.S. entry into the war in 1917, temperance was promoted as an American virtue, but it often served as a disguised form of anti-Germanism since many breweries were owned by German Americans. Haughtiness toward American culture, compared with

European literature and music, did not help the German-American profile.[9] German disappeared from school curricula.[10] Ohio's governor, James M. Cox, told his state legislature that the German language was "a distinct menace to Americanism."[11] German language books were censored in public libraries. Some school boards banned German literature and German music. By 1918, German church leaders had substituted the English version of their congregations' names for the German ones. German culture vanished as a part of American political culture.[12] In 1900, 600,000 students—4 percent of the school population—were learning German.[13] By the war's end, nineteen states had laws making English the exclusive language of instruction in schools, and some states excised German as an option in their schools' curricula.

The wartime propagandist Committee on Public Information published nine pamphlets in German, with such titles as *The Meaning of America, No Qualified Americanism,* and *Democracy: The Heritage of All.* The committee wanted German Americans to Americanize. Its pamphlet *American Loyalty* consisted of statements by American citizens of German descent espousing the virtues of American nationhood.[14] The number and circulation of German-language newspapers fell by 50 percent.[15] Three managers of the *Philadelphia Tageblatt* were sent to prison for printing antiwar stories. Acts of violence against German Americans grew from 1917, including one lynching.[16] Vigilante mobs set themselves up in numerous communities across the country and victimized, sometimes violently, German Americans for alleged disloyalty and un-Americanism. The German-American Alliance's branches began closing in 1917 and had all but disappeared by 1918. This trend did not stop a Senate investigation, instigated by Utah senator William H. King, in 1918. King suspected German Americans' loyalty, even those who had naturalized. King's bill to revoke the alliance's federal charter permitted two months of congressional hearings filled with hostile stories about the alliance and German Americans.[17] The special subcommittee recommended a revocation of the alliance's charter, a recommendation voted through the Senate on July 2, 1918, with House concurrence.

Aside from German Americans, the group most suspected of disloyalty were Irish Americans eager to exploit Britain's wartime hardship for their republicanism. The rebellion in Dublin on Easter 1916 had ardent support from Catholic Irish Americans, particularly the Clan na Gael in New York City. The clan raised funds for Irish republicans and orchestrated Sir Roger Casement's expedition to Germany in 1914 to win German support for the Irish rebellion. Many of the principals had traveled to or lived in the United States, including Eamon de Valera, who had been born there. (He avoided execution with the others because of his dual British-American citizenship.) The proclamation of independence issued by the nationalists on Easter Monday 1916 in Dublin cited the support of Ireland's "exiled children in America."[18] Irish-American republicans raised, in the five years after the rebellion, $10 million for the cause.[19] There was some censorship of nationalist Irish-American publications for their anti-British stances (for example, the *Gaelic American* and the *Bull* were denied access to federal mail), but little of the intense hostility experienced by German Americans befell the American Irish. Irish Americans were more assimilated by the time the United States entered the war. Lacking a distinctive language, they were less vulnerable to suspicion and criticism on this basis.

Both German Americans and Irish Americans were targets of the "100 percent Americanism" campaign. President Woodrow Wilson was joined by such luminaries as Theodore Roosevelt in condemning ethnic Americans' tepid nationalism. Wilson's exhortations to cast off group loyalties and subscribe to individualistic American nationalism were aimed at these Americans of Irish, German, and Italian descent. One of Wilson's strongest condemnations was delivered several days after the *Lusitania* sinking, and Wilson retained a suspicion of German Americans' collusion throughout the conflict. The American-Irish Historical Society, whose leaders were aware of the danger of appearing unpatriotic, made St. Patrick's Day a reminder of Irish-American contributions to the American Revolution and Civil War.[20] But the annual St. Patrick's Day parade and celebration, despite the recitation of oaths of allegiance to the United States on these occasions, was not enough to convince Wilson and others of Irish-American loyalty.

Other groups devised similar celebrations as they also came under suspicion. Sensitive about Norway's neutrality during the First World War, Norwegian Americans were keen to demonstrate their patriotism to the United States. Commemorative events were designed with this end in mind.[21] Polish Americans also held numerous commemorations in cities such as Chicago, which demonstrated their loyalties to the United States and to their home country. In Cleveland, the American-ization parade on the Fourth of July 1918 drew a crowd of 75,000, many of whom were ethnic immigrants eager to espouse loyalty to their new nation. They waved flags and wore red, white, and blue sashes embroi-dered with the inscription "America First." But ethnic groups also dis-played pride in their countries of origin by wearing native costumes or by displaying floats with national memorabilia.[22] Unusually, citizens of Cleveland wanted their war monuments to be inclusive and pluralistic rather than exclusionary. The mile-long Cleveland Cultural Gardens were built to celebrate both Americanization and the ethnic traditions making up American nationhood, diversity symbolized in the word *cultural* included in the memorial's title. The selection of symbols dis-played in the gardens was controlled by the Cleveland Cultural Gardens Federation, whose board had members from a range of (white) ethnic backgrounds.

But still fearful that nationhood was weakly established among many Americans, the U.S. government set up a national committee to orches-trate loyalty.

Forging National Identity

During World War I, the government established the Committee on Public Information (CPI) to instigate and promote support for the United States' war efforts.[23] In the CPI's booklet *Why We Are Fighting Germany*, Interior secretary Franklin Lane described America as "a living spirit" and asserted that it was "more precious that this America should live than that we Americans should live."[24]

Headed by Progressive George Creel, the primary aim of the committee's team of journalists, scholars, and artists was to engineer mass popular support for American participation in the Great War. Its work lacked the amateurish air of some fin de siècle Americanization and propaganda activities. Daily recitation of the Pledge of Allegiance was legislated.[25] And throughout the country, any expressions of hos-tility toward the American flag, no matter how casual or ironic, normally brought intense condemnation upon the perpetrator. Constitutional niceties about how the right of free speech included criticism of the flag received short shrift. Those defiling the American flag found themselves serving brief spells in prison. Indeed, wartime attitudes helped deepen the Stars and Stripes as a symbol of American nationhood. In this pre-radio era, the federal government paid for 75,000 "four-minute men" to visit public places, including churches and schools, to deliver patriotic speeches and news of the war's progress. As in 1898, war abroad was an opportunity to nation-build at home.

To muster support for the war effort, Creel's committee[26] opened offices in other countries, distributed publications defining America's role, submitted articles to the then-extensive foreign-language press in the United States (through its news division and *Official Bulletin*), and brought foreign newspaper reporters to America. The committee's reform-minded members embraced the Wilsonian aim to make the world safe for democracy. It propagated a one-people ideal of the American nation at home and abroad by stressing the freedom and democratic rights defended in the U.S. polity.

An advertising department at the committee undertook publicity campaigns in American newspapers and magazines to contrast America's democratic institutions and values with those of Germany's authoritarianism. The campaign distinguished democratic from hierarchy-based polities, a dichotomy with long-term implications for the United States' own nation-building. News content was controlled by the Division of News, which made every effort to influence the stories of print journalists, pressing reporters to write narratives hostile to the enemy and to stir up American nationalism. Under the division's watchful eyes, every news story about the war was censored or monitored at some point in its production; standardized information was circulated across the United States.[27] Powers established in the Espionage and Trading with the Enemy Acts of 1917 gave legal backbone to this regime of voluntary censorship. These powers were employed to tackle dissent about one-nation ideology and to help the "100 percent" view of an assimilationist ideology.

The Division of Civic and Educational Cooperation,[28] headed by an American historian of Germany,[29] coordinated patriotic exercises in high schools, turning commencement days into nationalist events. It distributed a vast array of works of popular scholarship, including *The*

War Message and *Facts behind It*.[30] Close to a hundred such pamphlets and booklets were produced by the division. The guiding aim was to encourage anti-German attitudes.[31]

The Committee on Public Information was an agent of American nationalism. It harnessed the energies of patriotic societies throughout the United States and planted nationalist sentiment where it was absent. The CPI's vision of democracy relied on that articulated by President Woodrow Wilson. Both the Fourteen Points and the president's speech upon entering the war were issued as pamphlets, which sold millions of copies and were translated into several languages. Beginning what was to become a historical theme, the CPI equated democracy with American ideals. The CPI's 300-page *War Cyclopedia: A Handbook for Ready Reference on the Great War* took a quotation from Woodrow Wilson to define Americanism as consisting "in utterly believing in the principles of America and putting them first as above anything that may come into competition with them."[32]

The CPI's bulletin, *National School Service*, published in 1918 and 1919, promoted national unity by setting out the duties of citizenship. It went directly to schools and parents.[33] Teachers supported the CPI's efforts enthusiastically. Indeed, the U.S. commissioner of education, Philander P. Claxton, observed, "There is no other group in our population so strategically situated for direct patriotic service as the teachers."[34] The bulletin contained a mixture of homilies on Americanization and stories about the war. Pupils were exhorted to help Americanize America, that is, to stir up ardent patriotism. The American way of life and democracy were exalted. As an instrument of patriotism, the bulletin was a further brick in the construction of American nationhood. Given the nationalist predisposition of teachers, it was, however, one which reinforced existing structures rather than creating new values.

African Americans rarely featured in nation-building initiatives and where they did, as in some propaganda films, it was in a limited and stereotypical way. Native Americans might as well have lived in a different country, despite the feats of enlisted Indians in the armed services.

The Creel committee's work extended abroad. Its foreign section established a worldwide network of foreign agents, who disseminated

American war aims and monitored what would now be defined as anti-Americanism. The rapturous welcome extended to Woodrow Wilson in Europe when he visited at the end of the war reflected in large part the success of these overseas agents in spreading information about America and promoting its way of life.[35] The section aimed to sow seeds to enhance America's appeal to European mass publics by contrasting and celebrating the United States' affluence and democratic openness with Old World hierarchies and austerity.

But this openness did not extend to democratic inclusion for certain groups at home or indeed abroad. As the next section discusses, in foreign policy, the United States was unwilling to break with a hierarchical view of the world's peoples.

A World Order without Racial Equality

Announcing American participation in the Great War to Congress in April 1917, Wilson identified the distinct purpose of U.S. policy. He declared:

> [T]he world must be made safe for democracy. . . . We entered the war as the disinterested champions of right. . . . we shall fight for the things which we have always carried nearest our hearts,— for democracy, for the right of those who submit to authority to have a voice in their own governments, for the rights and liberties of small nations, for a universal dominion of rights by such a concert of free peoples as shall bring peace and safety to all nations and make the world itself at last free.[36]

Wilson's language and war aims favored national self-determination, especially for small nations struggling to emancipate themselves from an external power. His vision was in line with a model of assimilative nationhood.

Wilson's stirring rhetoric led directly to the conception of a postwar global order of free and democratic states. This became a template for the Western world's struggle against undemocratic political systems based upon fascism, communism, or, indeed, as Wilson's Fourteen

Points made clear, imperialism. The president's capacity to recognize the newness of the Great War, which became known as the First World War, as an event in the international system and to compose an imaginative response to its novelty gave Wilsonianism its lasting quality.[37]

But Wilson's support of segregation at home clashed with the proposition that citizens had the right, as a consequence of submitting to authority, "to have a voice in their own governments." It was inevitable that his idealistic vision of a global order of free peoples would be used to confront the reality of a hierarchical domestic order in which African Americans in particular were segregated: pragmatism could not justify the overt conflict with ideals. This contradiction was seized upon by African-American leaders. The National Association for the Advancement of Colored People (NAACP) published its own Fourteen Point plan for achieving democracy in the United States, identifying a domestic equivalent for each of the points that Wilson had proposed as an international aim.[38] The NAACP exposed a weakness in the rhetoric and practice of American nationhood.

Nonetheless, World War I was a new kind of international engagement for the United States, completely different than, for instance, the expedition to the Philippines. Entering the conflict late, but with the burden of making the world safe for democracy, American soldiers proved an overwhelming presence in Europe. The United States' dominance, military and political, enabled President Wilson to orchestrate the postwar peace negotiations. Wilson's vision for the rebuilt nations of Europe and for the rights of new nations was one of states and individuals, not groups. Wilson's denouncement of hyphenated Americans and his conception of the United States' assimilationist one-nation ideology at home stemmed from his commitment to liberal democratic states based in individualism and his fear of group-based disunity.

He and other American leaders based their world vision on their conception of nation-building in the United States. Wilson's Fourteen Point agenda for a liberal world order, premised on establishing the dual principles of liberal democracy and national self-determination, did not include an assumption of racial equality, and his one-people rhetoric was not open to everyone. However, group-based divisions could not be kept at bay, since racial hierarchies were common in the United States and employed in other victors' language. At home, the Wilson administration entrenched segregated race relations in the federal government, fearful of upsetting white Americans and indifferent to African Americans' sensibilities or rights.

The paradox fostered by Woodrow Wilson's mixture of global liberalism and domestic racism was felt keenly by African Americans. In 1917, the year American troops were deployed in Europe, Black Americans who had moved to East St. Louis to work in wartime industries were set upon in a ferocious riot which cost forty lives. Fifty-eight African Americans were lynched that year. In the armed services, black recruits encountered racism and discrimination. They were assigned to segregated units commanded by white officers and quickly discovered that the units were employed principally in menial tasks, supporting, not engaging, in combat.

Negotiating the League of Nations showed just how important, internationally, divisions based in such group classifications as race were to American society and to the content of one-people American nationalism. In a widely reported speech delivered in New York, the Japanese ambassador to the United States, Ishii Kikujiro, called for the inclusion of a clause condemning racial discrimination in the league's founding document: "[W]hy should this question of race prejudice, of race discrimination, of race humiliation be left unremedied?"[39] He reassured Americans that such a measure would not be seen as an opportunity for unlimited Japanese immigration to the United States. This caveat did not preclude criticism of the ambassador's proposal.[40] At Paris, Wilson (egged on by his British colleagues) resisted the Japanese initiative. Some historians emphasize British fears for its empire as the main obstacle to the clause, but this underestimates Wilson's role. His views about the inferiority of peoples of color, expressed for instance in his consistent support of segregation, did not deviate from the prevailing scientific assumptions of the sort on display at the San Diego World Fair of 1915–1916.

The Japanese proposal came to a meeting of the League of Nations Commission, which was responsible for drafting the new organization's special tasks and was chaired by President Wilson. The Japanese looked to Wilson to deliver on his rhetorical commitment to an international order based in equality among peoples. Having failed in earlier discussions to budge Wilson's opposition to the clause, the Japanese delegate, Baron Nobuaki Makino, outlined his country's aspiration in a proposed amendment to the league's covenants: "[T]he equality of nations being a basic principle of the League of Nations, the High Contracting Parties agree to accord, as soon as possible, to all alien nationals of States [that are] members of the League equal and just treatment in every respect, making no distinction, either in law or in fact, on account of their race or nationality."[41]

The commission reconvened a month later at Versailles, and Baron Makino again advanced the justice of such an amendment.[42] President Wilson was warned by his chief of staff and confidant, Colonel Edward House, that passage of the clause "would surely raise the race issue throughout the world."[43] By this, House and his colleagues meant that existing systems of racial inequality in European states and empires, as well as practices in the United States, would become politically salient as critics of such systems argued for their abolition. Although it was supported by eleven of the seventeen delegations present, Chairman Wilson dismissed the clause on the grounds that equality was an implicit principle of the league anyway and, inventing a procedure on the spot, declared that unanimity was required for its adoption, a condition not invoked for two previous amendments. By "throughout the world," Colonel House can hardly have excluded politics at home in America.

The outcome was widely reported in the American press as a defeat for Japan and a victory for Wilson (the *Sacramento Union* headline read: "Peace Delegates Beat Japan's Proposal for Racial Equality").[44] Wilson must have felt some ambivalence, however, since he must have recognized that this was a poor start for the league. Although not an imperialist and a statesman with no imperial ambitions for the United States, Wilson was nonetheless not an advocate of racial equality and realized that if such a clause were included in the league's covenant, it would have profound implications for American politics—and he was certainly far more concerned about the rise of Bolshevism.

African Americans supported the proposal for a racial equality clause and lobbied the Japanese before the peace conference convened. The significance of Japanese ambitions lay in a historical perspective which viewed their nation—long, together with China, treated as inferior by

Western leaders—as potential rivals to Western power. Rejection of the amendment reinforced the view among African-American intellectuals such as W. E. B. Du Bois and James Weldon Johnson that without national representation of peoples of color in the league, racism would be unaddressed. Their criticism of Japanese imperialism, however, was rather muted.[45]

The failure of Wilson to resist British hostility toward a racial equality clause (and indeed Wilson's own lack of enthusiasm for such a measure) cast a long shadow abroad and at home. This policy would have knocked a hole in the imperial edifice and challenged the way in which language about group hierarchies and differences was employed politically.

As it was, this hierarchical language remained prevalent. Politicians and law makers in the United States often continued to see the world, during the interwar decades, in terms of "sensible white rule" versus primitive "yellow" or "brown" peoples. Domestic characterization of "Asian Orientals," the product of social scientific studies in the 1920s, privileged such language.[46] One senior U.S. Army staff officer's understanding of the Far East rested on enforcing white control of "yellow or brown races of limited development, the majority of whom are constantly stirred by sentiment or propaganda to throw aside Western control."[47] The secretary of State, Henry Stimson, accepted that the United States had to participate in "the white man's burden."[48] These comments, of course, reflect assumptions not just of Americans; they were shared by statesmen in Western countries keen to retain their empires and, for the most part, incapable of imagining how countries and peoples over whom they felt superior might overthrow them and formulate narratives of their history which lacked Western triumphalism as its culmination.

The Wilsonian declaration of self-determination threw a spotlight upon political regimes which failed to provide equal citizenship to all of their members. The failure of the Japanese proposal in 1919 made the struggle for racial equality a global rather than an exclusively American issue, something African Americans already grasped. One African-American professor at Howard University, Kelly Miller, presciently spelled out this implication of Wilson's principles: "[T]here exists among modern statesmen and publicists the complaisant delusion that they can indulge in universal declarations of the rights of man, while the ears of the weaker people are too dull to hear and their minds too feeble to understand. But when Pandora's box is once opened, it can never be closed."[49]

When Americanization interacted with patriotic needs, such as during World War I, the dynamics of nation-building were most intense. To secure the cause of one-people nationalism, political leaders disparaged ethnic loyalty as incompatible with American politics. In this setting, the war loosened ethnic affinities in the short term as white Americans rushed to be part of the "real" camp. Others were not yet afforded the opportunity for membership no matter how much they Americanized, and wartime nationalism underscored this exclusion.

Victory in 1918 prompted a wave of commemorations consistent with the type of nationalism the war had encouraged. In 1921 the Tomb of the Unknown Soldier was unveiled at the military cemetery in Arlington, Virginia, depicting ordinary soldiers as defenders of American democratic values. Eight permanent war memorials (six in Belgium, one each in France and Britain) were built by the War Department. In Newark, New Jersey, the sculpture *Wars of America* was unveiled in 1926. The sculpture consisted of forty-two figures representing American soldiers in all conflicts from the Revolutionary War to the Great War. In the artwork, soldiers are embraced by parents and family before departing for war; this figurative device bonded civilians and soldiers in the defense of a shared American nationhood. But only white soldiers were included, and even in this population doubts about German Americans endured.

The apparent pulling together and the sidelining of group loyalties achieved in World War I nationalism was less deep and more exclusive than it appeared at the time. This superficiality rested principally on the differential treatment of groups in the one-people ideology of American nationhood. As the chapters in part II will explain, this ideology was vulnerable to change but not in the way usually understood in narratives of American nation-building. On the contrary, a nonteleological reversion to groups was on the agenda, though few realized this at the end of the 1930s.

PART II ◈

I nternational influences are increasingly identified as a strong force impelling the United States to devise laws and institutions addressing civil rights violations and other sources of group discrimination.[1] This pressure centered on giving equal rights of membership and democratic inclusion to all Americans regardless of any group identity they proclaimed or found imputed to them. The reform of civil rights seemed to mark the arrival of individualism in the ideology of American nationhood. Yet group divisions and identities remained intact despite this set of reforms and despite the international pressures to shift to assimilated nationalism. It is this effect which is investigated in the chapters in part II.

All political ideologies of nationhood are necessarily unfinished since the future challenges that nation-builders will face are unpredictable. However, as World War II erupted in Europe, many Americans were confident that a form of assimilated nationhood had been achieved in the United States sufficient to the task of political integration and, in providing a standard for membership, capable also of accommodating future demands for inclusion: members of the polity were expected to assimilate, cast off group identities, and rally to the one-people creed. A government report in 1938 on "problems of a changing population" confidently reviewed the United States' success in integrating its different groups.[2] But as both wartime pressures and political events in the ensuing decades would demonstrate, this assumption was flawed.

With the great benefit of hindsight, it is plain that the demands of mobilization in the Second World War deeply challenged the presumption of equality promoted in the ideology of American assimilationist nationalism. This external engagement exposed group inequalities at home. Franklin Roosevelt's preferred form of address during this global catastrophe—"my fellow Americans"—rested upon an unrealized equality of membership. An irrepressible debate over internal membership commenced as national and international expectations about democratic inclusion advanced. The subsequent widening of membership did not, however, occur overnight or spontaneously. Nor did the struggle for individual rights implode group identities.

Why did the model of assimilationist nationhood in place by the end of the 1930s prove inadequate as a long-term solution for the American polity? The short-term sources of instability are readily identifiable. They include the burgeoning grassroots movements against discrimination and inequality of treatment orchestrated by African Americans and other groups, such as Latinos and Native Americans. The U.S. Supreme Court gradually accepted legal challenges to segregation, culminating with the *Brown* decision in 1954. The powerful new human rights regime created in the United Nations and disseminated through its Universal Declaration on Human Rights, a document which U.S. representatives helped to draft, proved a new set of influences and standards about equality and democratic inclusion to which critics of assimilationist nationhood could appeal.

But there is a deeper long-term reason for this instability, intrinsic to the ideology of American nationhood. The expectation, explicit for instance in Lyndon Johnson's Howard University speech in 1965 with which this book opened, that a condition of liberal individualism, the idealized melting pot, would be expressed in American nationhood clashes with the need to accommodate group-based demands for democratic inclusion. These group divisions are of such historical significance that they continue profoundly to shape American politics and conceptions of American nationhood. Instead of displacing group divisions and sources of identity, new arrivals in the United States ensure their reinforcement, revision, and reconfiguration. For instance, immigrants from Latin American countries find themselves lumped into a grouping called "Latino" in American public discourse. Their place in the American nation is defined as that of a distinct group rather than simply as individuals with rights of citizenship (or without rights). Even though the group Latino includes massive internal heterogeneity (contrast Cuban Americans with Mexican Americans, for example), cultural and political rhetoric presumes a delineated group whose membership in the nation rests on identification with that group. The parallel with nineteenth-century expectations about groups is striking; at that time, for example, all American Indians were categorized into a single entity.

Attention to group demands about membership accelerated after 1941, driven by America's international roles. Without this external context, the pressures to change the content of American nationhood would have been far weaker. The irresistible populism and equality of wartime helped international challenges to colonialism, a prelude to its eventual toppling. The ideological and political justifications for imperial power dissolved, including the spurious doctrine of racial hierarchy. The old mantra of the right to national self-determination revived, not only in respect to Western colonies but later in the century as an aspiration of those nations controlled by the Soviet Union. The UN was a decisive institution in this respect. Its Universal Declaration of Human Rights, adopted in December 1948, proclaimed "recognition of the inherent dignity and of the equal and inalienable rights of all members of the human family" and warned that no distinctions should be drawn among individuals in respect to race or other essentialist classifications. This formulation marked a shift from the right of self-determination for nations to a concern equally with individual rights within and across nations. The UN's charter made the protection of individual rights a priority. Eleanor Roosevelt, closely involved in drafting the UN's Universal Declaration, wrote in 1948, "[T]he conditions of our contemporary world require the enumeration of certain protections which the individual must have if he is [to] acquire a sense of security and dignity in his own person."[3] This message could not be limited to an overseas audience: it would have profound resonance back home too, adding to the pressures to address group-based discrimination.

Making American nationhood democratically inclusive entailed the enforcement of civil rights, redressing historical injustices, and revisiting the memories of Americans' national narrative. In each area, the content of one-people inclusion was engaged with and revised both in ways justified by reference to a shared ideology of American nationalism and in ways that recognized that cross-generational reconciliation is a key aspect of democratic nation-building. In other words, the role of one-people nationalism remained that of providing a political glue for Americans, but the content of the doctrine was stretched, modified, and challenged to make membership more inclusive for new arrivals. These modifications were never uncontested nor straightforward, and broadened membership in one sphere was sometimes qualified by contraction in some other respect. Such revisions lay out the nonteleological character of American nationalism: to conceive of the United States' national narrative simply as an unending movement toward liberal individualism is too limited a perspective.

In chapter 6, we will see how wartime mobilization against fascism and racism abroad inflamed racial and ethnic divisions at home and the difficulty of suppressing group-based issues in the political agenda. This struggle centered on the invalidity of retaining group hierarchies, which were based on dubious "scientific" doctrines, in the prevailing values of American nationhood. Chapter 7 examines the way in which the United States' role in supporting anticolonial movements and other expressions of democracy abroad linked the nation further with a Wilsonian doctrine of national self-determination. This connection should have intensified the domestic reforms shifting the values of American nationhood away from group hierarchy toward one-people democratic inclusion. It did have this effect to some extent.

But, as chapter 8 will show, while the confrontation between America's role as a promoter of liberal democracy abroad and its domestic inequalities was used by critics of the United States to reveal failings in its treatment of groups at home, in the long run this confrontation did little to erode the lines of division. America's nation-building has been an internal process differentiating among, and then accommodating across, group divisions and classifications. Consequently, the major international pressures for reform have worked to highlight deficiencies in the rhetoric of one-people solidarity but not in practice to render individualism the dominant ethos in America's ideology of nationhood.

6 ❖

World War II and the Challenge to Assimilation

World War II made America an international force and a global presence.[1] This role was bound to influence the domestic pattern of group divisions and inequalities. Principally, this international exposure and related external engagements sharpened awareness about group divisions within the United States. Those groups already excluded from complete membership mobilized in anger about their second-class citizenship when called upon to defend values abroad that were denied them at home. And Americans again found themselves differentiating internally between some citizens as full members, such as ethnic Americans, and others as unfit for this status, judging, for example, Japanese Americans to be doubtful members of the nation.

America's role as a wartime leader of liberal democracy and of the Western democratic tradition accentuated the significance of these conflicts about group membership. The United States led efforts to implant democratic institutions and values in postwar Germany and Japan and to build a new post–world war order centered on the United Nations and the accompanying commitment to human rights. All of these activities enhanced the international perception of American nationhood as a standard bearer of assimilated nationalism and liberal democracy. America's external propaganda initiatives also played this role by promoting the view that group hierarchies were of declining importance to the country's domestic politics.

Did this increased awareness of group inequalities, prompted by greater openness to international influences and pressures, succeed in making reform of civil rights and other aspects of group discrimination more substantial or in shifting American nationhood toward individualism? The next two chapters take up these issues. In this chapter, an account of how wartime intensified the political salience of group divisions in American society is first developed, followed by consideration of the way in which war mobilization also propelled the United States into a more significant global presence, increasingly vulnerable to international influences and scrutiny of its domestic practices.

War and Group Divisions

War mobilization is a classic occasion for one-people exhortations and appeals to set aside group demands in favor of collective effort. There was plenty of such rhetoric and a good deal of pulling together by Americans between 1941 and 1946. Yet there were powerful impulses in other directions. Japanese Americans found themselves outside the nation's membership physically, through internment, and African Americans had to reconcile the searing racism endured at home with calls to fight nations defined as enemies in part because of their racism. Combined, these and other tensions meant that the war years changed indelibly what constituted American nationalism as a doctrine able to integrate Americans around a shared vision of nationhood. The trajectory of assimilationist nationalism was fundamentally challenged, halting the apparent rise of melting-pot individualism.

"TO SHAKE UP WHITE AMERICA"

American failure to tackle domestic racial inequality prompted the novelist Richard Wright to write an essay in June 1941 entitled "Not My People's War."[2] Unlike W. E. B. Du Bois, who in 1918 penned an editorial in *Crisis* urging African Americans to postpone the pursuit of racial equality until the European war ended, Wright could now see no reason for blacks to participate in a U.S. war which might make no difference to their status in American society. It was this fundamental contradiction between mobilizing the country to defeat fascism and racism overseas while remaining a hierarchical society, wedded to codes rooted in ethnic, racial, and nationality differences, which World War II presented.

Wartime racism evoked a range of responses from African-American intellectuals and activists, some urging enlistment, others like Wright recommending against any accommodation with such racist institutions as the military. Paul Robeson stressed the continuity between Western indifference to Italy's seizure of Ethiopia in 1935[3] and the failure to address the position of African Americans. Nazism and racism were disturbingly indistinguishable: "[T]hey speak the same language of the 'Master Race' and practice, or attempt to practice, the same tyranny over minority peoples."[4] Malcolm X (or Malcolm Little, as he was then) avoided the service by telling the draft board he wanted to arm Black Americans to fight white society. Although the majority of African Americans ignored Wright's and Robeson's advice in 1941–1945, they did expect economic amelioration and civil rights. Membership in the NAACP increased tenfold during the war years, from 50,000 in 1940 to a half million members in 1946, organized through more than 1,000 local branches.[5]

Some Black Americans responded to this international opportunity by declaring a Double V campaign: victory against the foreign enemy, Japan, and the enemy at home, racial prejudice. The editor of the *Pittsburgh Courier* wrote, "[C]ertainly we should be strong enough to whip both of them."[6] A few weeks later, the *Chicago Defender* initiated a similar double war aim.[7]

Washington's political and military leaders feared that the Double V campaign would dilute the war effort. Writing from the British embassy in Washington, the philosopher Isaiah Berlin reported that many African Americans considered the war "a white man's conflict."[8] To counter this impression, the U.S. Senate's Foreign Relations Committee began openly to advocate independence for India, and the White House urged the British government to adopt a new approach. One African-American sociologist wrote in the middle of the war that "India and the possibility of the Indians obtaining their freedom . . . have captured the imagination of the American Negro."[9]

Decolonization and other nationalist movements placed American racism as not just an isolated peculiarity but as part of a global experience.

The struggle against imperialism in India, Burma, Africa, Malaya, the West Indies, and South America were all written about in the black American press.[10] The federal government's repeal of the Chinese Exclusion laws in 1943 and 1944, motivated by international calculations, seemed ironic to many African Americans, given the federal government's jejune initiatives to uphold racial equality and to end lynching.

Many Black Americans encountered employment discrimination especially in the defense sector.[11] Mobilizing this African-American economic pressure to achieve political gain by renegotiating the boundaries of political membership, the March on Washington movement led by trades unionist A. Philip Randolph extracted President Franklin Roosevelt's reluctant agreement to establish the Fair Employment Practices Committee in 1941 and to issue an executive order proscribing discrimination.[12]

Randolph's threatened protest was superbly timed. Uniting "the masses for a definite purpose,"[13] Randolph frightened the Roosevelt administration with his demands for access to defense jobs and equal opportunities in the armed forces. Frenetic negotiations between White House contacts and African-American leaders initially failed to halt the march, scheduled for July 1, 1941. Extensive discussions produced an acceptable draft executive order (despite opposition from the War and Navy departments) to establish a committee to enforce fair employment. To Roosevelt's relief, the protest was called off.

The March on Washington Committee[14] did not just lobby for better employment opportunities under federal supervision. It challenged the social order structuring African-American membership in the polity. The movement rejected the servile status imposed on African Americans by segregation. Randolph restricted membership in the organization to African Americans. But Randolph was promoting neither black separatism nor a back-to-Africa agenda.

Randolph believed that decisively and permanently to end the pattern of black-white relations protected in segregation required building self-esteem around a "pro-Negro" movement.[15] Randolph planned to "shake up white America."[16] Rather than conferences and meetings, this agenda required direct protest action of the sort he proposed: 50,000 to 100,000 African Americans marching down Pennsylvania Avenue in Washington, D.C., to demand equal rights at work and in the military.

In promoting the imaginative leap necessary to see citizens of color as equal members of the nation with all of the attendant rights of citizenship, Randolph took a crucial step toward reconfiguring American nationalism to be democratically inclusive. He forced the question: how can a one-people ideology coexist with group discrimination?

Wartime provided Randolph's moment for action but the question long outlasted the war. The struggle against Jim Crowism in public places was a logical extension of the March on Washington tactic and was endorsed, after Randolph's advocacy, by the movement's conference in Detroit in September 1942. The instigator of the Montgomery bus boycott in 1955, Rosa Parks, was a veteran of the March on Washington movement.

What proved in retrospect to be a turning point in the civil rights struggle for African Americans and therefore for the content of American nationhood was enabled significantly by the external engagement of the Second World War. Without this catalyst highlighting group divisions in America, change would have been even slower. For other groups, however, wartime meant a contraction of membership and a demonstration of the limits of assimilationist nationalism as a doctrine of inclusion.

INTERNMENT

On February 19, 1942, two months following the Japanese attack on Pearl Harbor, President Franklin Roosevelt signed Executive Order 9066,[17] interning Japanese Americans as a matter, in the judgment of War secretary Henry L. Stimson, of "military necessity."[18] Despite protestations of loyalty to the United States (the Japanese-American Citizens' League had lobbied intensely for the right to naturalize) and in the absence of material evidence of sedition, more than 100,000 Japanese Americans were forced to sell their property and relocate to assembly centers and then to confinement camps located in the United States' interior.[19]

The U.S. Supreme Court unanimously upheld the constitutionality of military curfew regulations imposed on American citizens under the war powers.[20] The government's submission to the Court about the threat posed by Japanese Americans was partial, thereby giving the justices an exaggerated view of the dangers posed by failure to intern.[21] In a second case,[22] the Court upheld the legality of evacuating U.S. citizens of Japanese ancestry, though three justices dissented, holding relocation to be unconstitutional. In his dissent, Justice Frank Murphy characterized the majority verdict as the "legalization of racism."[23] (Closer to the dissenters' view was the 1944 decision *Ex parte Endo*[24] which declared retention of a citizen by the War Relocation Authority [WRA] illegal, in the absence of a charge, once his or her loyalty had been established.)

Existing and overt racism and prejudicial sentiment toward Japanese Americans had erupted in the wake of the Pearl Harbor bombing. Those already suspicious of or hostile toward Japanese Americans, such as populist newspaper columnist Harry McLemore, white California farmers, and West Coast army commander John De Witte, expressed their views more virulently. De Witte, for example, objected to Japanese Americans' "racial" connections with Japan and Asia. Other politicians and commentators, such as Attorney General Francis Biddle and writer Walter Lippmann, were reluctantly drawn into an increasingly hostile environment in which the most vocal participants, inside and outside government, demanded internment despite the doctrine of habeas corpus.[25] Hysteria was whipped up with rumors about imminent invasions and fifth columnists. The cumulative effect was an undemocratic incarceration.[26]

Popular and academic depictions of Japanese people, seen as part of America's "Orientals,"[27] were harsh. Media coverage did not consider Germans of the wartime Third Reich a different species, even after disclosure of the Holocaust. Nazis were bad Germans,[28] which implied the existence of good Germans, whereas the prospect for such reformable Japanese was dim.[29] Contrasting perceptions of Germans and Japanese built on long-standing views. Not only had Japanese immigrants been singled out as one group purposefully to be excluded from easy entry to the United States whereas Germans were one of the few beneficiaries of the restrictive 1924 immigration law, but Japanese Americans were perceived as a security threat precisely because of their difference.[30] President Roosevelt encouraged "scientific" investigations of Japanese skull sizes. Experts hypothesized that the alleged temporal difference in the development of Western and Asian brains might account for the latter's badness.[31]

Wartime encourages simplistic portrayals of enemies, particularly as defending the nation is so critical. Its atmosphere sharpens the division between inclusion and exclusion. Japanese Americans immigrants were scapegoats and among those considered unassimilable, and this history provided a source of prejudices and stereotypes with which to characterize the Pacific enemy.[32] Just as sociologists in the 1920s helped construct an "Oriental American,"[33] so cultural anthropologists' research now provided an important frame of reference.[34] Experts and popularizers attributed a herd mentality to Japanese people. Japanese national character was described in terms of clinical and emotional maladies, of the sort common in arrested adolescence.[35]

Both first-generation Japanese Americans, known as Issei, who retained Japanese nationality because they were denied the right to naturalize, and their American-citizen children, known as Nisei, were interned. Issei and Nisei constituted 30 and 70 percent, respectively, of the 112,000 people directed by the War Department, under Executive Order 9066, to leave the West Coast. Many sold their possessions for ludicrously low sums. To demonstrate their loyalty, others had already destroyed any Japanese items that their families owned. They were permitted to bring only a small number of items with them; the rest of their property was stored in warehouses. All of this was done hastily and for many was a traumatic experience well depicted in Julie Otsuka's novel *When the Emperor Was Divine.*[36] One Japanese American recalled his wartime incarceration thus: "I couldn't believe this was happening to us. . . . This is the greatest country in the world. So I thought this is only going to be for a short while." It was not to be: "But after several months they told us this was just temporary quarters, and they were building more permanent quarters elsewhere in the United States. All this was so unbelievable. A year before we would never have thought anything like this could have happened to us—not in this country."[37] Internment signaled a sharp redrawing of the boundaries of membership permissible in an American nationhood described as one people.

After much lobbying from his own staff and the WRA, President Roosevelt did issue a statement on February 1, 1943, intended to reassure Japanese Americans. Rehearsing the ideology of one-people American nationalism, he proclaimed, "Americanism is a matter of mind and heart; Americanism is not, and never was, a matter of race or ancestry."

And in March, Roosevelt added, "[T]hese citizens of Japanese ancestry are no more enemy aliens than are citizens of Italian or German parentage."[38] These public interventions were not unmindful of America's international role as a defender of democracy, a role which had grown in significance as the war developed. But privately, Roosevelt's suspicion of Japanese Americans and his indifference to their fate was undiminished.[39] The president's action contradicted the speech's sentiment. Japanese Americans' disloyalty was inferred by many ordinary Americans. Internment strengthened this inference.[40]

Incarceration underlined the "another-nation" status of Japanese Americans at that time. This separateness seemed justified by their alleged "racial-ethnic" difference, which made them unsuitable for equal membership. Group hierarchical presumptions about membership in the American nation shaped this perception. In its group specificity, the executive order used government authority to override civil rights and to differentiate the terms of political membership. Attorney General Biddle later concluded that interning Japanese Americans but not German or Italian Americans reflected "the racial prejudice that seemed to be influencing everyone" and was based not on "the logic of events or on the weight of evidence."[41]

The camps closed in 1946. Because of continuing public hostility, the decision, from November 1944, to authorize the release of the internees was implemented cautiously and without any official statement. Aware of the antagonism facing returning Japanese Americans, Los Angeles's mayor, Fletcher Bowron, held civic events to celebrate American nationhood as inclusive. The city held a Franklin Delano Roosevelt Memorial and United Nations Rededication Program, which was attended by many Hollywood stars.[42] But such inclusive events were rare in the panoply of official expressions of patriotism. Japanese Americans' exclusion from the right to naturalize (until 1952) reflected and reinforced popular attitudes. And undoubtedly revulsion at wartime horrors perpetrated by the Japanese forces, often on American soldiers, was deep.

The conflict between the individualism and group politics of American nationalism is laid bare in this historical experience. As one incarcerated Japanese American wrote to a friend in 1942: "[T]ime and time again, I have argued that America is not a democracy for white people only. Was I wrong? God help us all if I am or was because what a future is in store for everyone in a false democracy!"[43] He was only half wrong.

Wartime internment showed how prejudices about groups could be mobilized to limit some members' rights despite a national rhetoric urging togetherness. It is how this language of one-people togetherness was used in wartime to which we now turn.

"A PEOPLE'S WAR, NOT A GROUP WAR"

Nicholas Ray's movie *Flying Leathernecks* (1951), set during the World War II battle of Guadalcanal, includes a scene in which a selection of the men's families are pictured at home receiving letters from their enlisted sons. These families are diverse—including Italian Americans, Native Americans, and Swedish Americans—and each is portrayed as staunchly patriotic. The same melting-pot story, limited to white ethnics, imbued the wartime movies Lewis Seiler's *Guadalcanal Diary* (1943) and Howard Hawks's *Air Force* (1943). The movies celebrate an American nationalism rooted in shared experience but genuflect to individualism and its defense. Their ethos was to show Americans from different groups working together to defend a one-people nation capable of fostering individualism. Writers and directors absorbed the wartime instruction to filmmakers that "there are still groups in this country who are thinking only in terms of their particular group. Some citizens have not been aware of the fact that this is a people's war, not a group war."[44] This language echoed Woodrow Wilson's homilies against hyphenated Americans in 1917.

In practice, the effect of wartime mobilization and propaganda on the United States' group-based polity was uneven.[45] This unevenness was however not entirely random. White ethnic groups such as German or Italian Americans were now in the "one nation," and on the basis of this integration many scholars predicted the decline and eventual elimination of group distinctions in American society.[46]

It was precisely this imagined future which group-based demands for democratic inclusion posed for nation-builders. Wartime presented a contradictory opportunity. Mobilization required channeling group diversity into a single purpose and thereby diluting group loyalties. Yet achieving that heightened togetherness benefited from a public acceptance of difference since this was part of what was worth fighting for.

In the years leading up to the war, some group-based divisions were less salient. The collapse of mass immigration dampened hostility toward European ethnic groups. This trend was picked up on by some federal law makers and politicians. A report on *The Problems of a Changing Population*, issued in 1938, went so far as to make group-based pluralism an American strength: "Americans have come to realize that while we do not have a wealth of cathedrals, fine carvings, old family customs, or a national folk music and literature, we do possess an abundance of cultural groups."[47] The report trumpeted a "new appreciation of cultural diversity," a view at variance with the more familiar rhetoric of assimilationist nationalism. While Americanization eroded many groups' values, there remained a sufficient "diversity of social values" to permit a "renewed emphasis on tolerance and experimentation in the realm of social relations."[48] Ironically, the report's authors commented favorably upon Japanese American assimilation.[49] They cited approvingly the Indian Reorganization Act (1934), under which Native Americans were offered tribal self-government mimicking U.S. constitutionalism on a microlevel.[50] However, the 1930s had not appreciably altered African Americans' position.

Although the new openness to ethnicity embraced Americans of German and Italian origin, Nazism did revive some hostilities toward Americans of German background. Nazi propagandists and apologists, such as the German-American Bund, were vilified. As one congressman declared, "[A]ny effort to organize Americans into a group or bloc based on racial lines, or as a result of intolerant views held toward other Americans, strikes at the fundamentals of our government."[51] This homily was delivered without irony, the speaker showing no knowledge of racial segregation. Most Americans descended from German or Italian immigrants had abandoned or suppressed their ethnic values and traditions during World War I or during later Americanization programs. German Americans were rarely seen as different from "real" Americans, which shows how the boundaries of membership in the nation change over time.

Other group divisions were unappreciated, and wartime did not hasten their acceptance. In June 1943 in Los Angeles, white servicemen attacked anyone wearing a zoot suit in the city's Mexican-American neighborhoods. For such citizens, there was scant evidence that the war was a "people's war."

African Americans encountered fierce racism and prejudice in the armed services. Rather than treating all draftees or volunteers as individuals, the U.S. armed services used group distinctions.[52] African Americans were consigned to segregated units. Puerto Ricans serving in the U.S. military during the Second World War were segregated into the 65th Infantry Regiment, partly for linguistic reasons, and were again segregated during the Korean War. A unit of volunteer Japanese-American Nisei, the 442d Combat Infantry Battalion, under white officers, was formed and became the most decorated unit in the army during the war. African Americans were segregated to preclude their assimilation whereas assigning Native American recruits throughout the armed services was intended to advance their integration.

Even the tepid guarantees to avoid discrimination and segregation of trainees, set out in the Selective Service and Training Act of 1940, were ignored by the War Department. Aware that the New Deal had largely failed African Americans, Franklin Roosevelt set out the model of gradual integration, which he anticipated in war:

> [W]e've got to work into this. Now, suppose you have a Negro regiment . . . *here*, and right over here on my right in line, would be a white regiment . . . Now what happens after a while, in case of war? Those people get shifted from one to the other. The thing gets sort of backed into . . . gradually working in the field together, you may back into it.[53]

The problem with this sanguine scenario was that so few African-American GIs were placed in combat roles that opportunities for such intermixing were rare. The "band of brothers" was white. A White House press release in October 1940 confirming the policy of Jim Crow segregation in the War Department was unpromising:[54] "[T]o make changes now would produce situations destructive to morale and detrimental to the preparation for national defense."[55]

The War Department was not eager to reform.[56] Even after the passage of the Selective Service Act of 1942, which beefed up these requirements, recruitment and training of African Americans was lackadaisical and hesitant. Proposals in the same year for modest inroads into segregation were rejected by the War and Navy departments. Chief of Staff George Marshall thought such measures would damage military efficiency and discipline.

African-American newspapers monitored conditions in the armed forces.[57] Their coverage ensured that the domestic and foreign experiences of black soldiers were relayed to African-American communities. The contradiction between mobilizing to defend democracy and the mistreatment of black recruits was a constant theme in reports. Editorials underlined the damage done to one-people nationhood by this incongruity: the war gave a new emphasis to this theme.

Black American recruits' infelicitous wartime experiences have been widely documented. White officers, often southerners, frequently abused their positions of authority in commanding African-American units; few black GIs were promoted; inadequately trained military police handled African-American recruits roughly, on occasion provoking riots;[58] segregated training facilities for white and African-American units were unequal; in the Navy, black enlistees were virtually restricted to positions serving white crews; the location of training stations in the South resulted in unpleasant, often violent, incidents; few African Americans served in combat roles, most working in service units; and, as in World War I, segregated conditions were transplanted to the overseas bases on which black GIs served, notably those in Britain.

At all levels of the military and in each service, white officers and recruits were the products of a society which had made African-American subjugation a cornerstone of its political culture for more than a half century, rationalized with spurious beliefs about natural group hierarchies. This prejudice had not been much disturbed even during the radical New Deal reforms in the 1930s. How could this set of circumstances fail to provoke a questioning, if not downright cynical, reflection upon the United States' mission in the Second World War to be, in Franklin Roosevelt's words "the great arsenal of democracy"?

Recognizing the electoral and political need for cosmetic improvement,[59] President Roosevelt appointed William Hastie, from Howard University, as civilian aide on Negro affairs to the secretary of War and promoted Benjamin O. Davis, Sr., to the rank of brigadier general. But

Hastie resigned after being frustrated in his efforts to weaken segregation in the armed forces.[60] His successor made some achievements largely because riots in training camps and defense industry cities pressured the government to act.

Close to 400,000 Mexican Americans served in the U.S. armed services, many winning medals for bravery.[61] In killing more than 100 Germans in the Krinkelt Wald (in Belgium), machine gunner Sergeant Jose M. Lopez, from Brownsville, Texas, struck down more enemy soldiers than any other member of the U.S. armed services during World War II.[62] The war strengthened Mexican-American political status in the nation by asserting their claim to equal membership. This mantle was picked up by the next generation to reach voting age and by the Chicano movement, which developed in the 1950s and 1960s among Mexican Americans to challenge assimilationist nationhood.[63]

Aside from sustaining historical forms of group discrimination at home, America's racism increasingly clashed with the image of American nationhood promoted abroad, both directly in its propaganda efforts and implicitly in its international roles. It is these tensions which the next section addresses.

War and America Abroad

Franklin D. Roosevelt, president between 1933 and 1945, was a long-standing internationalist. He had campaigned, as the Democratic party vice-presidential nominee in 1920, for U.S. membership in the League of Nations. Having steered a precarious path between neutrality and support of the Allies, Roosevelt now mobilized American forces in response to the "date that will live in infamy" (December 7, 1941). In the previous ten years, the United States had watched the League of Nations ignore Japanese expansionism, Italian imperialism in Ethiopia, German aggression, and the Soviet Union's alignment with Nazism. Such inaction turned American public opinion against interventionism. Toward Latin and Central America, the Good Neighbor policy aimed to support or install democracy. It had mixed results. Under his administration, independence of the Philippines from the United States was finalized, and policies toward Central and Latin America were noninterventionist (the United States pointedly did not invade Cuba in 1933 when a left-wing president challenged American material interests and withdrew troops from Haiti in 1934).[64] Echoing Woodrow Wilson's vision, Franklin Roosevelt proclaimed in Argentina, "[D]emocracy is still the hope of the world. If we in our generation can continue its successful application in the Americas, it will spread and supersede other methods by which men are governed."[65] Franklin Roosevelt now had a global stage on which to issue descriptions of America's professed self-presentation.

Two examples—America's support of anticolonialism and of racial equality at the United Nations and the United States' role in fostering democracy in the defeated nations of Japan and Germany—show how the United States' international image as an articulator and defender of liberal democracy intensified with the pressures of war and stoked expectations about the postwar order.

TURNING AGAINST COLONIALISM

The Atlantic Charter was the product of a meeting between Great Britain's Winston Churchill and President Franklin Roosevelt, held in Placentia Bay off the coast of Newfoundland in August 1941 to discuss joint war aims. Lend-lease was in place but the United States had yet to join the conflict. Rather, as Woodrow Wilson had made the United States' role in "saving democracy" a correlate of his vision of a liberal state system resting on national self-determination, so Roosevelt was thinking ahead to the terms upon which American intervention in the war could be justified to his voters at home. For President Roosevelt, the charter gave "meaning to the conflict between civilization and arrogant, brute challenge."[66]

From the beginning, the White House's draft of aims for the meeting specified anticolonialism, that is, the illegitimacy of imperial powers controlling colonies and the rights of colonial peoples to independence and self-determination. The final text had eight propositions, including sovereign rights and self-government for all peoples ("they respect the right of all peoples to choose the form of government under which they will live") and opposition to the undemocratic restructuring of territorial boundaries ("they desire no territorial changes that do not accord with the freely expressed wishes of the people concerned"). The significance of these principles for colonial peoples was endorsed by African-American leaders, including W. E. B. Du Bois and A. Philip Randolph.

For British prime minister Winston Churchill, the Atlantic Charter's anti-imperialism was a difficult pill to swallow. Even before the Japanese attack on Pearl Harbor, the British political elite had feared that the United States would make independence for India a condition of American participation in the war. They wanted to get the leader of the Labour party, Clem Attlee, to make a speech, aimed at Americans, justifying imperial policy in India, believing that such a left-wing source would help bolster the British imperial case.[67]

An editorial in the *Bombay Chronicle* described the charter as a "Magna Carta of the World" which would apply to India.[68] Churchill simply rejected this implication.[69] In 1945 at Yalta, Churchill would only sign the U.S.-drafted Declaration on Liberated Europe on the condition that citing the Atlantic Charter had no implications for the British Empire.[70] Roosevelt warned the British prime minister that "as a people, as a country, we're opposed to imperialism."[71] The charter plainly precluded a mechanical reconstitution of the old order.[72] Roosevelt despaired of Prime Minister Churchill's expectation that imperialism would be restored: "Dear old Winston will never learn on that point."[73]

For Roosevelt, restoration of the colonial order was unimaginable, a view expressed in the charter and subsequently in the founding of the United Nations. When the major powers (Britain, the United States, the Soviet Union, and China) jointly issued with twenty-two other countries on January 1, 1942, the declaration of the United Nations, it embodied the principles of the Atlantic Charter.

The Atlantic Charter had symbolic importance. Despite his anti-imperialism, President Franklin D. Roosevelt was unwilling to exert much pressure on imperialistic countries to reform. This reluctance disappointed African Americans, including members of the NAACP who, from the late 1930s, emphasized the transnational comparisons and links between their domestic circumstances and those of people of color in other countries. Fearing to upset allies, Roosevelt's silence when the British arrested Gandhi and others in August 1942 revealed the limits of America's anti-imperialism: high on rhetoric and symbolism, it too often lacked punch. Nonetheless, the United States wanted to be seen as anti-imperialist. The NAACP's Walter White told Roosevelt, "[O]ne billion brown and yellow peoples in the Pacific will without question consider ruthless treatment of Indian leaders and people typical of what white peoples will do to colored peoples if the United States wins."[74] By the founding meetings for the United Nations, the United States had yet formally to condemn colonialism although the Atlantic Charter did so pretty clearly.

The principle of racial equality had been lost at the founding of the League of Nations. Many of its advocates were determined to prevent a similar omission from the United Nations. It required U.S. support. In April 1945, those attending the San Francisco conference to draft the United Nations' charter could not ignore the subject. Walter White, for one, thought this was the opportunity to establish an equality clause and to link it with decolonization as well as domestic reform in the United States. As the *Chicago Defender* editorialized in 1945, "[T]he Negro is the colonial of America."[75] The war's end coincided with a growth in racially motivated attacks. How America acted at the United Nations would therefore be important for the ideology of American nationhood at home.

From the outbreak of the Second World War, Walter White placed African Americans' interests in a global context, connecting them with other struggles for racial equality. He urged President Roosevelt to declare support for Indian independence. As White wrote to a colleague, "I have been screaming my head off for the past eight or ten years . . . that the United States had better wake up to the significance and the danger of this anti-white, anti-colonial revolt."[76] With a committee headed by William Hastie drafting proposals, the NAACP had spent four years in preparation for the United Nations' foundation.[77] Du Bois became closely involved in this preparation, rejoining the association, from which he had resigned in 1934. White aligned the NAACP and the cause of racial equality with that of anticommunism.[78] He judged that demonstrating American patriotism and anticommunism in equal measure was a prerequisite to civil rights reform.

Both the NAACP and the Council on African Affairs (founded in 1937 by Paul Robeson) implored the Truman White House to make anticolonialism an issue at the planning meetings for the United Nations. By associating America with equality abroad, additional pressure mounted for this standard to be achieved back home.[79] Criticism of European imperialism was widespread in the black press, including the NAACP's journal, *Crisis*. NAACP members greeted with alarm Winston Churchill's Iron Curtain speech in which he identified a division between the communist and democratic worlds. In calling for "a special relationship between the British Commonwealth and Empire and the United States,"[80] the new order would most probably have "disastrous effects upon the fate and fortunes of colored peoples."[81]

The association and other organizations, such as the March on Washington movement, the Council on African Affairs, and the National Council of Negro Women (headed by Mary McLeod Bethune), all saw in the Atlantic Charter's eight principles the basis for racial equality in the United Nations' charter. In creating an international consensus, they wanted to link diasporic black communities in a shared leap forward in the achievement of equality. White maintained, "[T]he race question in the United States [is] part and parcel of the problems of other colored peoples in the [world]."[82] This interpretation of the diasporic ties between African Americans and blacks in Africa and the Caribbean eschewed the old back-to-Africa project (Garvey's UNIA had long since disappeared) and instead urged a united front across state boundaries to challenge racism. But at the UN founding meeting, there were no mechanisms to ensure colonized peoples' representation, a point Du Bois made to the State Department throughout 1944 and 1945. And of eight officially appointed members of the United States' delegation to San Francisco, none was black, an omission immediately protested by African Americans. This protest paid off. Secretary of State Edward R. Stettinius, Jr., agreed to appoint an NAACP consultant to the U.S. delegation, a role filled by Walter White and Du Bois[83] and, later, by Mary McLeod Bethune.

The NAACP representatives all agreed that inclusion of a racial equality clause and an anticolonization position at the United Nations would be potentially beneficial to the domestic struggle for civil rights. As Walter White declared en route to the West Coast, he and his colleagues aimed "to induce the San Francisco conference to face what is one of the most serious problems of the twentieth century—the question of race and color."[84]

African-American demands for an equality clause to be included in the UN charter had widespread support from other countries. China pressed a similar priority. But the U.S. secretary of State conveyed American unwillingness to support such a resolution or one declaring the rights of colonized peoples. Repeating its stance of 1921, Britain shared this opposition. The NAACP initiated a huge lobbying campaign to compel the U.S. delegation to accept the legitimacy of such a clause. Association leaders convened a conference on colonialism in New York[85] and surveyed 151 African-American organizations about their expectations for the proposed United Nations. The association coordinated with a large number of delegates, official and unofficial, who represented peoples of color from around the world.[86] America dropped its opposition to the equality clause. Agreeing to the resolution, Stettinius acknowledged, with understatement, that the association's pressures "have not been without effect."[87]

Recalling the fate of the League of Nations in the United States, the State Department was keen to build support for the new international organization domestically, not least because the UN Treaty would face stiff opposition to its ratification in Congress. Internationally, the United States' emerging conflict with the Soviet Union made America's leaders eager to retain ties with the larger Western European countries, most of which planned resolutely to retain their colonies (for instance, the Dutch in Indonesia).

In this setting of countervailing ideological and political pressures, inclusion of the equality clause was a major achievement. It made the United Nations an international forum opposing race discrimination, which could be cited by domestic reformers. The United States' agreement to a human rights platform was one it acceded to in significant part for pragmatic reasons to secure its role in the emerging postwar order by tying itself closely to liberal democratic values. Nonetheless the significance of the clause as a stance against doctrines of group hierarchy could not be overlooked.[88] This aspiration was a commitment at one with the values of the United States' own founding documents as interpreted by one-nation enthusiasts. It projected the image abroad of America as a polity wedded to the defense of individualism and civil rights. This perception was complemented by its role as a promoter of democracy among the defeated nations.

Both Japan and Germany were authoritarian and repressive societies. They had to be rebuilt with democratic institutions and sentiments on terms which banished, at least formally, racial hierarchies. The United States, the leader of a victorious Western alliance with all of the legitimacy this provided, led this operation. It did so as a nation with a deep historical experience of group hierarchies, yet this history was largely kept separate from the United States' foreign image, which projected a liberal individualism with a Wilsonian commitment to nations' self-determination.

Led by General Douglas MacArthur, the United States administered the defeated Japanese nation between August 1934 and April 1952, setting up new institutions of governance.[89] The task was defined in terms drawn from traditional American views about "Oriental" societies and their quasi-feudal structures. The Americans were arguably "benevolent reformers."[90] An international military tribunal opened in Tokyo in January 1946 composed of judges from the eleven countries with which Japan had been at war. By November 1948, the tribunal had found twenty-six senior Japanese war figures, including soldiers, civil servants, diplomats, and one politician, culpable of waging aggressive war and responsible for war crimes. Seven were hanged, the remainder imprisoned. Controversially, the tribunal chose not to try the Japanese monarch, Emperor Hirohito, on the grounds that his removal would hinder the transition to a postwar society based in democratic values.

Paralleling the war crimes trial was the drive to democratize Japan. Freedom of expression was instigated by MacArthur in his "civil-liberties directive" of October 4, 1945.[91] Other liberalizing measures included voting rights for women, broadening school curricula, initiating union rights, strengthening local government, and decentralizing the police force. These measures were to broaden and deepen civil society by removing or undercutting the main features of a society perceived as quasi-feudal. A new constitution, its content infused with U.S. political institutions and the new postwar international human rights regime, consolidated the changes and also disallowed the country from resorting to war to resolve international disputes.

Wartime experts on Japan had explained Japanese behavior in terms of a servile mentality passed from generation to generation, which precluded questioning orders from those higher in the social hierarchy. These views made the possibility for social reform or democracy in postwar Japan seem remote. But other specialists, influenced by behavioral science, argued that systematic reform could change a society and its people over time. A group of left-wing Asia "specialists" argued that reform from below—or at least reform of Japanese society—and replacement of the imperial order held the possibility for democratization.[92] Such aspirations diverged from that of most Japan experts, who recommended restoring significant parts of the old order and considered ordinary Japanese people unprepared for democracy-building.

The new undersecretary of State, Dean Acheson, appointed in August 1945, aligned himself with those experts and views committed to an overhaul of Japanese society in order to implant democracy. This important choice meant that the United States was taking a nonhierarchical approach abroad which it had yet to follow in its domestic policy toward all groups based on race, ethnicity, or national background.

MacArthur's radical democratization plans made plain the international community's view that the prewar order had to be replaced with pluralist institutions and protection of individual rights. These measures could foster a civil society capable of producing and sustaining democratic institutions. The prewar antidemocratic generation was pushed aside from decision-making positions. Reform required an exceptional concentration of power in the postwar U.S. occupation forces and their commandant, Douglas MacArthur.[93] Not surprisingly, American culture was presumed to be and was presented as superior to that of the defeated people, and this approach not infrequently translated into prejudicial and racist attitudes toward the Japanese.

The U.S. forces set up a propaganda regime to instill democratic values among the Japanese. This initiative focused on the education system (which is always a key medium of reform)[94] and popular culture. The propaganda complemented the constitutional changes. Textbooks were examined by Americans for compatibility with democratic values (passages celebrating Japanese militarism or nationalism in old texts were blacked out by students under their teachers' guidance), and a steady fare of prodemocracy messages was drummed through the media of newspapers, radio, and films. Both schools and many aspects of popular culture were partially Americanized to spread democratic values and sentiments. Community-based activities helped to broaden participation and develop civil society. Adult education classes gave instruction in the habits, values, and consciousness correlated with democracy. These all stressed the rights of citizens as individuals. Still, the new American framework for democracy-building in Japan retained the emperor as the head of state and left much of the civil service in place, providing continuity with Japanese culture and tradition which may have made the shift to democracy more palatable for some citizens.

Despite the overall aim of implanting democracy, there were overtones of benevolent paternalism and particularly of domestic American attitudes toward "Orientals,"[95] whose experiences as immigrants in the United States had included plenty of discrimination. This was a contradiction for U.S. foreign policy: its own practice of nationhood rested on distinctions among groups of citizens beneath the rhetoric of being one nation. Ordinary American soldiers not only drew upon these domestic expressions of prejudice and caricatures of the Japanese, but were encouraged to combine them with views of a victorious nation civilizing a backward people. This approach was unlikely to have helped them think that reform of the boundaries of membership at home was urgent.

The U.S. engagement with postwar Germany had the same aim of instilling democracy, but administration of the new polity was divided among four powers (one of which, the Soviet Union, quickly enforced a geographically isolated state). Attitudes toward the vanquished Germans differed: many on the Allies' side viewed Germany as a democracy which had tragically veered from a liberal democratic tradition but was capable of being restored to that trajectory. Holding a dichotomy between the German people and the Nazi Germans had been a plank of wartime propaganda and public discourse.

As the scale of the regime's death camps became known and as the villains were scrutinized at Nuremberg, this distinction looked tarnished. Privately, President Franklin Roosevelt had dropped the dichotomy as untenable. Roosevelt observed, "[W]e have got to be tough with Germany and I mean the German people, not just the Nazis."[96] Treasury secretary Henry Morgenthau wanted Americans to be taught to "hate Germany."[97]

His tougher attitude inclined Roosevelt toward a postwar policy to curb German militarism and to punish the country's military and civilian elite, who were responsible for the war and genocidal actions. Intelligence reports, based on interrogations of German prisoners of war, found little grasp of democratic values ("eighty-five percent have no conception of democracy") nor aspiration to build them.[98] Not making his new views public, Roosevelt nonetheless based planning for the postwar period upon his hardened judgment about the indissoluble links between Nazis and the German people, and as the war continued, attitudes among American voters toward Germans' culpability stiffened. But in terms of public discourse and language, the potential for the German people to restore democracy prevailed, helped by the implicit and at times explicit assumption that Germans, at heart, were "just like us," unlike the "different" Japanese. German Americans were assimilated in the American nation to an extent still unimaginable for Japanese Americans, and they were not treated as a distinct group. Such views created a twofold agenda for the four powers occupying Germany from June 5, 1945: war crimes trials for the Nazi leaders and the deNazification of German society both to expel the evil past and to create the conditions for democratic sentiments to flower.

The international military tribunal, made up of members from the United States, Britain, France, and the Soviet Union, convened in Nuremberg between November 1945 and October 1946. Of the twenty-four leading defendants, three were acquitted and the rest sentenced to death or life imprisonment; another 185 prominent Nazis were tried; and tens of thousands were interned. The tribunal established precedents about human rights and crimes against humanity in international law, including the UN's Convention on the Prevention and Punishment of the Crime of Genocide (1948). This support of democratic values stretches through to the Geneva Protocol (1977), the UN Security Council's War Crimes Tribunal in The Hague (1993), and the International Criminal Court (2002).

Although democratic institutions had failed to prevent Nazism, they did constitute a tradition which might have aided reconstruction. But democracy-building was constrained by the scale of Nazi entrenchment in German society: millions of Germans had belonged to the Nazi party or related organizations.[99]

The Cold War conflict shaped these democracy-building efforts. The division of Germany into two countries, one affiliated to the democratic West and one to the communist East, soon made de-Nazification less urgent than ensuring an ally in the Cold War. The dilution of de-Nazification from 1948 on meant that in practice former Nazis retained or returned to their civil service positions. The attempts at cultural change and educational reform varied in the four zones. Radio, print, and films were all mobilized to support the democracy-building exercise. American cultural influences were pervasive in postwar West Germany and designed to assist the entrenchment of democratic values. The education system, as in Japan, was reformed to make these values fundamental.

These contrasting exercises in implanting democratic institutions each had the United States as leader, though more so in Japan, where it had exclusive authority. In both cases, American practices and values were important models for the new regimes as they developed political arrangements to respect individual freedoms and human rights. And in both cases, education was an important medium of change as it had been in the United States' nation-building interventions at the turn of the century. But in contrast to those earlier episodes in the Philippines and Puerto Rico, postwar involvement in Japan and Germany presumed democratic inclusion and anticipated reversions to self-government and autonomy, an expectation consistent with the United States' self-image as an anti-imperialist nation committed to promoting democracy internationally. It is an expectation that President George W. Bush cited in his September 7, 2003, address to the American people on U.S. policy in Iraq: "America has done this kind of work before. Following World War II, we lifted up the defeated nations of Japan and Germany and stood with them as they built representative governments."[100]

War mobilization amplified both the scale and depth of the inequalities and prejudices faced by groups based on race, ethnicity, and national background in American society and the association internationally between the United States and the defense of liberal democracy. These two effects seemed to place international influences increasingly at the center of America's domestic struggles about and revisions of how to define the terms of membership in the nation. The settlement reached by the end of the 1930s looked wanting: the United States could hardly become leader of Western liberal democratic beliefs without evaluating the implications of this ideological role for a domestic version of nationhood that sustained group inequalities.

As a society, America entered the Second World War calibrated with hierarchies based in race, ethnicity, and national background. Despite the defeat of Nazism, hierarchical presumptions did not evaporate overnight among Americans. There was continuity in the "enemy" presented by war mobilization. Most strikingly in respect to Japanese people but also echoing earlier attitudes toward German and Italian Americans, the delineation of wartime enemies fitted with established views about who belonged and who did not belong in the American nation. While white Eastern and Southern European ethnics, notably those who were Catholic, gained a new acceptance as did American Jews, other exclusions persisted. War mobilization made these group divisions more complex and reshaped some of the main lines of cleavage but did not expel them from American nationhood.

It is likely that the spurious claims of "racial" and "eugenic" science would have lost credibility in the 1940s and certainly by the 1960s as scientists rejected as fundamentally flawed the genetic assumptions of this framework. But the defeat of Nazism and the exposure of the Nazis' evil manipulation of "race" hastened this demise. For American nationhood, the Second World War both facilitated more tolerant views of ethnic identity in U.S. society and forced changes to the segregationist political order: the former was already under way, although the latter might not have occurred for many years or even decades without this exogenous shock. The diverse senses of belonging expressed in American nationalism were reformulated to be more inclusive as ethnicity was renegotiated to be a virtue instead of a defect; segregation, in its multiple forms, was challenged though not much dented. Each of these effects meant acknowledging the practical and political limits of assuming that the ideology of American nationhood was one of individualism and that group fissures were invisible or vanquished. Thus, as the nation fought a war to defend freedom, group divisions, expressed in a variety of ways from intergroup violence to internment for one group, continued to divide the country.

Any wartime sense of unity was fragile as the more astute politicians, such as Harry Truman, appreciated. Powerful exclusionary pressures endured. This was a great paradox of the war's significance for group divisions. Nominally fought to defend individualism and to defeat fascism, of necessity wartime rhetoric and war aims drew upon doctrines of hierarchy.

Retrospectively, the effects of World War II seem decisive as a source of change in the context of America's ideology of nationhood, though these influences did not lead to immediate reforms. The efforts of A. Philip Randolph's protest movement and publicity about segregation in the armed services pushed group inequality onto the political agenda (certainly for the postwar administration of President Harry Truman). But linked with vilification of Japanese Americans, segregation permitted the routine maintenance of assumptions about group hierarchy with which the United States entered the war to survive more richly than the conventional narrative of America's national story would imply. To many at the time, the ameliorative effects of war appeared limited. This reflected a paradox about the war's effects: having fought to defeat fascism and Nazism, the United States' triumph appeared to be a triumph for the model of nationhood—celebrated in melting-pot individualism and assimilationism—with which it entered the conflict. But it was this very liberal individualistic model of American nationhood which reformers at home and critics observing from abroad wanted changed, because it overlooked the obvious group discriminations equally present in the nation.

7 ◈

America Abroad at Home

International Pressures and Nationhood

Since the 1950s, American nation-builders' sensitivity and responsiveness to international criticism of their failure to live up to the standards of assimilationist nationalism and democratic inclusion at home, which they championed abroad, intensified. Did this sensitivity and responsiveness make America adopt more just and nondiscriminatory policies toward those groups defined by race, ethnicity, and national background? It certainly contributed to reform, as the discussion below explains. But, as the next chapter recounts, it did not break the group divisions themselves and replace them with liberal individualism.

International influences helped to shift American nationhood from group hierarchies and the associated so-called scientific doctrines in several ways. First, the United States' international promotion of liberal democracy permitted discriminated groups at home to point to the contradiction of opposing racist doctrines abroad without enforcing civil rights at home; with the creation of the United Nations, there were new forums for this protest. Second, these international contrasts imposed direct political pressure on nation-builders to improve the treatment of groups. For instance, the discriminatory experiences in Washington of black diplomats who were representing new states was a significant headache for the State Department and tainted America's support of anticolonialism. Third, some reforms, for example, the new immigration law enacted in the mid-1960s, were in significant part determined by the United States' concern about international criticisms of the former discriminatory system, in this case, the national origins system enacted in 1924. The way in which these sorts of influence functioned is examined in this chapter.

The United States' vulnerability to international criticism and scrutiny began decisively during World War II. But it was President Harry Truman's administration (1945–1953) which watched the rapid restructuring of the postwar world from an alliance of victorious states into a bipolar rigidity. This Cold War dichotomy made America's promotion of liberal democracy an ideological struggle. The Truman Doctrine (launched in respect to Greece and Turkey) was forged in the atmosphere fueled by Winston Churchill's gloomy Iron Curtain speech. George Kennan's recommendation for a policy of containment, as an anti-Soviet strategy, guided the State Department and the White House. This policy implicitly assumed a singular conception of American nationhood centered on individualism, an unpromising setting in which more fully to appreciate group distinctions or the claims of groups historically discriminated against. The White House decision to support the Greek government's fight against communists, in 1947, made America central in the democratic world's struggle against communism. Indeed, President Harry Truman declared, "[T]he free peoples of the world look to us for support in maintaining their freedoms."[1] It was a unilateral intervention. The infirmity of the United Nations and the timidity of other Western democracies in the face of military aggression made plain the United States' global role in the post-1945 world: no longer restricted to its own Western hemisphere, the United States had to look east, west, and south in its role as a defender of democracy.

This perception of Western weakness shaped the National Security Council's influential (and at the time confidential) paper NSC-68, setting out U.S. foreign policy aims and means for the unfolding Cold War.[2] The best that could be done in the face of European weakness was to offer global leadership, fiscal and military support (as the United States has done widely), and organizational integration through the North Atlantic Treaty Organization (NATO). The same NSC paper rejected an isolationist stance for pragmatic reasons, concluding that the Soviet Union and China would exploit such withdrawals, and for psychological reasons, including the "imponderable, but nevertheless drastic effects on our beliefs in ourselves and in our way of life of a deliberate decision to isolate ourselves."[3]

The NSC paper's authors celebrated the defense of a free society because "the idea of freedom is the most contagious idea in history,"[4] a proposition echoing President Truman's conclusion that Allied success in 1945 was the "victory of liberty over tyranny." The NSC added:

> The fundamental purpose of the United States is . . . to assure the integrity and vitality of our free society, which is founded upon the dignity and worth of the individual. . . . The free society attempts to create and maintain an environment in which every individual has the opportunity to realize his creative powers. . . . For the free society does not fear, it welcomes, diversity. It derives its strength from its hospitality even to antipathetic ideas. It is a market for free trade in ideas.[5]

There were numerous comparable formulations of these values by politicians and policy makers. Plainly a complement to the external Cold War strategy of containing communism, this framework emphasizes individualism.[6] But the commitment to "diversity in a free society" anticipates the continuing tension between assimilationist nationalism and demands for democratic inclusion in a one-people ideology.

Cold War pressures strongly influenced African-American activists. The intense patriotism and ideological mobilization of these years made criticisms of U.S. policy politically very costly for those making them. Under this pressure, the integrationist NAACP reaffirmed its anticommunism. But the international ideological struggle between communism and democracy also presented an opportunity for change. The association felt bolstered by President Truman's speech at a rally it organized at the Lincoln Memorial in June 1947. The president conceded the need to demonstrate "that we have been able to put our own house in order" as a prerequisite of global leadership.[7]

Some African Americans, such as Paul Robeson, did not mellow their critique of American policy, but they were a minority within the Black American community. McCarthyite denouncements accentuated the political and personal costs of the Robeson stance. Opponents of civil rights reform were quite willing to smear civil rights activists as communists, as all too many reformers discovered. The NAACP, led by Walter White, and the Council on African Affairs, led by Robeson among others, now took separate trajectories shaped by distinct agendas and different readings of the international context for domestic reform.

A New Forum for Group Rights: Global Pressures

From the mid-twentieth century, the United States' global presence put it at the center of the shift to the international human rights regime. This positioning reflected back into American society. As President Harry Truman's secretary of State, George Marshall, averred, "[S]ince it is a major objective of the foreign policy of the United States to promote world-wide respect for and observance of civil rights, our failure to maintain the highest standards of performance in this field creates embarrassment out of proportion to the actual instances of violation."[8] Given that Marshall had himself defended segregation in the military, this statement showed a shift in his attitude and in his appreciation of the changed expectations about democratic inclusion and equality in the postwar world order.

An early expression of the new post-1945 internationalist agenda and its significance for domestic policy came in President Truman's decision to establish an investigative committee on civil rights. To act as the leader of the free world and a bulwark against communism required not only acknowledging the interests of new, recently decolonized nations. It meant reform at home. Truman issued Executive Order 9981, which desegregated the armed services and established an investigative presidential committee into equality of opportunity in the military as steps in this direction.

Translating civil rights into enforceable policy was not easy. In 1954, the Supreme Court's judgment in *Brown* to desegregate schools provoked 100 congressional representatives and senators to sign a motion rejecting it. Senator James Eastland defended segregation for its protection of his biological conception of race: "[E]very race has both the right and the duty to perpetuate itself. All free men have the right to associate exclusively with members of their own race."[9] This language obviously implied a hierarchy of groups defined by race.

The Loyalty Day parades, orchestrated in the 1950s by the Veterans of Foreign Wars (VFW), illustrate how anticommunism mediated international pressures for breaking with group hierarchies in domestic politics. Millions of Americans turned out on the weekend before May 1 to counter communist marches and to celebrate patriotism. The rallies demonstrated that "the great mass of American people are loyal to the principles of Americanism."[10] For patriots, racial inequality was a blemish but not a major flaw. In celebrating American nationalism, these events ignored the burgeoning demands for democratic inclusion.

But ideology, politics, and history were calling time on the racists and hierarchists. The post-1945 world could not repeat the errors of 1919 and disregard the need firmly to embed racial equality as a standard of international behavior by states: failure had permitted the rise of Nazism. Even if a state such as the United States had wanted to resist this trend, it would have been able to do so only in the short term, given the powerful forces for democratic inclusion.[11]

Nor could this international priority be kept out of domestic politics. The ideology of one-people American nationalism faced mounting international pressures, both ideological, such as the language of human rights, and political, such as the civil rights movement, to be inclusive. These pressures arose very much in the United States' own self-presentation of its democratic values from the Second World War onward. One key forum for this projection was the United Nations.

THE UNITED STATES AT THE UNITED NATIONS

The defeat of Nazism and fascism seemed to render race an unacceptable category for deployment in political debate or in policy decisions. Though it has hardly vanished from popular and official discourse in America (or other societies), nonetheless since the middle of the twentieth century, political and legal rejection of group-based hierarchies as publicly acceptable ways of talking about or engaging with the world's peoples either nationally or individually has steadily mounted. These changes were far from automatic. For instance, throughout the 1950s and 1960s, Canada and Australia administered "whites only" immigration policies, intentionally to keep out immigrants from Asian or African countries. This blatant racism was quite bare-faced given wartime memories. Concurrently, these two countries maintained harsh policies toward their native and aboriginal peoples. The United Nations was a key forum in promoting this new attitude, making the rejection of group distinctions fundamental to the Universal Declaration on Human Rights adopted in 1948. Other UN principles, such as the two International Human Rights Covenants and the Declaration on Granting Independence to Colonial Countries and Peoples (1960), strengthened an international environment that was respectful of individual rights and scornful of government policies dependent on racial distinctions.[12]

The United States was in a dilemma at the United Nations, publicly committed to upholding former colonial states' rights but reluctant to push this line too strongly. The United States' often low-key response to colonial peoples' rights and its resistance to granting the United Nations power to intervene in domestic jurisdictions were disappointments to African Americans such as Du Bois, Robeson, and Walter White. For White, this position weakened the "bold moral leadership" open to the United States.[13] Even the United States' support of independence for UN trusteeships (where a mere 3 percent of colonial peoples would reside) was precarious. Ralph Bunche, an adviser at the State Department, shared the NAACP's alarm about the United States' stance and tried to get the Australian delegation to propose a tougher position for the United Nations' charter. This strategy failed. But the United Nations' condemnation of South Africa, in January 1947, for its racist treatment of Indian workers seemed a harbinger of change. Failure to prevent this vote of censure alarmed the U.S. delegation.

Reformer Mary McLeod Bethune equated colonial peoples' position with that of African Americans living under segregation and disfranchisement: the "Negro in America [enjoys] little more than colonial status in a democracy."[14] It was this parallel which, for many civil rights reformers, gave U.S. policy abroad such resonance for politics at home and made international politics a pressure for change in American politics.

Initially, the new UN clause prohibiting discrimination because of race had little impact on African Americans' daily lives. It was of symbolic interest, since the postwar reality in the United States was a newly invigorated world of segregation. The casual brutality meted out to African-American veterans and citizens as the war ended showed that while many Americans may have wanted global security, expunging racism at home was not a priority. If civil rights did not exist abroad, this weakened their prospects at home since racism rested on the common doctrine of group hierarchy, which the war was supposed to have demolished.[15] As the future Supreme Court justice Thurgood Marshall gloomily told the NAACP's first postwar annual meeting, "[T]he war against fascism has done nothing to break down the vicious system of second-class citizenship in our own country and in many ways has allowed home-grown Fascists to grow in stature."[16] Marshall's comments underscore how far from spontaneous or automatic the break with group hierarchy would be in the postwar decades.

Balancing the dual needs to express patriotism and to advance Black Americans' rights, the NAACP saw the United Nations as a forum in which to internationalize the domestic struggle for civil rights.[17] The association submitted a petition on American racism to the United Nations in October 1947. Penned by W. E. B. Du Bois, *An Appeal to the World* condemned America's failure to treat African Americans equally. The petition exploited national and international connections as a trigger for civil rights: "[I]t is not Russia that threatens the United States so much as Mississippi; not Stalin and Molotov but [Senators] Bilbo and Rankin; internal injustice done to one's brothers is far more dangerous than the aggression of strangers from abroad." The problems affected America's role as a liberal democracy in the international community: "[T]he disenfranchisement of the American Negro makes the functioning of democracy in the nation difficult; and as democracy fails to function in the leading democracy in the world, it fails the world."[18] Du Bois succeeded in getting his petition accepted by the head of the United Nations' Commission on Human Rights, John Humphrey.[19] The NAACP looked to other UN members for support.

The NAACP's document was widely discussed. But having learned from its earlier failures, the American delegation to the United Nations ensured that the petition failed to garner enough votes to be considered before the United Nations' Subcommission on the Prevention of Discrimination and the Protection of Minorities. With this decision, America compromised its commitment to the new international regime and diluted how international pressures might have driven reform at home. State Department efforts stopped any direct response to it at the

United Nations. But the petition was a publicity coup and made suppression of the United States' "race issue" impracticable.[20]

The decision to prevent the petition from being discussed in the United Nations' subcommittee required American delegate Jonathan Daniels to construe a very limited view of the United Nations' powers.[21] It was Eleanor Roosevelt, a member of the NAACP board as well as a member of the U.S. delegation at the United Nations, who had to defend America's opposition to Walter White and his colleagues. She argued that the association's petition would simply have advantaged communist opponents of the United States led by the Soviet Union's team at the United Nations. The political cost of holding communist sympathies was at its height. The NAACP was anxious not to appear excessively critical of the United States.[22] Du Bois dissented from this timidity, and his path separated from that of the association. As an ardent campaigner for civil rights at home, Eleanor Roosevelt was the ideal person to represent this rationale to African Americans since her reformist credentials were impeccable.[23] But even she could hardly disguise how the United States' line struck a blow against the fight for civil rights at home.[24]

Within a week of the United Nations' rejection of the NAACP's petition, President Truman's Committee on Civil Rights published its report, *To Secure These Rights*, which laid bare the same issues and the urgent need for reform. Thus the State Department's machinations at the United Nations hardly helped to erode the salience of group divisions in American politics, which was driving civil rights reform, though it did limit some of its airing internationally.

The United States' attitude toward colonialism remained a sore point for African Americans and a frequent source of frustration and disappointment. American opposition to the Anglo-Franco invasion of Suez in 1956 (effectively scuppering the operation) made clear where the United States stood in respect to such colonialist escapades.[25] And the values formalized in the United Nations' charter and ethos meant that the writing was on the wall for colonial arrangements. But U.S. foreign policy was not exclusively aimed at promoting democracy. Having agreed, in December 1960, to support a resolution condemning colonial arrangements, President Dwight Eisenhower reversed himself after special pleading from the British and instructed the U.S. delegation to abstain (joining such countries as France, the United Kingdom, Belgium, and South Africa).[26] This decision disappointed the U.S. delegation to the organization and seemed to temper the capacity of the United Nations to advance civil rights.

America's ideological commitment to democracy promotion was always balanced with a strategic, security-defending imperative in foreign policy. These two aims—the ideological defense of democracy and the strategic defense of national interest—sometimes correlated (for example, defending Western Europe against communism), but on other occasions the two principles clashed. The resolution of this conflict was usually in favor of the strategic interest over democracy promotion (a conclusion which U.S. policy toward Latin American countries, such as Guatemala, the Dominican Republic, and Chile, in the Cold War years implies). Such mixed motives are not always intrinsically bad, but they can have unattractive aspects, for example, America's support of undemocratic regimes sat uncomfortably with a formal espousal of individual rights. And the United States' wartime support for anticolonial movements in Africa did not extend to challenging South Africa's apartheid or Rhodesia's racist regime, other than tepidly, for several long decades.[27]

These mixed motives worried civil rights reformers because it meant a further focus on American nationhood as an individualistic model, neglecting its group-based complexities. African-American lawyer and member of the National Council of Negro Women Edith Sampson defended the U.S. government as the Cold War unfolded. Identifying herself as an "American,"[28] Sampson suffered discrimination like many other African Americans, but rejected communism. Sampson was an ideal representative, in the State Department's view, of the United States at the United Nations, where she criticized the Soviet Union's use of labor camps. From the 1960s, however, Sampson's speeches gave lukewarm support for American nationalism as she found the pace of domestic change timid.[29] Typical of many African Americans, Sampson eschewed the unflinching critique of American democracy developed by Paul Robeson and W. E. B. Du Bois,[30] whose critiques deeply influenced the black power movement. To black nationalists such as Malcolm X, the United States' exposure to and participation in an international human rights regime had all too little influence on domestic American politics, where group hierarchies still prevailed. This was certainly true of daily life as experienced in most American cities, including Washington, D.C.

DIPLOMATIC WASHINGTON

The State Department helped to present American values and beliefs to the world. This role assumed unexpected dimensions in the new anticolonial, post–world war order as countries with predominantly black populations achieved statehood. There were two principal diplomatic effects: increased inspection of who served in the State Department's ambassadorial positions and concern about how well diplomats from black nations were treated in the United States. Both posed unanticipated challenges.

In the forty-year period from 1949 to 1988,[31] only nineteen Black Americans rose through the ranks of the Foreign Service to the rank of ambassador (although other African-American ambassadors were drawn from outside the service).[32] State was hardly atypical in the U.S. federal government, but its role in foreign affairs made these statistics germane to the external presentation of the American nation. As one diplomat who found himself confined to a round of limited postings, told the personnel department: "[Y]ou're not only discriminating against us [African Americans] in the Service, but you're exporting discrimination abroad in the Foreign Service."[33] It sent an external signal about this group's position in American society. Black diplomats were delegated exclusively to Haiti or Liberia and the so-called Negro circuit—the Canary Islands, the Azores, or Madagascar.[34] In 1958, Congressman Adam Clayton Powell, Jr., concluded that the virtues of the "American way of life" were unrecognized in Asia and Africa: "[I]t is not being sold because there is a road block at the highest peak, and the road block is in the Department of State."[35]

NAACP reformers and the personnel director of the State Department met to improve African-American representation, but progress was slow. The association often doubted the commitment to change. It was difficult for some federal officials to accept that discrimination might contribute to the patterns of underrepresentation. The appointment of an African-American ambassador to a communist state, to somewhere in Western Europe, or to a newly decolonized Asian country could only have complemented the United States' efforts at democratic self-presentation and challenged communist propaganda. State's international role meant that its presentations at the United Nations were crucial and its articulation of American values closely scrutinized as representative statements.[36]

Black diplomats stationed in Washington, D.C., encountered discrimination.[37] Their experience made headlines in the foreign and national press. In 1948, the ambassador from Ethiopia was ejected from his box at a public ceremony because of his color. In 1961, the ambassador from Chad couldn't get a cup of coffee at a diner on Route 40 in Maryland. He was on his way to present his credentials to President John F. Kennedy.[38] Such incidents occurred too in New York City, where the United Nations was located. Many airports operated segregated restaurants.

With seventeen new states established in Africa alone in 1960, the number of black diplomats encountering racism and discrimination presented a growing crisis. The State Department was at its wit's end as it issued a stream of contrite missives.

For newly appointed diplomats, these encounters must have seemed surreal. Black diplomats posted to America found themselves part of a group commonly experiencing discrimination. But in contrast to the position of African Americans, black diplomats were empowered by their status as outsiders because the U.S. government had to respond to their experience of discrimination. Their ability to induce executive action by the U.S. government was a direct expression of international influences for better treatment of groups defined on hierarchical scales.

There was a further irony. Unlike its Western allies, the United States was not an imperial power accountable to the members of a set of former colonies who demanded reparations from the imperial center. Rather, the United States' leaders had, from the collapse of its Philippines engagement, eschewed imperialism and had made the termination of colonialism a wartime aim and an ethos for the United Nations.

The State Department first arranged for officers to chaperone black foreign dignitaries during their visits to the United States. It then established the Special Protocol Service Section to design measures to ease discrimination against black diplomats.[39] The problems continued, and the section lacked sanctions to do much more than request an end to discrimination by, for example, real estate companies.[40] The Protocol Section managed to pressure the presidentially appointed District of Columbia Board of Commissioners to issue a fair housing regulation in December 1963, thereby sidestepping Congress.[41] Advocating the regulation, Secretary of State Dean Rusk told the president, "[I]t is of great importance to our foreign relations that action be taken promptly to end housing discrimination in Washington."[42]

Motivated by a mixture of strategic calculation and personal commitment to equality and compelled by the politics of anticommunism to address external criticisms of American society, reform-minded bureaucrats took advantage of the Cold War to achieve modest but incrementally important changes. This initiative was one additional medium to bring international expectations about equality of treatment into the domestic struggle for an end to group hierarchies in American nationhood: America's group distinctions influenced these key exposures to international influences. The Cold War also presented a challenge to those officials responsible for representing and defending the image of U.S. values and institutions abroad since they wanted that image to be one of individualism, not group division.

Projecting a New Image of American Nationhood

Controlling and shaping the global image of the United States and of its political institutions and values put a considerable strain on propagandists in the State Department and other agencies. They were keen to project a positive picture of America's ideology of nationhood without conceding too much about the dilemmas of group injustices. In addition to their own propaganda efforts, these concerns led to a good deal of policy activity and monitoring of how Americans presented their country abroad.

Overseas visits by eminent African Americans critical of civil rights alarmed the U.S. government. The Truman administration embargoed Paul Robeson's passport in 1950 and suspended his right to travel.[43] The U.S. Information Service (USIS) placed an article critical of Robeson in the NAACP's journal *Crisis*.[44] William Patterson, chairman of the

Civil Rights Congress, also had his passport seized and was denied the right to travel overseas.[45] The U.S. State Department tried to engineer cancellations of Josephine Baker's appearances in Latin America, including Cuba (where she was arrested but released without charge).[46] A talk by Baker in Stockholm in March 1956 on American race politics, attended by an audience of 5,000, including the Swedish prime minister, generated wide discussion in the Swedish press about the unequal rights of African Americans.[47] African-American congressman Adam Clayton Powell, Jr., a representative from New York, often criticized Baker's actions as overly critical of the United States.

These incidents derived from a common but fundamental problem: the United States' failure to enact and enforce laws upholding the constitutional rights of all of its citizens equally. By highlighting domestic political debates about the criteria for democratic inclusion and equality of membership in the U.S. polity and the protections rightfully accorded to members, this failure opened an opportunity for foreign criticism of America. It was the Soviet Union, the standard bearer of an alternative political system, which made the most of criticizing the United States' group-based discrimination. The Soviets made the Birmingham, Alabama, church bombings in May 1963 "a historical indictment of America's Negro problem."[48] Soviet propagandists were selective in their use of American material, plainly more interested in U.S. failings than in evidence of any amelioration.

To counter such international criticism, the United States publicized advances in civil rights. President Truman's executive order (in 1948) desegregating the armed forces was widely publicized. The U.S. Information Agency (USIA) distributed the decision to desegregate schools in the *Brown* case (1954), underlining its significance for the civil rights of Black Americans. But even codifying reform created new problems and further opposition. In September 1957, nine African-American children were denied entry to a white school despite judicial orders to admit them; the state governor failed to use his powers to enforce desegregation, thereby requiring intervention by the Eisenhower White House. This crisis at Little Rock, Arkansas, received daily coverage internationally.

National commemorations during the 1950s inevitably promoted a one-people American nationalism. Celebration induced a complacency at a time when the external world saw the need for change in the ideology and the practices of that ideology to recognize group-based rights. The commemorations could not camouflage the pressures, at home and abroad, for civil rights reforms. In October 1957, a survey of opinion in Brussels, London, and Paris found that 71 percent, 65 percent, and 61 percent, respectively, of respondents considered that "Negro-white relations" in the United States seriously harmed America's image.[49] By 1963, almost 80 percent of Americans held a similar view.[50] Fifty percent of British respondents to a USIA survey thought most Americans opposed equality.[51] (Even as late as 1978, for European elites, America featured disproportionate racism and discrimination, and they perceived a nation still divided along group lines.)[52]

Dwight Eisenhower's vice president, Richard Nixon, grasped the importance of how U.S. values were projected overseas.[53] After a tour of African states a year before the Little Rock crisis, he warned that the United States could not "talk equality to the peoples of Africa and Asia and practice inequality in the United States."[54] After the brutal treatment of protesters in Birmingham, Alabama, Uganda's prime minister wrote to Kennedy protesting that the attacks arose because the victims were black. He made the contradiction between mistreatment of African Americans and the United States' democratic leadership explicit.[55]

Where the federal government and executive were seen to counter— or attempting to counter—racism, the foreign response was positive. National political leadership could make a difference to the United States' international image. President Kennedy's speech on civil rights in June 1963, delivered to a nationwide television audience and anticipating the Civil Rights Act passed a year later, marked a shift in his administration's commitment. When President Lyndon Johnson addressed the graduating class at Howard University in June 1965, he was speaking not just to an American audience but to an international one. Johnson's speech signaled a fundamental reform in the definition of the membership of the American nation: membership was no longer to be demarcated by race or, he implied, by other indicators of group difference. He conceded that group politics had fostered "separate nations" within the United States.

In throwing off colonial powers, the leaders in the new democracies in Africa and Asia were following the dictum laid down by Woodrow Wilson in 1919, recognizing "the right of those who submit to authority to have a voice in their own governments." This political egalitarianism was observed by African Americans.[56] Malcolm X returned to the United States after his tour of newly independent African states in 1965 to found the Organization of Afro-American Unity modeled on the Organization for African Unity. But the America to which he returned was still locked in a furious struggle to break the grip that group hierarchies retained on its national life.

GROUPS WITHOUT HIERARCHY

To outside observers, U.S. efforts to support democracy abroad conveyed the image of an internally integrated nation. Group divisions were presented as either at an end or of no significance in the American nation. Yet the potency of group hierarchies was observable in the struggles over civil rights. This contradiction surfaced at the world fair convened in Brussels in 1958 on the theme of "A World View, a New Humanism."[57]

The guidebook for the U.S. exhibit at the Brussels fair reinvented the United States' group divisions. It celebrated ethnic and racial diversity as essential to American nationhood. Instead of the old melting-pot image, the guidebook included a map of the United States adorned with citizens of foreign origin dressed in ethnic costumes, holding hands from coast to coast. The New York City image included groups of German, Irish, Syrian, and Belgian citizens living harmoniously.[58] The picture conveyed an American nation comfortable with the coexistence of diversity and unity around a set of common one-people values though with a selective view of which groups were included. This openness to diversity and group bonds was beginning gradually to influence textbooks, particularly for history, used in public schools. The conventional narrative of American history as a story of successful assimilation was balanced with one that acknowledged intergroup differences and valued the voluntary retention of ethnic values and identification. Steadily, the image of the American nation as a melting pot of individuals was succeeded by one presenting a compendium of diverse groups. The Brussels event offered an opportunity to present these more comfortable images internationally. However, just as U.S. society was on the brink of a domestic revolution to extend civil rights, so these tensions below the surface erupted in respect to the world fair.

The Department of State[59] considered the Brussels World Fair an opportunity to counter international criticism of civil rights in America and to demonstrate how democratic inclusion was under way. The advice of a team of distinguished scholars, led by the MIT economic historian W. W. Rostow, and the U.S. Information Agency aided preparations.[60]

The U.S. exhibit included a display on "Unfinished Business" dealing with segregation. "Unfinished Business" sat alongside exhibits displaying the vibrancy of American society, its cultural richness, and its scientific advances. But Rostow's planning committee was adamant that segregation be acknowledged internationally as a blemish and something which the American nation was tackling; this blemish would be tempered by including examples of desegregation. The organizers sensibly anticipated hostility from southern congressional representatives, especially since it was a more honest treatment of unequal citizenship than the fare commonly projected by the USIA.

Even before the fair opened, South Carolina senator Olin Johnston labeled the exhibit a "propaganda fiasco" while Georgia's senator, Herman Talmadge, was apoplectic at such an international apology for racial discrimination.[61] A State Department official visited the exhibit and removed a photograph of an African-American man dancing with a white woman; a photograph of a multiracial group of children was also judged unsuitable.[62] Undersecretary of State Christian Herter recommended closing the exhibit on the anodyne grounds of its "poor craftsmanship" and failure to present "a balanced story" about segregation.[63] Despite laudatory appraisal by European newspaper editors, who admired its self-critical style as an indicator of the openness of American democracy, the exhibit was removed before the fair opened to the public.

The elimination of the offensive exhibit did not assuage critics. President Dwight Eisenhower convened a meeting about the display. He ruled that "there is no reason in my judgment why we should not put our best foot forward at an exhibit such as this."[64] The material on segregation was replaced with material about American public health. This change incurred further criticisms, not least from some Republicans, addressed to Secretary of State John Foster Dulles and Eisenhower about the popularity of the segregation exhibits with European audiences as well as the anticipated criticism from African-American newspapers. A letter from ten of the young Americans working as guides at the exhibit in Brussels, addressed to President Eisenhower and printed in the *Congressional Record*, applauded the success of the original "Unfinished Business" exhibit as a crowd pleaser which, as a "powerful type of inverse propaganda," often prompted those programmed in anti-Americanism to change their attitude.[65]

The very process of presenting American values and institutions abroad clearly generated unexpected complexity about how best to portray the content of American nationhood. Despite the decisive Supreme Court ruling in 1954 outlawing segregation, the mind-set of group hierarchy had fervent defenders four years later. Even in this international setting, the United States' opposition to colonialism and its leading role in promoting postwar democracy could not displace this tension. Shifting the group hierarchies of American nationhood was far from automatic. Too many politicians thought in terms of such hierarchical group-based language. But for reformers, this international criticism made reform all the more urgent.

INFORMING THE WORLD

During the Second World War, the Foreign Information Service, soon known as the Voice of America, began work.[66] The Office of War Information (OWI), headed by Elmer Davis, became an umbrella agency for all government information activities, foreign and domestic.[67] The U.S. Information Service, renamed the U.S. Information Agency in 1953, was the OWI's overseas arm. Information libraries were established in twenty-eight foreign countries; magazines and pamphlets were written and distributed; exhibits were created; and foreign journalists were brought to the United States. Hollywood was coopted into the propaganda effort through the OWI's Bureau of Motion Pictures. RKO was persuaded not to rerelease *Gunga Din* (1939) because of its depiction of racial subservience in India under the British Empire, and the bureau worked with script writers to inject propaganda into movies such as Darryl Zanuck's biopic *Wilson* (1945).[68]

The USIS sponsored overseas trips by jazz artists, an initiative praised both in the visited countries and in Black American newspapers. The artists, such as Dizzy Gillespie, were aware of the ironies of their tours. As a motive, they often cited support among blacks in the diaspora rather than the promotion of American nationhood.[69] Louis Armstrong refused to tour after Arkansas governor Orval Faubus deployed the National Guard to obstruct desegregation at Little Rock.

From the 1950s, the State Department became responsible for providing governmental information and promoting cultural activities abroad. The urgency of these propaganda tasks grew with the Cold War.[70] The newly named Office of International Information and Cultural Affairs financed student exchanges and funded American libraries overseas. A new information program helped efforts to defuse anti-Americanism among elites abroad (and has been cited as a model in the "war against terrorism").[71] The State Department could end exchanges and cultural relations with countries that failed to reciprocate.

The renamed U.S. Information Agency (USIA) administered an overseas program. The USIA's aims were uncomplicated, as one memorandum explained: the "underlying purpose of the information program is to enhance the security and well-being of the American people"[72] (though this did not make it immune from Senator Joseph McCarthy's committee on un-American activities, which challenged the selection of books in overseas USIA libraries—a curious action for a country promoting its cultural openness in contrast to communist states).[73] The USIA subsidized initiatives by universities and foreign publishers to promote American values, complementing the intellectual propagandizing of the influential Congress for Cultural Freedom in Western Europe.[74]

The USIA focused on information for mass publics rather than culture for elites in its propagation of American values abroad. But cultural containment, the promotion of artistic and creative values enjoyed in the West, part and parcel of anticommunism, remained an integral if less visible aspect of the United States' Cold War strategy. The USIA considered cultural engagement a crucial element in the battle for ideas fundamental to the Cold War: if America and Western countries in general could be shown as centers of the avant-garde creative arts, this would illustrate how liberal democracy enhanced individual expression.[75]

To counter the myriad images of group strife from Little Rock in 1957 to Malcolm X's assassination in 1965 and Martin Luther King, Jr.'s murder in 1968, the USIA and other agencies strove to portray a positive view of group politics in the United States. State and USIA worked to counter such critics as Josephine Baker and Paul Robeson and to coopt, if possible, distinguished Black Americans to its cause. Target audiences included colonial peoples in African countries who were closely interested in how the United States treated its citizens of color. In 1956, the USIA put out *The American Negro Today*; it was translated into numerous languages, including Russian. The forty-page booklet compiled positive foreign news reports about the Supreme Court desegregation decision. Rather than portray the desegregation of the armed services as a change forced on the federal government, this was described as "the great experiment of 'integration,'" and the authors seemed unable to rise above a patronizing tone: "[I]f decently treated and trained, Negroes can fight as well as any man."[76]

These often complacent accounts of civil rights were inadequate guides to the civil rights struggle in the American nation, challenging the individualistic ideology of one-people nationhood: unsurprisingly, the image projected abroad was one of positive change.[77] But the level of foreign reportage and criticism required rebuttal and countering with some often dubious claims. In a 1963 publication on African Americans, the USIA assured readers that the level of voting participation among this group was significant.[78] From the mid-1960s, real legislative reform could be cited in USIA publications, and the movies it financed, *The March* (1964) and *Nine from Little Rock* (1964), were praised for their accuracy. International pressures did not create these legislative changes, but such laws would be seized upon by those promoting a more positive image of American nationhood abroad.

The connections between domestic and foreign policies tested State Department officials whose instinctive approach was to isolate the two arenas and to downplay any linkage. Thus the connections drawn by African-American critics about the effects of domestic racism upon perceptions of the United States abroad were commonly overlooked by the department or dismissed as communist anti-American propaganda.[79] The State Department did its best to keep these international influences and pressures out. But politically the department was compelled to respond, and in propagating a new image of American nationhood, it contributed to appreciation of the group diversity of U.S. society at home. The traditional individualistic presentation was contradicted on an almost daily basis by reports of the struggles for equal rights undertaken by groups that felt marginalized in the American nation. This pressure forced changes in the 1960s, some examples of which we will now consider.

Revising Groups and Nationhood

M ajor reforms to the place of groups in American nationhood oc-curred in the 1960s. The most familiar measures are the Civil Rights Act (1964) and Voting Rights Act (1965). The momentum of these and other measures benefited from international influences, as nation-builders were alert to the sort of external scrutiny and criticisms out-lined earlier. This can be seen further by examining the reform of immigration policy and the new status of Native Americans.

IMMIGRATION POLICY

Together with de jure and de facto segregation, the national origins immigration system was a powerful expression of popular belief in group distinctions. This belief had strong advocates in America. Presi-dent Franklin Roosevelt wanted an appropriate "racial" mix in postwar immigration patterns, a view which harked back to the eugenic argu-ments that fueled the 1924 immigration law rather than looking to a future in which such influences would be illegitimate.[80] In 1952, Con-gress enacted legislation over President Truman's veto, affirming na-tional origins. But as an expression of membership, the national origins system looked embarrassing after a war in which participants sought to end the use of such distinctions in politics. It took twenty years to abandon.

Successful reform came during President Lyndon Johnson's admin-istration (1963–1968). For Johnson, the national origins system dispar-aged "the ancestors of our fellow Americans" and "needlessly impedes . . . our foreign policy."[81] Johnson condemned the system as "incom-patible with our basic American tradition." Many supporters of reform tied their advocacy to civil rights reform. Secretary of Labor Willard

Wirtz explained this link between the abolition of national origins and the concurrent transformation of civil rights, telling Congress that such discrimination had "no place in a free and democratic society."[82] Secretary of State Dean Rusk was especially embarrassed by the continuing restrictions imposed upon persons from Asian countries or, in the parlance of the period, what he called "Asian stock."[83]

Both the Kennedy and Johnson administrations approached reform gingerly. They proposed a phased change, assuring congressional opponents that neither the number nor the composition of immigrants, in terms of countries of origin, would change significantly. Both claims were doubtful. The national composition of immigrants was likely to change since many countries with low quotas had long waiting lists of applicants seeking visas whereas those countries with high quotas often failed to fill them.

Even at this stage, some members of Congress openly defended the national origins system precisely on the grounds that its quota system permitted America to determine its cultural or "racial" composition, a position redolent with the assumptions of group hierarchy. This argument stalled reform for twenty years after World War II. Rusk was grilled by opponents in Congress who were wedded to the national origins aims of racial and ethnic balance (commonly buoyed by particular constituency interests against reform). In *Our Immigration Laws—Protect You, Your Job and Your Freedom*, one organization warned voters that unless they lobbied Congress, legislators would repeal the "safeguards against [the] radical distortion of the nature of the American population."[84] Traditionalists defended quotas as a means of retaining America's "true" heritage. The Daughters of the American Revolution feared that reform would "drastically alter the source of our immigration."[85] The American Coalition of Patriotic Societies lauded national origins for its guarantee "that the people who come in shall be a reflection of those who are already here."[86] Johnson personally assuaged the varying concerns of members of Congress about the reform.

The act abolished national origins quotas from July 1, 1968, and ended the Asia-Pacific Triangle provision. The bill gave all Western Hemisphere countries, such as Jamaica and Trinidad, which had gained independence since 1952 nonquota status. The previous restrictions embarrassed the United States' international image as a liberal democracy.

Relief was palpable in President Johnson's press statement welcoming the House Judiciary Committee's passage of the bill, which was followed by its passage in the Senate two months later. Johnson celebrated the law as the redemption of "the pledge of this nation to posterity—that free men have no fear of justice, and proud men have no taste for bias."[87]

President Johnson signed the bill on October 3, 1965. Rich with one-people symbolism, the signing ceremony was held on Liberty Island under the upraised arm of the Statue of Liberty in New York harbor, before an audience packed with famous immigrants, politicians, and representatives from immigrant organizations and publications.[88] The publishers of ethnic magazines for Chinese, Finnish, German, Hungarian, Italian, Latvian, Lithuanian, Norwegian, Polish, Slovak, Spanish, Swedish, and Ukrainian Americans, among others, were invited. Lyndon Johnson declared that by ending the "undemocratic" national origins system, the new law "repairs a deep and painful flaw in the fabric of American justice." The law abrogated exclusionary racial and ethnic boundaries in America's immigration regime. The discredited national origins quota was "un-American," in Johnson's words, because it "violated the basic principle of American democracy—the principle that values and rewards each man on the basis of his merit as a man." The hierarchical assumptions about race, ethnicity, and national background upon which it had rested were untenable, scientifically and democratically.

Yet in his own rhetoric, Johnson could not resist retaining and indeed celebrating a mythic account of America's immigration history, conflating involuntary immigration with those migrating by choice and glamorizing a frontier narrative of America's political development, thereby writing out the violent displacement of Native Americans from the nation's historical memory. Deploying this one-nation rhetoric, Johnson misleadingly asserted that "our beautiful America was built by a nation of strangers. From a hundred different places or more they have poured forth into an empty land, joining in and blending in one mighty and irresistible tide."[89] Such a whitewashing was at variance with President Johnson's own speech at Howard University, also in 1965, welcoming

African Americans, as "another nation," into the membership of the American nation. His narrative of American history ignored the reasons for the enactment of the Civil Rights and Voting Rights acts in 1964 and 1965.

For Johnson, one of many nation-builders, the one-nation rhetoric had a key political role in American nationalism. It anticipated the dissolution of group bases of identity into a liberal individualism—a future Johnson wanted to announce as much to international as to domestic audiences. The narrative provides a story line, apparently open to all individual Americans, through which they can accommodate themselves and their distinct histories, transcendent of group ties and therefore of any group-based injustices, and achieve full membership in a nation whose ideology celebrates that unabashed individualism. This transformation has still not really occurred.

FROM WARDS TO MEMBERS OF THE NATION

Johnson's reference to America as "an empty land" rehearsed the most conventional and tired narrative of American nationhood. Most worrying, this account overlooked Native Americans. Like other groups, Native Americans mobilized in the postwar decades to challenge this narrative and to demand greater rights of membership in the nation.

For American Indians, the 1941–1945 war was an assimilationist experience. Half of all Native American men living on reservations had either enlisted or been drafted by the war's end.[90] Native American war heroes were nationally acclaimed.[91] Others left reservations for war-industry jobs in urban areas. The combined effect was profoundly to alter Native American perceptions of America, their view of the possibilities for participation in American society, and their view of tribal self-government. Recognizing these changing attitudes, Congress implemented a strategy of "termination"[92] to end the notion of Native Americans as wards of the federal government (though in practice it created new opportunities for Native American lands to be sold off).

These developments set the stage for American Indians to negotiate a new type of membership in the American nation. The new status was acknowledged by both Presidents Lyndon Johnson and Richard Nixon. Johnson told Congress, in 1968, that "we must affirm the right of the first Americans to remain Indians while exercising their rights as Americans," and two years later Nixon announced that the "special relationship" would be protected in parallel with greater autonomy. The National Indian Youth Council orchestrated protest fish-ins to highlight how valuable natural resources seized from Native Americans had been to U.S. prosperity.[93] The council's actions won American Indians access to fish in their "usual and accustomed grounds." Their protests coincided with growing international recognition of liberal democracies' failure to treat their first peoples fairly. The eighteen-month occupation or "reclaiming," which began in November 1969, of Alcatraz Island in San Francisco Bay by a group of eighty activists (who cited the terms of the 1868 Treaty of Fort Laramie, giving American Indians the right to discarded or unused federal property which they had previously owned)[94] was a critical moment for many American Indians who wished to retain their heritage *and* to belong to the American nation. One young woman recalled: "[F]or the first time . . . I was proud to be an Indian.. I grew up in an all white area. It was very difficult. You were constantly struggling to maintain any kind of positive feeling, any kind of dignity. Alcatraz changed all that."[95] The "New Indians" and the red power movement had arrived.

Education policy damaged this generation and their parents. Whether in boarding or day schools, education had severed them from their own communities. Many could not converse in their own languages. The replacement of this system with one which integrated Native American children into regular schools produced new dilemmas. Many public school–educated young Native Americans felt alienated and cut off from their parents' world.[96] So despite nominal equality of membership, Native Americans' status within the American nation often appeared to be marginal or peripheral.

In the 1970s, militant Native American protests organized by the American Indian Movement (AIM) drew attention to the historical injustices perpetrated upon this community within the United States. Though termination policy was halted and reservations guaranteed, real amelioration was negligible. Entrenched inequalities prompted the occupation of the Bureau of Indian Affairs (BIA) in Washington (after a march on Washington by Native Americans led by the Trail of Broken Treaties movement)[97] and the siege at the village of Wounded Knee,

South Dakota, in 1973. The conflict between AIM and the FBI at Wounded Knee was intense and bloody.[98] Native Americans held protest marches in Washington, D.C., in 1978 (taking seven months from February to August) and again in 1994.

All of these events took place in an international context increasingly favorable to the rights of indigenous or aboriginal peoples, a trend which culminated in a UN declaration in 1994 on the rights of indigenous peoples. American Indian militants played to this global setting. Charged with illegally occupying and damaging property at the village of Wounded Knee (between February 27 and May 8, 1973) and causing injury to a federal officer, two AIM defendants, Russell Means and Dennis Banks, made their trial a public forum for both domestic and international audiences in which to rehearse the treatment of Native Americans in the United States and the government's failure to respect treaty rights (such as the Treaty of Fort Laramie, 1868). Means proclaimed to the courtroom: "[I]f I do not have treaty rights then my unborn and my children might as well right now become white people and forget, forget the traditional values and traditional ways because if we don't have treaty rights, we don't have any rights at all."[99] The defendants were acquitted.

This generation of Native Americans rejected the benign aims of the New Deal era when the pro–American Indian John Collier was commissioner. They deconstructed what they judged to be the Indian Reorganization Act's (1934) patronizing presumption about American Indian cultures. The president of the Association on American Indian Affairs, Oliver La Farge, dismissed the act as an "arcadian solution," which confined Native Americans to "a delightfully communal, antiindividualistic way of life upon the land, securely islanded in the ocean of our alien culture."[100]

Several decades later, as Indian criticism of federal policy intensified, the self-determination aspirations of the Collier era again became fashionable among American Indian leaders. In the former Indian Affairs commissioner's own words, the 1934 act offered "recognition that Indians, like everyone else, needed to organize, to function as individuals through groups of their own devising, and to make their own choices as to way of life."[101]

Native Americans pursued equality within American society but held steadfast to their group identity. This strategy offered a significant widening of the content of the American nation: American and Native American. In practice, self-determination meant the establishment of separate tribal groups, often more approximate of business organizations than autonomous governments but with distinct identities. This pattern has continued.

The United States' international role in defending democracy helped to trigger the democratization of American nationhood.[102] Through overseas engagements as an advocate and defender of liberal democracy, the United States' domestic treatment of some groups in American society was held up to intense foreign scrutiny and found to be inadequate. Decolonization and new international expectations about human rights intensified this scrutiny and its political significance. International tensions and foreign enemies, particularly totalitarian communists, provided the impetus to the new direction in U.S. foreign policy in the third quarter of the twentieth century. Communism created strategic and political challenges for policy makers, forcing both short-term and more considered responses. But the content of American foreign policy was not simply pragmatic. It genuflected to and articulated presumptions drawn from policy makers' understanding of American nationhood and its sources. A secular society mobilized an ideology of individualism and self-determination articulated through its founding documents in the service of protecting the Western democratic tradition.[103] Openness to criticism was key to this ideology. That openness, though often resented by assimilationist nationalists, was exploited by adversaries of the United States to publicize the group divisions in its society. The United States' success in addressing these group cleavages paradoxically strengthened the importance of its democratic institutions to American nationhood and consolidated the values promoted in its presence abroad: it helped the surge to democratic nationalist inclusion at home. Americans were reminded of their own anticolonial origins and the democratic expectations that this history had imparted.

These global pressures have been influential since the close of the Second World War. Writing for President Truman, the National Security Council, in its NSC-68 report, had concluded: "[W]e must lead in building a successfully functioning political and economic system in the free world. It is only by practical affirmation, abroad as well as at home, of our essential values, that we can preserve our own integrity."[104] This construction, dictated by enmity to totalitarianism, echoed both Woodrow Wilson's vision for a liberal world order and Franklin D. Roosevelt's wartime aims (and, indeed, anticipated language used by Presidents Ronald Reagan and George W. Bush).[105]

Politically and diplomatically, the Cold War could not be waged without some initiatives from America's nation-builders to improve civil rights and institutions at home to counteract group-based discrimination. These measures were presented as ways of providing individualism for those Americans experiencing injustice or inequality because of their association with particular groups; in practice, such reforms did not dissolve but instead recast the lines and political significance of group distinctions.

While the United States' presence and force in both the Second World War and the Cold War showed that it was an effective defender of liberal democracy, the seeds of its image in this role were laid during Woodrow Wilson's presidency and especially in his declarations about the intent of U.S. foreign policy during and after the Great War. By the conclusion of conflict in 1945, its role as a defender of democracy was integrated with a conception of America's moral leadership. As the essayist Henry Luce declared: America's internationalism "cannot come out of the vision of any one man. . . . It must be a sharing with all peoples of our Bill of Rights, our Declaration of Independence, our Constitution. It must be an internationalism of the people, by the people, and for the people."[106] Yet this Lucian image of "the people" was a strikingly individualistic one: it overlooked the important group hierarchies, identities, and divisions integral to how the ideology of American nationhood had developed over 100 years.

This projection of an individualistic, liberal, democratic world posed questions about democratic inclusion at home. How adequate were the founding documents as a model of integration? What implications followed for nation-builders of Luce's celebration of the Founding Fathers? No leaders in Washington would ever challenge the individualism presumed in American nationalism, but this individualism was in practice inseparable, as a guide to American politics, from deep group divisions. Making the nation democratic meant recognizing this intertwining.

It is striking how many initiatives to broaden the boundaries of membership and to realize democratic inclusion for historically marginalized groups only succeeded after decades of struggle in domestic and international arenas. Thus, there were ardent defenders of national origins as the basis for immigration policy in the 1960s and 1970s. And although the State Department had to ease the racist conditions facing black diplomats in Washington, it could concurrently withhold Paul Robeson's passport and ignore the demands of the NAACP that African Americans be promoted in the U.S. Foreign Service. The struggles of Native Americans further unpacks the uneven boundaries of membership in the American nation; American Indians paradoxically had to establish their distinct group identity as a basis for inclusion within the boundaries of the American nation. Group divisions did not dissipate. Latent in these group divisions and struggles over equality of membership was a politics divided in group terms, not the often anticipated erosion of group-based divisions into an individualistic nation. It is this latent potential which became the politics of multiculturalism.

8 ◆

Renewing the American Nation

In the second half of the twentieth century, the main propensity in international approaches to nationhood was to accord rights to individuals as individuals and to reject doctrines employed to distinguish among the members of a polity in terms of any group ascription they may hold or which is imputed to them. This pressure aided reformers struggling for civil rights in the United States, and between the 1940s and 1960s a package of measures was enacted by the U.S. Congress, upheld by the courts, and supported by presidents to break with America's historical mistreatment of some citizens because of their group membership. What this international pressure did not do was to effect an eradication of group referents, based on race, ethnicity, or national background, as determinants of classification in American public discourse and government policy. The reforms to the content of membership in the American nation have not made it a more individualistic ideology nor transformed it into a postethnic cosmopolitanism, despite the international influences to do so. Examining the reasons for this resistance provides a means to better understand the sources of American nationalism and how it develops over time.

Reform of American nationhood took place in a political setting deeply wedded to group referents in nation-building for a variety of historical and institutional reasons. Nation-builders have compelling political reasons to invoke a one-people ideology of American nationhood linked with rhetorical flourishes to individualism. It forms a renewable solution to the political divisions rooted in cultural diversity. But at the heart of the unfolding narrative of this ideology are the self-perceptions and consciousness of groups' histories held by their members. It is these histories which shape and configure the American nation because they are the filters through which Americans perceive their nation. In consequence, international influences mostly acted as pressures to excise group-based discrimination rather than as prompters to question the very place of group divisions in American nationhood.

On occasion, international influences for change were stalled or diluted by deliberate obstruction. The last chapter showed how the State Department succeeded in stopping an NAACP initiative at the United Nations designed to bring the position of African Americans to international attention. But there are more fundamental mechanisms ensuring that group identities and differences continue to structure the practice of American nationhood. Groups perform political roles, helping to integrate new arrivals in the American polity, an activity in no way diminished with the growth in transnational ties among many groups in America and their countries of origin. These political roles are greatly enhanced by the way in which existing institutional and government policies function with the presumption of group classification. One recent example nicely conveys this pattern: many universities have racially and ethnically themed graduation ceremonies at which the members of one group defined by race or ethnicity in a graduating class hold a dedicated ceremony.[1] Opponents of such events charge that they increase separatism for many students; supporters cite them as a way of enhancing intragroup support for members at a university. Either way, such events are striking instances of self-segregation comprehensible only in terms of America's historical tension between individualism and group divisions: for some groups, winning equality of membership still means acknowledging and sustaining, voluntarily, how vertical and horizontal divisions derived from race, ethnicity, and national background operate in the American polity. Democratic inclusiveness rests upon a community of groups likely to be renewed and reshaped over time but whose dissolution is improbable.[2]

These characteristics of American nationhood as a group-based ideology and practice reflect how *internal* the process of nation-building has been in the United States. Certainly, international influences have prodded nation-builders at key moments, alternatively embarrassing them because of discriminatory practices or encouraging reform to present a stronger image of the United States' liberal democracy abroad. But these international influences have been mediated into domestic nation-building through two key legacies: the historical legacy of a nation built on hierarchical assumptions about fitness for membership and having always to deal with the consequences of such distinctions and the legacy of being and remaining a multicultural nation.

The American nation is a multicultural one in at least two senses. Its citizenry is, and has always been, composed of a profound diversity of peoples in terms of Americans' own use of race, ethnicity, and nationality distinctions: despite the rhetoric of one-people nationhood, it is the terms of membership of these groups that fluctuate historically, not the presence of the groups.[3] The scale of America's group diversity is striking.[4] Compare the concatenation of nationalities in a city such as Los Angeles (including Americans of Korean, Mexican, Filipino, Vietnamese, Chinese, Japanese, Indian, Latino, Russian, and European origins) with the overwhelmingly white population of a town like Staunton, Virginia, President Woodrow Wilson's birthplace.[5] Indeed, the experiences of small-town white America compared with that of culturally diverse urban America are barely reconcilable. Even this distinction masks significant trends like the growth of the Latino population in midwestern states such as Iowa and Ohio. But they constitute a single nation, if one with group-based divisions, all claimed as part of one-people nationalism.[6]

Second, this diversity significantly influences American politics because group identities are strongly held and recur, and because of the way in which politicians structure appeals to definable groups in the electorate. But a group-based nation inevitably strains the contours of one-people membership because the members of some groups either reject the notion of a common narrative of inclusion or find themselves treated as marginal within any such shared narrative. This dialectic of inclusion and exclusion is why the development of American nationhood is so open-ended and why the rhetoric of "one nation" is so elastic.

This chapter examines three ways in which this narrative of American nationhood continues to unfold in a nonteleological fashion shaped by historically formed group divisions and government institutions. First, the way in which the American nation absorbs new members reveals how pivotal are group categories and communities to this process. Second, how the legacies of earlier injustices perpetrated upon some citizens enter the politics of nation-building is discussed with examples drawn from the experiences of American Indians and Japanese Americans. And last, the way in which government policies and institutions, such as the Census, structure public discourse in terms of group identities based on race, ethnicity, and national background is reviewed.

New Members and Nation-Building

A year before he signed the immigration reform law of 1965 to end national origins as a policy, President Lyndon Johnson reasserted the individualism of American nationhood: "[W]e are all Americans. We are one nation—one people."[7] Yet the new age that Johnson's speech wished to inaugurate in immigration reform failed to materialize in one significant sense. Americans still talk about immigration in terms of specific groups, ethnicities, and nationalities (increasingly linked with religion) retaining, if unwittingly, the language of national origins.[8] Why is this the case?

There are contingent reasons. During electoral campaigns, strategists of all parties employ ethnic, racial, or nationality distinctions as a key organizing premise with, for instance, increasing attention now paid to Latino voters. Other factors recycle historical grounds for group classification, for instance, hostility to a foreign language or immigrants' failure to acquire competence in English or the efforts of some ethnic groups to exploit the diversity visa program set up under the Immigration Reform and Control Act (1986) to reproduce the national origins biases. Another important factor is how America's enemies abroad are found in certain groups at home—a category which has shifted greatly over time. We have seen the examples of German Americans during the First World War, Japanese Americans during World War II, and most recently Arab and Muslim Americans as the "war on terrorism" is pursued. The rights of legal aliens have been chipped away piecemeal in judicial interpretations of the Patriot Act, which was enacted after the terrorist bombings of September 11, 2001.

But the central reason for the retention of group language is the rhetorical tradition of celebrating immigration as a defining American value and as a primary source of nationhood renewal. This celebration has group overtones. What makes the group appeal powerful is the historical categories through which immigrants are conceived and perceived. These categories are rehearsed and in part revised to relate to new groups of immigrants and to traditional problems of nation-building. Historically, immigrant groups pose specific challenges to nation-building, a concern of enduring significance. This is easily illustrated by how Latino and Asian American immigration is discussed.

Both the scale of Latin American immigration and the expansion of the Latino population are confirmed in the Census of 2000. One study calculates that non-Latino whites were, by the end of the 1990s, a minority in the United States' 100 largest cities. The same 100 cities collectively increased their Latino residents by 3.8 million between 1990 and 2000. According to the Census, Latinos comprised 12.5 percent of the American population compared with African Americans' 12.3 percent, Asian Americans' 3.6 percent, and Native Americans' 0.9 percent. Latinos numbered just over 35 million Americans, compared with 34.5 million African Americans, an increase of 50 percent over the Census of 1990. Mexicans made up half of the increase in Latinos. With existing patterns of immigration and the birth rates of resident Latinos, naturalized and alien, it is anticipated that this population will continue to grow during the next several decades. In some cities, Latinos constitute a significant proportion of the population, for instance, they are 46.5 percent of Los Angeles, 65.8 percent of Miami, and 91.3 of Brownsville, Texas. In other parts of the country, the Latino population is minute.

Intellectuals and politicians discuss the "Latinization" of the United States. A crude description, it is also unhistorical in that such a term overlooks the substantial patterns of migration to the United States since the nineteenth century.[9] The wartime *braceros* program, in place between 1942 and 1964, brought in up to 100,000 Mexican contract workers annually. Mexicans are especially associated with the category of illegal immigrants.

One way in which this Latinization trend is appropriated in public discourse about nationhood is through a concern with language competence. Recent immigration has reignited the significance of language, especially bilingualism, in American nationalism; more than 40 million Americans do not speak English as their first language at home. Speaking Spanish distinguishes Latino immigrants as a group, as it has done historically.[10] Spanish connects Mexican Americans to many other Latino groups, including Puerto Ricans and immigrants from Latin and Central America. It maintains and diffuses a Latino influence into America, an influence resisted by those who insist a nation must be united in a common language. Such opposition to Spanish is not new. New Mexico was denied statehood until 1912 because of the prevalence of Spanish. The ban on Spanish in California schools was ineffectual in the early part of the twentieth century, and both southern California and New Mexico had effectively segregated school systems. As late as the 1960s, children were reprimanded in schools in the Southwest for speaking Spanish, which was punishable with "Spanish detention."[11]

Bilingualism is a challenge to nation-building, although it has been practiced in some form since the nineteenth century. Most commonly, immigrants have been encouraged to learn English yet at times counterpressures have encouraged acceptance of operating in two languages. The Bilingual Education Act of 1968 addressed the problems of Spanish-speaking children in schools and legitimized the bilingual initiative. It also provided an opportunity for the Nixon presidency to woo Latino voters to the Republican party (with limited success). The Office of Civil Rights pioneered a campaign of bilingual education for children formerly classified, principally because of poor language performance, as mentally backward. In 1974, the U.S. Supreme Court found, in *Lau v. Nichols*, that failure to provide school instruction in children's languages (in this case, Chinese) violated their constitutional rights. Native Americans took advantage of this legislation to establish bilingual education programs (though many other Native American children attend regular high schools).

Some critics of bilingualism object in principle to its dilution of the American nation's single language; other critics come from those who have experienced it.[12] The former often promote a more general anti-immigrant perspective. California's Proposition 187, in 1994, imposed state limits on immigrants and their rights (receiving support from whites by two to one and opposition among Latinos of three to one). Several states, including California, Arizona, Colorado, and Florida, have made English their official language. But given the number of non-English speakers, this measure is tilting at windmills. When even a conservative Republican president willingly speaks to voters in Spanish, bilingualism is unlikely to contract (and in Texas, the two candidates seeking the Democratic gubernatorial nomination in 2002 held a debate in Spanish without controversy).

Thus bilingualism renews the meaning of membership compatible with American nationhood: it means that membership does not require, in practice, single-language competence. Language helps to maintain group distinctions: in a state such as California, where many residents receive their news from ethnic newspapers or broadcast outlets, these ethnic media help to maintain immigrants' ties with their home countries. This consequence challenges old-fashioned assimilation. Although language presents a potential for political division, the efforts of restrictionists and ardent nationalists to mobilize, in the 1990s, a narrower definition of the "one people" foundered. Formulating and projecting a historically narrow notion of America's one-people nation faces remarkable barriers in the current multinational composition of the population, but such an agenda always has supporters willing to wait for an appropriate political opportunity to advance their cause. It would be foolish to pronounce its demise.

Federal and state government reluctance to revert to Americanization programs enhances the retention of group identities. An international culture supportive of human rights, including the rights of migrant workers, in principle sets limits on what such measures can include. Increasing numbers of migrants hold dual nationality—a category which grew substantially in the 1990s, since about ninety countries permit dual nationality and, traditionally, the United States does not investigate whether its citizens hold another passport. For many individual migrants, whether or not they hold dual citizenship, integration into American society remains an experience structured along existing lines of group distinctions, distinctions rooted in ethnic, racial, and national classifications.

That language need not separate a group from membership is suggested by the experience of Puerto Ricans. Puerto Ricans are an intranational community. On the U.S. mainland, Puerto Ricans retain self-contained communities and strong ties with their homeland. The population is Spanish speaking and therefore occupies a distinct enclave in the U.S. polity: if Puerto Ricans are assimilated as a group, it is as a Spanish-speaking group. When Congress passed (overturning President Woodrow Wilson's veto) the literacy test for foreigners applying for citizenship in 1917, a clause had to be attached exempting Puerto Ricans by making them U.S. citizens irrespective of English competence. The vast numbers of non-English-speaking Puerto Ricans who settled in the United States, particularly in New York, from the 1940s occasioned another anomaly. The Voting Rights Act of 1965 included a special Puerto Rican clause, applicable to New York state alone, preventing the state from denying voting rights to any citizen whose education had been at a school in which the main language was other than English.

The most recent (December 1998) referendum in Puerto Rico opted to retain membership in the American nation. However, the traffic between the island of Puerto Rico and the mainland has exploded. In 1946, there were 135,000 Puerto Ricans in New York City. By 2000, 3.8 million Puerto Ricans lived in the United States compared with 2.8 million on the island itself. But this Puerto Rican community is bilingual. The Spanish language has not been sacrificed despite the primacy accorded English as a means of sustaining an assimilated border between the island and the mainland. But this endurance of Spanish has not been easy nor automatic. Language has been used to interact with other Spanish-speaking Hispanics and to define Puerto Ricans' relationship to the American nation. Puerto Ricans' cultural world is Latino dominated; they have been at the forefront of social movements demanding that public agencies use bilingual media in issuing information.

Asian Americans make up 11 percent of California's population, 13.1 percent of Seattle, 11.9 percent of Detroit, and 17.6 percent of the Queens borough of New York City. The term *Asian American* is an unsatisfactory hybrid which throws together the different cultures and traditions of, among others, Chinese, Filipino, Japanese, Asian Indian, Korean, Thai, and Vietnamese national backgrounds.[13] An invention of census takers, it subsumes close to sixty different subgroups. Attempts to establish distinctive political attitudes in such a heterogeneous group are of mixed value.[14] As a category, *Asian American* masks significantly varying experiences of American nation-building—experiences which are for the most part kept marginal from the national memory.[15] For instance, while it is widely known that both Chinese and Japanese communities were segregated by the 1920s, there is less knowledge as to why: these communities arose not as separatist choices but because of the restrictive conditions imposed by American society. Some Asian immigrants still feel outside the nation. A forty-year-old Vietnamese woman, for instance, reflected on her status: "[H]ow can I feel I am American? If you say you are American, you must look American. . . . That means being white. . . . Even if I get citizenship, I cannot say I am American. I am still Vietnamese with American citizenship. I cannot say I am American."[16] This self-description expresses the way in which some Asian Americans, historically and more recently, have felt themselves to be outsiders in the American nation. It could be balanced with testimony from immigrants who feel quite comfortable as members of the nation. What is important is that both negative and positive stances exist and have political consequences for how some Americans define themselves as members of the nation.[17]

Part of the reason for these different attitudes toward belonging is that Asian Americans have been subject to oscillating public presentations. On some occasions, they have been identified as a "model minority," praised in order to shame other groups' failure to prosper; at other times, the loyalty of Asian Americans has been challenged, for instance, the portrayal, in the 1990s, of some Chinese-American scientists as spies, and the association of Japanese Americans with a rival economic power has been used against them.[18] Among the tens of thousands of Chinese immigrants arriving since the 1960s many, particularly women, have had to take low-paying jobs in unskilled sections, such as the garment industry, working with fellow Chinese immigrants. This involvement in the enclave economy has made group identity salient for these immigrants and makes a sense of ethnic cohesion stronger than one based in economic class: a historically important role of group divisions in American nation-building has been to camouflage class tensions.

Residentially segregated Chinese New Yorkers present a classic group, based on immigrant identity and experience, that is presumed not to wish to assimilate.[19] The same pattern applies to first-generation Korean immigrants who interact principally with other Koreans, speak Korean at home and at work, and observe Korean customs. Second- and third-generation Korean Americans are unlikely to be so segregated but remain attached to a distinctive community, organized for instance in its own churches, Protestant but Korean speaking.[20] (This religious segregation slots into a much wider pattern observable in the different churches attended by African Americans and white Americans, despite a shared religiosity.)

The use of group language to describe immigrants has a significant political consequence for how nation-building and group diversity interact. Description of Asian and Latino immigrants as distinct groups maintains their opposition to American citizens despite being a part of the American nation. While employment of the phrase *new immigrant* to Asian Americans and Latinos is ahistorical, that ahistoricism begs investigation.

A key way in which the American nation's values and beliefs form and renew over time is through a selective historical memory which excludes a significant part of the United States' own history. This selectivity is a strength and a liability. It offers an exaggeratedly inclusive historical record: Americans can point to the many nationalities and ethnicities integrated into American nationhood. The weakness of selective memory is an obstacle to understanding the strength and importance of historical injustices: an implicit and, for some, explicit culture necessarily defines the "new immigrants" as foreign and in need of assimilation because they may be a threat to the nation as presently constituted. And it illustrates why to be genuinely inclusive one-people nationhood must be group sensitive: the rhetorical celebration of immigrants as a source of renewal too often conflicts with group-based practices.

In many respects, America has entered a new world of migration, for instance, in the growth of transnational links. For migrants from a village in the Dominican Republic living in a borough of Boston, their interconnected lives form a "transnational village."[21] Comparable transnational arrangements exist among migrants from Mexico, Jamaica, Haiti, and El Salvador (a trend helped in some cases, such as for Mexicans, by their governments' acceptance of dual citizenship). These communities are not only an expression of choices among their members to retain and solidify homeland ties. They are also responses to the often hostile conditions of immigrant life and a means of forging a safe niche within a wider process of nation-building from which the migrants often feel excluded. But, for some Americans, such transnational links represent threats to the renewal of American nationhood, not new sources of enrichment.

But transnationalism itself reflects legacies of the way in which individualism and group loyalties have developed in the United States and continue to shape newcomers' encounters. Latinos, for instance, experience racial discrimination, observable in the residential segregation of a city such as Boston. This encourages them to retain a stronger sense of solidarity and group identification than might have been expected, as one Dominican explains: "I will always be a minority in Boston. No matter how much money I make, I will never be considered a full-fledged American. People will always treat me as an outsider."[22] Discovering that being Puerto Rican singled them out as members of a group (as perceived by other Americans) came as a shock: "[O]nce on the mainland, I realized I was an 'ethnic,' a discovery that baffled me. . . . During my eighteen years in the United States, ethnicity has structured my experience."[23] Thus the choice to connect transnationally reflects in part being an outsider: it dilutes the unsettling experience of migration.

What was once seen as distinctive about Puerto Ricans' experience— their transnationalism and bilingualism—has become a more familiar experience for other groups in American society that retain close links to their home countries and speak their own languages but integrate into the American nation. It illustrates the way in which group diversity has to be reconciled with nation-building in a one-people ideology. It places limits on the drive to build an individualized core in American nationhood, yet it is mostly overlooked in celebratory accounts of the nation's immigrant values. The internal dynamics of nation-building explain this pattern. These dynamics also shape how historical injustices impinge upon enduring debates about membership.

The Costs of Nation-Building

The standard narrative of American nation-building expects group injustices to fade away and grievances to heal with the passage of time. This certainly occurs in respect to some groups' grievances, and

America's capacity to transcend its past helps this process enormously. However, some senses of injustice have not evaporated, frequently kept alive by parents telling children about the past mistreatment they or their ancestors endured or awakened by revelations about past policies. By strengthening their affinity with and loyalty to the group, this cross-generational legacy affects citizens' sense of membership in the polity and how others perceive them.[24] It sets an agenda for politics. Being a law-based and litigious society enhances the opportunity for compensation seeking and indeed partly fuels it.

Nonetheless, these sorts of demands about and reconciliations with the past are not just exercises in compensation. They are significant in showing how internal is the process of American nation-building: there are international influences complementing these internal dynamics (notably, the increased attention to the rights of first peoples in all settler societies), but the details of cross-generation reconciliation and of compensation are nationally specific.

Americans are often surprised by the persistence or reemergence of group demands in their national politics. Issues which many assumed had been resolved or evaporated decades ago can reappear as apparently settled boundaries of membership and community rights are reopened, leading sometimes to demands for restitution or to the creation of new group-based divisions. Few thought of Japanese Americans, in the 1950s and 1960s, as a group warranting redress for wartime internment, yet this compensation was achieved in the 1980s; a similar view may develop regarding some of those interned after the terrorist attacks of 9/11. The demand for reparations for slavery seems arcane and surprising to many: surely, many voters conclude, the Civil War ended a century and a half ago, and with its conclusion died the question of slavery. But the century after the Civil War ended coincided with a version of American nationhood and patriotism which camouflaged this legacy in U.S. politics or rather camouflaged the place of African Americans in this legacy.[25] For some descendants of slaves and for other Americans who worry about this legacy, the issue of reparations has real purchase.[26]

These challenges to revise the boundaries of internal membership, to enrich senses of belonging, and thereby to renew the American nation take several forms. Proponents of change are motivated by the ways in which the language and practice of group distinctions, often associated with inequalities, shape nation-building in America. First, there are revisions to give or withhold from some groups the rights of citizenship. The wartime treatment of Japanese Americans illustrates the latter while African Americans' fight for civil rights is an instance of the former. Enlarging inclusion is the most familiar type of revision and dominates the conventional narrative of America's shift to democratic inclusiveness. But revision can also be exclusionary as some Arab Americans have recently found and as judicial rulings about legal aliens since the Patriot Act of 2001 and the president's executive order issued on November 13, 2001, permitting detention and military trials for noncitizens accused of terrorism, attest. Second, boundary revision can involve some specific redress, remedy, or compensation for an identifiable violation of legal rights or for a historic injustice. The success of Native American claims about treaty violations is a case of such revision. Third, boundary revision can be undertaken to anticipate and preclude future inequalities or violations. Measures taken under this ambitious strategy can also themselves become sources of future conflicts about group membership and the parameters of democratic inclusion. Affirmative action policies are a case in point: their rationale is to improve the future prospects of those eligible for these benefits, but their implementation stokes existing lines of group cleavage and, for some Americans, forges new tensions. Minority-majority electoral districts are equally fraught.

Common to each type of boundary revision is a shared assumption: group hierarchies are an inadequate basis for a genuinely inclusive ideology of nationhood given America's community of groups. Yet Americans' and America's beliefs about group hierarchies have a deep hold on the nation. Indeed, the endurance of group distinctions in itself encourages the retention of hierarchical assumptions, usually with fixed views about the unsuitability of some groups to be full members. Compensation and reconciliation measures are designed to deepen the affected individuals' and groups' sense of belonging and membership in the one-people nation by expunging and recognizing the damage of earlier episodes in nation-building. To move forward as "one people" requires remembering how group diversity and nation-building have been inadequately reconciled in the past.

Understanding the demands and effects of boundary revisions returns us to President Lyndon Johnson's speech at Howard University in 1965, introduced in chapter 1. Johnson made justice for African Americans a federal priority, as a response to the historic injustice experienced by these citizens or their ancestors. But the implications of his address were wider than simply setting an agenda for African Americans. Unintentionally, the speech cast a light on many aspects of the nation-building process and on how membership and international influences, especially as a consequence of America's standing as a model of liberal democracy, mediated the content of nationhood; and the speech conveyed, though perhaps in ways the president failed to appreciate, just how far the boundaries of membership would need to be revised to make democratic inclusion of equal importance to assimilation in American nationalism. Thus, although his speech addressed the circumstances of African Americans only, it had implications for Native Americans, Mexican Americans, and other groups historically distinguished by race, ethnicity, or national background.

This historical legacy touches on unexpected aspects of Americans' historical narrative. For example, the familiar idea of America's national parks has to be revisited as the country takes account of how such apparent wilderness areas came into federal possession. As the American Indian Luther Standing Bear commented, "[O]nly to the white man was nature a 'wilderness,' and only to him was the land 'infested' with 'wild' animals and 'savage' people."[27] The sense of "American wilderness" is a luxury based on the deprivation of Native Americans' land rights. Such challenges to settled arrangements about membership and conventional views about historical claims of groups arise because, historically, American nation-building placed democratic inclusion on a back burner.

Building an assimilationist model of nationhood stored up questions about membership in the nation for future generations. For instance, ethnic Americans of European background, such as Italians, Germans, Poles, or Russians, whose traditions were discarded as they were educated in English, later searched out their languages and ethnic heritages. A long-term effect of immersion in American values was the stirring, in later generations, of an interest in their ethnic origins. Such motives prompted the Polish-American Chicago congressman Dan Rostenkowski to sponsor the National Ethnic Heritage Act in 1968. The act funded the study of those national and ethnic traditions pushed aside in the first half of the twentieth century. The program has been used by many groups to explore the United States' multiple traditions. The self-description as a hyphenated American has been revived as a badge of proud self-identification, not as a term of opprobrium used by the state's leaders. Anticipating a permanent settlement in the content of nationhood underestimates the tendency for issues about nationhood and democratic inclusion to move in and out of political significance and to be reshaped in the process. The balance between nation and democracy can differ over time and across states. Even within a one-nation ideology, there are significant varieties competing for dominance, for example, the Nation of Islam's vision of American nationhood differs from that of most other Americans.

Democratic inclusion heralded important changes in groups' membership in the nation, measured by their sense of belonging and not just by the possession of rights relative to their historical experiences. For instance, by the closing decades of the twentieth century, American attitudes toward American Indians had undergone a 180-degree change: the number of Americans claiming Native American ancestry had exploded, doubling in the decade between the Censuses in 1990 and 2000 (to 4.1 million). Having devoted most of the nineteenth century to the extinction of Native Americans, followed by their Americanization in the first half of the twentieth century, American Indians were now accorded center stage in the United States' newly discovered cultural plurality: indeed, California's celebrity governor, Arnold Schwarzenegger, felt entitled to criticize the wealth some Native Americans had accumulated from their casino outlets. Congress honored Navajo "code talker" veterans from World War II for their wartime work, yet the Navajo language they used had been banned among Navajo children in prewar schools, a nice instance of how nation-building often involves dismantling and reconfiguring existing institutions.

Some compensation is monetary. Examples include Mississippi's agreement to spend $500 million to help remedy the inequalities of its segregated university system[28] and the decision to pay reparations to survivors of the race riot in Tulsa in May 1921, which left at least forty African Americans dead.[29] Mexican Americans deported from Los Angeles during the economic crisis of the 1930s have initiated a lawsuit against the city seeking compensation on behalf of the estimated

400,000 expellees.[30] Lawyers working for groups of Black American workers, such as black farmers, have won compensation for long-standing discrimination by federal programs and agencies.[31] Finding justice for victims of civil rights protests in the 1960s has taken thirty to forty years on occasions. In some cases, the process continues.[32]

The Alaska Native Claims Settlement Act (1971) established a framework through which Native American claims upon their former lands could be addressed. The act paid $962.5 million to Native Americans and ceded 45 million acres to them. Under the act, the state was divided into regions with a corporation representing Native Americans in each region and an additional corporation to represent those who had left the state whether compulsorily or by choice. The settlement framework presents an opportunity both to atone for historic injustices in respect to the disputed territory and resources and to reach terms for future agreements. The 1971 framework has been used to settle other federal-tribal disputes.[33] There are many additional territorial claims pending as a new generation of tribal lawyers investigates the impact of forgotten treaties and deeds. Financed with revenues from licensed gambling and bolstered with an invigorated sense of cultural membership in the American nation, law school–educated Native American political leaders challenge apparently settled territorial agreements, unearthing a litany of broken treaties. The Iroquois, now represented by the Oneidas in New York and Wisconsin, have challenged rights to 250,000 acres in upstate New York.

The common demand by Native Americans is a return of land. But other sorts of demands exist. After a U.S. Army investigation of the Wounded Knee attack on Sioux people declared the 1890 encounter an "episode" rather than a massacre, South Dakota senator James Abourzek (Democrat) introduced a bill to pay $1,000 each to descendants of the Sioux people killed at Wounded Knee (which would have totaled $600,000). But the bill disappeared in committee.[34]

Affirmative action is probably the most familiar example of a compensatory measure.[35] It was implicit in the speech given by President Johnson in 1965 in Washington, D.C. While civil and voting rights paved the way for political equality, these measures were insufficient to integrate "another nation," Johnson concluded, without programs to address the social and economic inequalities created by racial inequalities.

Lyndon Johnson recognized that formal freedom—the rights and opportunities which had been withheld from African Americans—was an entitlement and a necessary prelude to integration but was not in itself sufficient.[36]

Since the late 1960s and particularly since the Supreme Court rulings in *Duke* (1971) and *Bakke* (1978), affirmative action has been part of public and private sector policy to achieve proportionate representation of minorities and women and to remedy past discrimination.[37] It divides voters, often bitterly. The Clinton White House defended affirmative action policies,[38] and in George W. Bush's administration Secretary of State Colin Powell has publicly stated his support for them. But most Republicans oppose the policy and for the University of Michigan admissions cases taken by the Supreme Court in the spring of 2003, President Bush filed an amicus curiae brief opposing the use of race in admissions decisions. The Court found by a 5–4 vote that it is permissible to use race as one factor in making admissions decision to ensure diversity but struck down by a 6–3 vote race as a basis for specifying quotas by giving an applicant's race a set of points. Judicial and political debate about affirmative action centers increasingly upon the definition of "diversity" as an aspect of American nationhood, the core of group politics.

The historical grounds for affirmative action are often misunderstood. It is the way in which group divisions developed which gives the policy resonance as a form of redress consistent with nation-building. The issues that affirmative action tackles will not vanish, in no small part because of how these issues impinge directly on American nationhood.[39] Two examples illustrate this point. First, part of the reason for reliance upon group language in discussing post-1965 immigration is the eligibility of many immigrants for affirmative action policies.[40] How affirmative action enlarges certain rights of membership is contested. This is an unanticipated but nonetheless real consequence of the group divisions in the American nation and not simply a strategy for enhancing minority rights.[41] The same entitlement has made counting the size of each Native American tribe financially consequential since federal money for health care and education is tied to the size of a tribe. Second, if the American nation were a color-blind nation, then the need for race to be a factor in public policy decisions such as affirmative action would end. But it is neither color- nor group-blind. And indeed it has never been such: group identities have shaped or limited opportunity for too many people since the nineteenth century.[42] One example of this color- or race-biased legacy is the emergence of reparations for slavery as a political issue.

For many African Americans, slavery is a historical event with deep resonance about their place in the American nation.[43] The end of the Civil War presented an opportunity for the United States to recompense former slaves for their involuntary transplantation to the United States and for their exploitation in its economy's interests. The promise, made to African Americans who had been slaves, of a homestead in the new union proved hollow.[44] That the federal government might have adopted a more generous view toward former slaves is suggested by the terms of the Homestead Act, enacted in 1862. It offered free title to 160 acres, from January 1,1863, in the public domain of the West to white settlers who resided and improved the land for five years. Of course, this policy relied on taking land from Native Americans. In the 1880s, a number of writers argued that the federal government should compensate African Americans for the costs of slavery, with ownership of land cited as the ideal recompense.[45] The contrast with the recent example of Zimbabwe, where the twenty-first century has begun with a brutal state-orchestrated process of land reclamation from white farmers, is striking; in comparison, nineteenth-century American plantation owners fared lightly. But the failure to act imaginatively in the 1880s made for a profound failure in nation-building as a process of democratic inclusion and equality.

The movement to win monetary reparations for slavery has intensified, not abated.[46] It rests on the proposition that to compensate for the effect of enslavement on Black Americans, there should be special tax rebates, individual repayments of a half million dollars, or a public fund to help disadvantaged communities. Although bills have been introduced in Congress (more than ten by Congressman John Conyers alone) for such reparations schemes and unsuccessful efforts to sue the federal government have been pursued, until the 1990s the prospect of reparations was distant. It has now attracted support from civil rights groups,[47] activists, and many African Americans and is increasingly part of an international movement. Ten cities have passed resolutions calling for federal hearings into the impact of slavery. The Democratic party's 2000 election manifesto included a clause supporting the establishment of a federal commission to study the legacies of slavery. President Bill Clinton apologized for slavery, and some companies have followed suit, usually offering contrition for selling insurance policies that reimbursed slave owners for financial losses when their slaves died. The *Hartford Courant* in Connecticut apologized for profits made advertising the sale of slaves and the capture of runaways.[48] A California law requires insurance companies to reveal any slave insurance policies they may have issued.

Some supporters of reparations cite a psychological motive which originates in the ideology of one-people American nationalism. Advocate Randall Robinson writes: "[U]ntil America's white ruling class accepts the fact that the book never closes on massive unredressed social wrongs, America can have no future as one people." Without the provision of "just compensation" (not simply affirmative action), Robinson contends, the negotiation of African-American membership in the U.S. polity is incomplete.[49] His views echo those of A. Philip Randolph when Randolph organized the wartime March on Washington. Like Robinson, Randolph wanted the boundaries of who was included within America's "one nation" comprehensively revised to resolve the biased treatment of some groups in its formation.

The movement for reparations for slavery has coincided with altering memories of the Civil War. Until as recently as the 1950s and 1960s, this conflagration was seen as a "good war" and the role of slavery in its gestation downplayed or ignored.[50] Instead, popular memory evoked folksy images of white Confederate and Union veterans meeting to swap anecdotes at Memorial Day celebrations. Such celebrations excluded the 200,000 African-American soldiers and sailors who had enlisted in the Union army and who were crucial to the North's victory. The centennial remembrance of the Civil War did little to dislodge this image and only much later was a memorial to black veterans erected in Washington.

The interest in reparations thus not only reflects slavery's legacy but also links contemporary issues in American nationhood to the endurance of group divisions.[51] It speaks to one form of nationhood renewal. But there is no real sign yet that reparations for slavery will be established. The contrast with redress for Japanese Americans' wartime internment is striking.

Few Japanese Americans spoke openly about compensation as they reintegrated into American society after wartime internment.[52] Some worried that demanding recompense might ignite anti-Japanese sentiment. This attitude changed, however, as anger about the unconstitutional incarceration mounted and as some associated the experiences of internment with discrimination.[53] Confidence grew among former camp inmates about both the justness of compensation and the need for American society to confront its wartime policy of internment as a form of national catharsis. For many Japanese Americans, this issue gradually became a necessary step in determining their own complete membership in the nation by repairing an earlier episode. One former internee observed, "[I]t is not what it means so much to me, but it is what it will mean to my grandchildren. The history books will show what happened. And my grandchildren will not grow up in the mainstream of America being stereotyped as enemies during time of war."[54] In 1988, the Civil Liberties Act, signed by President Reagan, apologized formally to Japanese-American citizens, and in 1990 surviving internees received the first monetary compensation.[55]

The buildup to the law's enactment was lengthy. The Japanese-American Citizens' League (JACL) declared a Day of Remembrance for incarceration for the Thanksgiving weekend in 1978. It organized a two-mile-long cavalcade of vehicles to journey from Seattle, Washington, to the Puyallup Fairgrounds, formerly home to 7,200 Japanese Americans as Camp Harmony.[56] Participants wore a yellow name tag to replicate those worn by internees.[57] Nine years after the Day of Remembrance, in 1987, an exhibition, "A More Perfect Union," at the Smithsonian about Japanese Americans during World War II included exhibits on internment and the achievements of recruits in the decorated 442d Regimental Combat Team. The organizers received hostile mail about the exhibition. Veterans' organizations opposed compensation.[58] From 1974, Congress included among its number Representative Norman Y. Mineta from California, who as a ten-year-old had himself been incarcerated. Mineta recalled, "[Y]ou have to imagine how we felt looking up at the guard towers, knowing that their guns pointed not outward but in, at us."[59] He was joined four years later by another former internee, Congressman Robert T. Matsui (and both were preceded by Hawaiian Democratic senator Daniel Inouye). In 1976, President Gerald Ford revoked Executive Order 9066 and declared the wartime internment "wrong."

The nine-member Commission on Wartime Relocation and Internment of Civilians, established by President Jimmy Carter to investigate the case for compensation, held eleven hearings to packed audiences in ten cities and retrieved records from the National Archives.[60] Emotional individual testimonies conveyed enduring senses of injustice. Some witnesses defended incarceration, but the commission's report, *Personal Justice Denied*,[61] unanimously found a "grave injustice" and recommended compensation.[62] Although some members of Congress objected to redress either on principle or because of their constituents' opposition,[63] the Democrats endorsed redress in their 1984 manifesto. Framing the issue as one of government violation of constitutional rights to equal treatment gave redress an appealing cloak and made the issue squarely one about membership in the nation.

A formal apology was delivered by President George Bush in October 1990 at a ceremony in Washington, D.C., at which the attorney general met with nine Japanese-American internees (the oldest of whom was 107) and gave each a check for $20,000. At this public exercise in cross-generational nation-building and renewal, Bush's language invoked the ideology of American nationhood: "[I]n enacting a law calling for restitution and offering a sincere apology, your fellow Americans have, in a very real sense, renewed their traditional commitment to the ideals of freedom, equality, and justice."[64]

Compensation and restitution enhance membership and belonging. These measures demonstrate how the ideology of American nationalism can be remolded to address neglected aspects of democratic inclusion. What one historian writes about Chinese and Japanese Americans can be generalized in numerous group directions: "[T]hinking about Orientals has always been thinking about what it means to be American."[65] Thinking about the problem of democratic inclusion and membership is a way of conceiving American national identity and how the country's nation-building has often rode roughshod over some groups and members. The process is more open and egalitarian than it has been historically, but the process itself is not novel.

A century ago, few Americans thought of the historical treatment of Native Americans as a blemish on the nation's history. Yet changes in international conceptions about the rights of first peoples and openness to group diversity induced a new perspective. Likewise, many Americans in the 1940s were indifferent to the rights of their fellow Japanese-American citizens and enthusiastic about their confinement. A half century later, these citizens had been transformed into a "model minority" whose complete membership in the U.S. polity seemed unquestionable, with many Americans unaware of Japanese Americans' historical experience. That sense of membership has been consolidated by restitution, which also helped to expel the historical charge against Japanese Americans of disloyalty and un-Americanism. But this advance does not obviate the place of group distinctions in how Americans measure their nation.

Measuring the Nation

Measurement is central to nation-building. By collating information about Americans in group terms, censuses compile the data with which to map group boundaries, measured as percentages of the population. This process commonly accentuates the presence of groups by renewing Americans' perception of whom makes up their nation. The collected data encourage public discussion of group trends. Populist newspaper headlines put race, ethnicity, and national background at the center of public debates and discussions about the content and meaning of American nationhood.

While judicial rulings (and international opinion) now deny any legitimacy to race as a meaningful biological category, government policies continue to differentiate among American citizens by race and ethnicity, principally in the shifting categories specified in the censuses taken every ten years.[66] This is the irony of American history: the fantasized version of a pure, individualistic past clashes with the group-based divisions expressed and acted out in government policy.

Data reliability is crucial because of the retention of "race" as a category in public policy, for instance, in affirmative action. In the same year as the Civil Rights Act, 1964, the Federal Interagency Committee on Education was created.[67] This ad hoc committee, with members from several federal departments later involved in administering affirmative action (such as Justice, Housing and Urban Development, and the Equal Employment Opportunity Commission), reviewed and revised Census classifications. The committee had to be sensitive to the political consequences of racial classifications in federal censuses and departmental rules. Subsequently, a directive from the Office of Management and Budget (OMB) in 1977 specified four racial classifications (American Indian or Alaskan Native, Asian or Pacific Islander, Black, and White) and two ethnicities (Hispanic Origin and Not of Hispanic Origin).[68] This classification scheme set the terms under which groups could seek official recognition for entitlement to group-based federal benefits.[69] The OMB's directive was modified in 1980 to include subcategories in the Hispanic and Asian/Pacific Islander categories. A further review resulted in the recommendation to include "multiracial" beginning with the 2000 Census.[70] In that Census, close to 2 million respondents (1,877,248) checked more than one racial category. Nationally, 2 percent of the 281.4 million Americans labeled themselves as belonging to more than one race; 5 percent of African Americans chose this option. The Census categorization shows the entrenchment of race language within the sinews of American nationhood.[71] Census categories will always be contested and reformulated; for example, many Latino Americans reject the description "Hispanic" because of its association with Spanish imperialism in Latin America, and they seek its replacement with Latino (just as the category "Negro" became "Negro or Black" in 1970 and "Black, African American, or Negro" in 2000). But in the short term, these categories measure the nation in groups.

Racial self-description, introduced by the U.S. Bureau of the Census in 1960, seems both to legitimate the concept of race and to cloud its sociological and historical specificity. But enumeration by race is not just a mathematical exercise in objective measurement. It is a political task. Apart from a few mavericks, scholars are universally agreed on the concept's emptiness: it has no scientific meaning and sheds no light about differences among people. However, whether deployed politically, socially, or demographically, it is a category articulated by us as citizens and members, law makers, and commentators and then embedded in policy and daily life.[72] Yet agreement about this duplicity has made only a marginal impact on political language and culture.[73] The use of race in political discourse is undiminished. Thus the intellectual rejection of any essentialist notion of race has had no effect on its continued employment in politics and policy. This paradox in American public life pops up in Danzy Senna's novel *From Caucasia, with Love*, in an exchange between the sisters Birdie and Cole, whose father is black and whose mother is white: "'[Pops] says there's no such thing as race.' [Cole] shrugged. 'He's right, you know. About it all being constructed. But that doesn't mean it doesn't exist.'"[74]

The language of group distinctions changed in American nationhood as scholars and politicians tried to eschew race, a change encouraged by international condemnations, such as that by UNESCO, of race as a legitimate category. Often nation-builders substitute the term *ethnicity* on the assumption that it is an impartial term. This is curious since the sociological and historical construction of "ethnicity" does not differ fundamentally from "race." There is no reason to think of ethnicity as in any sense more natural or less contestable than race. In a historically white society like the United States, expressing an ethnic identity can be an individual choice rather than a category imposed upon the individual.[75] It has a certain political convenience. But use of the term has not been accompanied by critical reflection about its genealogy. "Nationality" also rests upon the ability to distinguish different nations, groups, and histories, but the bases of these distinctions—language, religion, a shared past, appearance, and so forth—are all identifiers because they have been chosen as such. There is no neutral system or language of classification to mark people as inside or outside a "natural" identity. Indeed, all three terms—race, ethnicity, and nationality—conflict fundamentally with the assumptions of individualism and individual rights which democratic inclusion promotes.

There is now a plethora of constitutional, legislative, and monitoring institutions in place to identify and ideally resolve group-based discriminations. As an obligation of subscribing to the UN Committee on the Elimination of Racial Discrimination,[76] the United States is supposed to end racial discrimination at home. As with Census classifications, this obligation relies upon the retention of group definitions. Indeed, in its own report for the committee, the United States acknowledged group-based discrimination: "[I]ssues relating to race, ethnicity and national origin continue to play a negative role in American society. The path towards true racial equality has been uneven, and substantial barriers must still be overcome."[77] Yet much federal policy is pitched to the salience of group divisions in the American nation. For example, the National Park Service published a thematic framework in 1994 designed to "ensure that the full diversity of American history and prehistory is expressed in the National Park Service's identification and interpretation of historic properties."[78] It was a response to fresh understandings of American history and a rejection of the service's founding framework (1936), which celebrated a narrative of the "stages of American progress." Such group-based revisions about America's history of nation-building litter federal policy.

Numerous daily incidents remind some Americans that they are not simply American citizens.[79] Rather, they are Americans whose citizenship and identity is defined or measured, in the eyes of other Americans, by their group membership. Immigrants from the Dominican Republic living in Boston report their surprise, given their own self-definition, at being classified as people of color by most Bostonians.[80] In the fall of 2001, an eighteen-year-old African-American student at the University of Alabama was denied membership in any of the fifteen all-white sororities on campus; it was the second year she had applied. None of the sororities had ever admitted a black member.[81] The Supreme Court had to decide in December 2002 whether the Ku Klux Klan ritual of cross burning was a permissible exercise of the group's freedom of speech. In its fifteen-part series "How Race Is Lived in America," the *New York Times* documented encounters between people of color and whites in the United States.[82] The newspaper's uncritical retention of the term *race* suggests how embedded its reporters judged the term to be. Gerald Boyd, one of the editors responsible for the *New York Times* series, found in his newspaper's articles a stark portrayal of the way in which racial distinctions shape African-American experience: "[R]ace is out there, time and time again. And if you're not careful, it's going to reach out and slap you and knock you down in some way and you'll never be able to get up from it. . . . [T]o give whites and race so much power is to me incredibly destructive and counterproductive and hurts."[83] Relentless residential segregation by ethnic groups, the separate worlds of television channels and churches for black and white

Americans, or separate ethnic and racial university graduation ceremonies hardly help to arrest these patterns, although many are designed to erode the significance of group-based inequalities.[84]

Group distinctions extend to the way in which foreign policy lobbying occurs. Such foreign policy lobbying is significant because of the United States' global power and because of the multitude of groups of different national backgrounds that have been absorbed into America through immigration. Organized into groups representing particular ethnic, national, or racial groups, many Americans lobby intensely for foreign policies preferential to their countries of origin, whether to support or overthrow existing regimes. Refugees from communist countries were admitted during the Cold War years, and many became ardent supporters of the United States' anticommunist foreign policy.

Unexpectedly, the decline of anticommunism has enhanced the lobbying opportunities for ethnic groups, by opening up a wider set of ends in foreign policy.[85] During the Cold War years, nation-building was intimately linked with the United States' foreign policy of anticommunism. Lobbying by such groups as Cuban Americans, the World Jewish Congress, and Greek Americans in alliance with Armenians has increased since 1989, as has African Americans' interest in Haiti and Irish Americans' support of U.S. involvement in Northern Ireland. Mexican Americans' concerns influenced the 1990 Immigration Act (and the earlier 1986 Immigration Reform and Control Act), and Mexican-American pressure for further reform continues. Examples of ethnic lobbying to impose or rescind the use of economic sanctions in foreign policy are plentiful, for instance, the pressure from African Americans to impose tougher sanctions on the apartheid government of South Africa before Nelson Mandela's release from prison.

For many of these ethnic and national groups, such as Cuban Americans or Chinese Americans, the commitment to modifying conditions in their home countries is part of their self-identity, and because they think this change can be achieved in part through U.S. influence, there is a powerful motive for their loyalty to the American nation (though some scholars see these pressures as a traditional and continuing threat to the nation's political unity). This is one illustration of how American nationalism is infected with group distinctions of the sort many expected to fade by the close of the twentieth century.

The aspect of foreign policy in which this influence of a domestic group's lobbying is now most often noted is the United States' Middle East policy, in part because America is seen as the most influential presence in the region able to support or to withhold support from the key local actors. This power makes the domestic conflicts arising from relevant groups' interests potent. Israeli and Jewish Americans have been more successful in influencing America's self-perception and its foreign policy than have lobbyists for Arab countries or Palestinians. The diasporic connections between Jewish Americans and Israelis are deep and the visibility of this linkage has grown since 1967. One reason for this influence is the United States' projection of an image of liberal democracy, which gives it an affiliation with other democracies, such as Israel. Since Woodrow Wilson's presidency, the wish to strengthen other liberal democracies as part of a liberal world order has influenced U.S. foreign policy.[86]

The United States' ties with Israel appear firmer now than they did during the early Cold War years. President Harry Truman realized that supporting the new Israeli state, in 1948, would have domestic implications but considered it an appropriate step further to crush anti-Semitism. And Truman's Republican successor, Dwight Eisenhower, supported Israel but not without influencing its policy. He insisted that Israel return Egyptian territory seized after the Suez crisis in 1956. These presidents and their successors, Kennedy and Johnson, feared appearing one-sided in their Middle East policy. However, since the Israeli triumph in the war of 1967 and the election a year later of Richard Nixon to the presidency, American support of Israel has been steadfast,[87] despite occasional American rebukes of Israeli actions in Palestine.[88]

But the success of Jewish Americans in interweaving U.S. and Israeli policy has effects on the group bases of American nationalism. Such a cornerstone of foreign policy sets up its antithesis, as Arab and Muslim Americans find themselves lobbying for a revised Middle East policy and in the process sharpening the lines of ethnic and national group divisions within the American nation. Traditionally, Republican voters, Arab Americans have shifted from that party to the Democrats since the 9/11 terrorist attacks, while Republicans have found increasing support among Jewish-American voters.[89] Such structural influences on

American politics, based in an intertwining of domestic and international politics, help emphasize why group distinctions appear inherent to the definition of American nationalism and reveal the challenge of retaining one-people nationhood. Can American Jews and Arabs continue to agree on membership in these circumstances? These pressures matter more than in other countries both because the existence of group divisions is far more entrenched and because the United States is a superpower.

M easuring the nation every decade in a census which retains group categories ensures widespread knowledge about these cleavages and invites public discussion of their significance. It permits observation of the nation's renewal by measuring new arrivals but also fans old distinctions because that measurement is done using categories of enormous historical weight.[90]

The renewal of nationhood is complex and multilayered. For some scholars, a submerged white nationalism is more politically potent than commonly acknowledged,[91] while others argue that electoral appeals shaped by reference, whether negative or positive, to norms about racial equality have significant resonance with voters. Politicians (often at the gubernatorial level) call upon subtexts and implicit codes, which violate the presumptions of racial equality, to win white voters.[92] But explicit racial appeals are rare and unlikely to succeed, despite significant divisions between African-American and white American attitudes exhaustively reported in opinion surveys over many decades.[93] This reticence conveys how great a cultural sea change has occurred since the 1960s. There are plenty of scars, however, as the furor in December 2002 over Senator Trent Lott's ill-phrased testimonial to Strom Thurmond's support of racial segregation attests.

The change has not marked the end of black nationalist mass ideology, traceable to nineteenth- and twentieth-century activists, which rests in shared beliefs about the need for greater economic and political influence by African Americans and a desire among some to pursue some separatist institutions.[94] This ideology continues to be balanced, however, with judgments about what are realistic aims and the desire to assimilate in the American nation.[95] Many African Americans, especially those in middle-class occupations and income category, live both in a national culture historically structured to marginalize them and in strong group-based communities, as residential and church segregation confirms. In other countries, these divisions would be exclusively class-based. It is a modern form of Du Boisian double consciousness. This pattern is not limited to African Americans. It is also observable among other groups, notably Muslim Americans.[96] But the circumstances of these options, in the post-1960s decades, have changed: the dominant culture and institutions can no longer be unresponsive to racial injustices and group discrimination but must address them as core demands of nation-building, and the continuing ties of community are enjoyed by choice and preference and not simply as a response to an exclusionary culture. As reactions to 9/11 showed, the retention of group-based identities does not seem to weaken membership in and commitment to the one-nation ideology. The war against Iraq has further galvanized this one-people ideology at a national level, illustrated by the way in which some American soldiers, notably those who had not yet naturalized, were celebrated by the nation.

Attacks on America normally heighten Americans' sense of unity and belonging to one nation. But this effect is pronounced or deflated according to how individual citizens behave toward one another. If there are groups of citizens whose ethnicity or national background renders them vulnerable to association with the external enemy and that connection is drawn, then any fresh unity is damaged.

The September 2001 attacks stirred up some such internal group divisions (there has been harassment of some Arab Americans, complaints about detention, and an increase in hate crimes).[97] Patriotic sentiment was expressed by all groups.[98] The Immigration and Naturalization Service's initial decision to fingerprint certain visitors only, from twenty-five mostly Muslim countries, threatens to foment group conflicts and divisions, however; it has been criticized by Muslim-American groups and civil libertarians, who argue that if the system applied to all visitors, it would not be discriminatory. Selective application of a law means discrimination. Under a law passed during the Second World War, for reasons of national security, immigrants or tourists from specified countries can be photographed and fingerprinted on arrival. The State Department is unenthusiastic about the proposal because of the likely damage to the United States' external image. More generally, while the violation of civil liberties on the scale of Japanese-American internment has been eschewed by the powers enacted in the Patriot Act of 2001, despite the federal government's approval of secret military tribunals for accused terrorists,[99] increased phone tapping and e-mail reading powers have reversed the long-standing trend to enlarge the civil rights of Americans as a corollary of democratic inclusion. Legal aliens, for instance, have been one group affected by this new legislation with the U.S. Supreme Court's affirmation of their constitutional protection, stated as recently as the summer of 2001, set aside. To historically minded critics of America's democracy-building record, the confinement of detainees in Camp X-Ray at the U.S. Naval Station in Guantanamo Bay, Cuba, is troubling and violates Convention III of the 1949 Geneva Convention relative to the Treatment of Prisoners of War. For supporters of the martinent policy, those detained are not POWs but "unlawful belligerents" ineligible for Convention III protection,[100] whose status in international human rights law has yet to be established.[101] The exercise is a reminder of how the boundaries of membership can contract and expand over time. It is hard not to believe that aspects of this post-9/11 response will set future nation-building issues of the sort recounted in this chapter.

The 2001 terrorist attacks seemed to elevate religious sources of division to new significance. But the constitutional separation of church and state limits the potential for religion to become a source of group-based policies (though it did not, of course, historically preclude religious discrimination toward, for instance, Jews or Catholics). This separation enables groups to practice their religions uninhibitedly and to weaken any hierarchy of religions. The significance of separating church and state was underscored after September 11, 2001. President George W. Bush visited a mosque in Washington and, speaking to Congress, the president told Muslims, "[W]e respect your faith. It's practiced freely by many millions of Americans and by millions more in countries that America counts as friends."[102]

In historical perspective, the unexpected and sudden political exposure of Arab Americans in the United States is consistent with the way in which group divisions, rooted in race, ethnicity, or national background, have periodically fueled the content of American nationhood.[103] American nationhood was achieved by an immense struggle for inclusion and, as I have emphasized, such a struggle never really ends despite an ideology of shared one-people nationhood. This struggle has been long, complex, and arduous. Political leaders have had to accept that rather than liquidating group identities (or groups themselves), it was necessary to harness them into the one nation. On occasion, as with Puerto Ricans, this incorporation even required conceding the right to a first language other than English (though the possibility of Puerto Rico being admitted as a Spanish-speaking state would be a tougher test). This broadening created, in turn, models of and expectations about democratic inclusion for other groups in the U.S. polity: membership in the nation changes over time in response to new circumstances, reconsiderations of the past, and redefinitions of rights.

Such historical renegotiations are the authentic expression of immigrant values. Immigrant culture is not simply an expression of America's classlessness and openness. It operates as a continuing reference point for making decisions about membership in the nation and the terms of that membership and ultimately serves to renew American nationhood.

America's experience as a great multiethnic democracy affirms our conviction that people of many heritages and faiths can live and prosper in peace. Our own history is a long struggle to live up to our ideals.

—GEORGE W. BUSH, *National Security Strategy*

Conclusion

America's Post-Multiculturalist Settlement

Modern American nationhood can best be described, I propose, as an ideology of *post-multiculturalism*: the wide acknowledgment of group distinctions combined with a state struggling to ensure that government policies do not accentuate hierarchical divisions among groups based on race, ethnicity, and national background, a struggle which is rich in historical connotations and which can no longer presume a teleological narrative toward melting-pot individualism. It is "post" in that the demands commonly advanced under a multiculturalist agenda are now quite modest ones. Necessarily, and as the discussions in the previous chapters serve to warn, this post-multiculturalism should not be considered in any sense the final version of American nationhood, simply its present incarnation. Nonetheless, it is an incarnation which can be understood only by an appreciation of how the ideology of American nationhood developed since the early twentieth century, and it proves to be a resource for politicians leading the United States internationally. It also constitutes a language that few nation-builders can ignore in any articulation of America's future.

The Post-Multiculturalist Settlement

If they had been asked to characterize American nationhood, few of his predecessors in the White House, except perhaps Bill Clinton, would have employed President George W. Bush's description of America as a "great multiethnic democracy." Even Lyndon Johnson, the president who openly acknowledged the "separate nations" physically present within the American polity yet politically excluded, emphasized the prospective shift to a national ideology of individualism and the associated erosion of group ties. Bush's words are closer to the reality of America's post-multiculturalism, that is, the combination of a group-calibrated nation and an empowered state.

Post-multiculturalism describes the present settlement that has been reached in American nationhood, a settlement attained in the light of the two arguments advanced in the preceding chapters. It is an American version, distinct in several respects, of the great European invention of the Enlightenment: nationhood and the associated package of rights and obligations enshrined in citizenship.[1] First, America's one-nation or one-people nationalism masks powerful group divisions among Americans arising from ties rooted in race, ethnicity, and national background, sources of identity imposed upon the groups' members as much as assumed voluntarily. These ties and loyalties are far deeper and pervasive than in comparable Western democracies for historical reasons examined in preceding chapters. Second, the persistence and renewal, if at times unwittingly, of group divisions in the American nation preclude the transformation of American national identity into the long-dreamed-of Hartzian liberal individualism because these divisions are embedded in the nation's ideology and political fabric. Furthermore, managing the conflict between group-based demands for democratic inclusion and the expectations of a one-people nationalist rhetoric privileging individualism has resulted in a strong state in the United States, that is, a federal government holding the legal power and authority to design policies mitigating the negative effects of group divisions on American society.

As the preceding chapters have documented, the United States' policies toward immigrants and its marginalized groups have changed dramatically across the twentieth century. Federal policy has come to accept that American society is multiethnic and culturally diverse and that this diversity has to be recognized in public policy (for instance, through bilingual education programs or compensatory schemes to overcome historical injustices toward certain groups, including affirmative action and reparations). The impetus for this policy change has been historical and political: the enduring failure of a narrowly focused melting-pot conception of Americanization, of the sort triumphant in the interwar decades, to be inclusive. As Supreme Court justice Thurgood Marshall remarked in 1978, "[T]he dream of America as the great melting pot has not been realized for the Negro; because of his skin color he never even made it into the pot."[2] This historical mistreatment of African Americans demanded redress. America had also to consider its historical policy toward other groups, including American Indians (granted citizenship in 1924 and eligibility under the Bill of Rights in 1968), Chinese Americans (excluded from immigration from 1882 until 1944), and Japanese Americans (excluded from immigration in 1908 and unconstitutionally interned during World War II). Injustices toward some groups continue, as the last chapter illustrated. The policy articulated during the years 1917–1945 of intense Americanism had affected Americans of Eastern and Southern European origin, who had to divest the traditions and values of their nationalities (symbolized by Woodrow Wilson's wartime reproach to immigrants that to Americanize properly they had to "individualize"). All of these efforts permitted the engagement with cultural diversity apparent in the closing decades of the twentieth century, a propensity intensified by the significant growth in Latinos and Asian Americans and a greater realization of how the United States' group boundaries and divisions comprised its nation.[3] In the Census of 2000, Americans were invited, for the first time, to identify themselves as multiracial, an option more than 2 million took. It is a tentative step toward transcending the dominant black-white paradigm of American cultural pluralism, a step which has yet fully to infiltrate public discourse of the sort used by the country's nation-builders.

Nonetheless, as President Bush's description shows, America's current generation of nation-builders accepts the reality of multiculturalism. But multiculturalist expressions or "cultural wars" no longer shape and divide the country's politics in a way many commentators, from the Left and the Right, complained about in the 1980s and 1990s, and indeed in terms of influencing government policy, the United States' multiculturalism is modest compared with, for example, national policy in Australia or Canada. Multiculturalism just *configures* its politics, serving as a source of routine exchanges as much as stimulants to conflict. What can be termed the post-multiculturalist era offers a settlement of competing visions of nationhood within a successful state. It shows how, for a modern liberal democracy, state-building is of equal importance to nation-building: *state-building* here means transcending group identities and managing secessionist or sectarian visions of nationhood with an ideology, orchestrated by the state's leaders and maintained in public rituals, broad enough to permit strong group identities to endure within a legal framework upholding the rights and obligations of citizenship. The problems of state- and nation-building are commonly discussed in respect to the tragedies of post–Cold War or developing countries' efforts at state-building, such as the messy disintegration of communist Yugoslavia, but they pose a general challenge for modern democracies. Most leaders in Western democracies still aspire to assimilationist nationhood as France's 2004 law banning Muslim head scarves attests. America's post-multiculturalist settlement is a powerful and functioning alternative to the narrowly assimilationist trajectory, though a path periodically tested by immigration and by America's self-presentation abroad as a strong state which invariably defines some groups at home as adversaries of the one people. Such language episodically interrupts public discourse, as interpretations of the Census compilers' documentation of the growth of Latino and Asian-American populations testifies.

My emphasis on how enduring group divisions shape the content of American nationhood differs from standard narratives of American political development such as that presented by David Hollinger, introduced in chapter 1. Hollinger develops an argument about the ideology of American nationhood incorporating "individuals from a great variety of communities of descent" on egalitarian terms. In this approach, group divisions are expected to evaporate over time as a postethnic ethos and practice unfolds.[4] The expectation that a process equivalent to a melting pot will drive all Americans into a cosmopolitan postethnic identity in which the lingering commitments of race, ethnicity, or national background have vanished is fanciful. The very condition of being a successful state despite a wide diversity of group identities is that these identities are permitted to endure, to reform over time, and often to be joined by new group-based members; and as the preceding chapters have illustrated, such identities frequently intensify as a result of government policy making distinctions among citizens. Post-multiculturalism is not the same as postethnic cosmopolitanism since postethnicity assumes the dissolution of the group ties which we have seen remain central to how Americans understand their fellow citizens, perceive their society, and above all perceive new arrivals. Failure to recognize the post-multiculturalist settlement encourages an exaggerated view of America's individualism: the continuing insistence, in much public rhetoric, that people are judged as individuals in fact obstructs the creation of a genuinely inclusive nationalism appreciative of the country's community of groups.

A second influential account of American political development is set out by the historian Gary Gerstle. Gerstle finds that American nationhood reflects the struggles pursued by civil rights reformers who, in alliance with labor organizations and reformist politicians, eventually wrenched control of the political system from the forces of conservative and historically southern-dominated racists. Gerstle dissects the conflict between "racial" and "civic" nationalisms in U.S. political culture, the contradiction between them imploding in the 1960s, when civil rights were entrenched.[5] The problem with this sort of account is that it retains the assumption of a progressive shift toward some sense of "complete" nationhood, overlooking the potential for future group eruptions. The political scientist Rogers M. Smith, whose writings provide a third perspective on American nationhood, does not assume a progressive shift in American nationalism over time. In his interpretation of American citizenship laws, Smith finds an oscillation between liberal and illiberal ideals and practices, which have coalesced into a set of multiple traditions representing legacies of different groups in the U.S. polity. To advance their ends, politicians and political organizations endorse, Smith argues, ascriptive and hierarchical principles dominant at particular historical periods; these doctrines compete with egalitarian and nonascriptive claims about American nationhood's beliefs and values. Political endorsement of ascriptive rules secured assimilationist nationalism by defining groups out of the nation, whether on grounds of race, ethnicity, or nationality; struggles on behalf of the excluded thus displaced hierarchical laws. But to understand the influence of such non-egalitarian and exclusionary values, it is not sufficient to examine the political expressions of competing ideologies. As we have seen throughout this book, government policy was of equal importance with ideology in shaping group identities. Indeed, in many respects, government policy fixed the lines of group distinctions and defined the ideology of nationhood. It is from the interaction of government policy and group-based pressures that the making and remaking of American nationhood occurs. Though Smith recognizes the danger of illiberal ideology resurging, he maintains that the ethos of American nationhood can be harnessed to facilitate a shared political community committed to individualism.[6] This argument assumes the capacity of liberal individualism to transcend group identities when these identities in fact remain intact. The argument developed in this book shows that all three sorts of accounts of American nationhood underestimate both the international pressures and the continuing significance of group divisions in debates about the nation. It is more productive to recognize these forces and their persistence in post-multiculturalism.

This group diversity is profound and continuing. Census data suggest a post-multiculturalism in the American nation, that is to say, a distribution of diversity in terms of groups defined by race, ethnicity, and national background across the country. There are important trends hidden in this aggregate picture. For instance, close to a million white Americans have left metropolitan Los Angeles since the early 1990s for other states in the nation. California both receives waves of new immigrants and watches native-born Americans move elsewhere; other large immigrant-receiving states, such as New York, Florida, Illinois, and Texas, have some comparable trends of losing white native-born Americans to other less-diverse states, such as Colorado, Georgia, and North Carolina, though these last two states have also attracted relocating African Americans. These broad trends could be taken as a reflection on how unhappy or discomforted some Americans, especially native-born ones, are with the reality of group diversity in the post-multiculturalist era. Such discomfort is consistent with the patterns discussed in this book of how, throughout the twentieth century, Americans have perceived and classified others through the lenses of race, ethnicity, and national background. It may be that the projected growth of the populations of Latino and Asian Americans will mean the dissolution of concepts such as race and ethnicity in public discourse and will make such distinctions irrelevant. But this will require a shift in the very concepts employed in the Census and in government policy.

Furthermore, group tensions often appear as a negative presence in American politics. There are sporadic group-based acts of violence such as the lynching of African-American James Byrd, Jr., by three whites in Jasper, Texas, in 1998. President Bill Clinton identified both racial profiling by local police forces and the disproportionate number of African Americans and Latinos in the prison population as matters of grave concern. The disturbances in Cincinnati, Ohio, in April 2001 when the death of an African American was blamed on the police reflected the prevalence of racial profiling there. Intergroup tensions, often driven by race hate, persist. Many Arab Americans have felt vulnerable in post-9/11 America.[7] One scholar warns controversially, but in a historically consistent way, about the impact of Latinos on American society, judging them a force for the dilution of America's core values.[8] These incidents signal how group distinctions often still mean that some Americans experience inequality of membership in the American polity, and this mars the narrative of American nationhood as a progressive shift to liberal individualism. Group-based incidents epitomize the experience, spelled out by Lyndon Johnson in his 1965 Howard University speech, of "other nations" whose rights are trampled over in the construction of American nationhood. It is for the resolution of such conflicts that Americans look to their state.

The Strong State at Home and from Abroad

The post-multiculturalist juxtaposition of a group-calibrated nation and a strong state is profoundly challenging to our dominant perception of the United States. The American state is a successful institution integrating its diverse peoples around a flexible, often challenged and revised, but mostly maintained ideology and language of a one-people nation. But the United States is not a nation in the most conventional sense of one which equates a single national identity with a single state. The American nation is uniquely a nation of groups, whose members are able to support a common vision of their nation as a state internationally despite the domestic group divisions. American nationhood is built on a community of groups more than individuals in spite of the national ideology of one people. Being a strong state unites Americans across this community of groups: the state enforces a political solution to group lines of division. Its strong presence is a correlate of cultural diversity. This community is therefore much more than a Tocquevillian land of voluntary associations; it is a nation of strong and in many ways separate communities, which for the historical reasons examined in this book form along lines of race, ethnicity, and national background to a greater extent than in comparable liberal democracies.

Although much of America's struggles about democratic inclusion and the terms of membership within its ideology of nationhood have been expressed around groups making demands, such struggles have often been resolved in individualistic terms. Members of groups appeal to individualistic rights as the basis for securing equality of membership and democratic inclusion. The rhetoric of nationhood presumes such individualism to be protected beneath the umbrella of a one people. This puzzle makes the state seem less present in American society than in fact it is; it gives the state a much more definite role in defining the good life than Americans' political culture would suggest. This public role is commonly considered much weaker in the United States than elsewhere. For example, in a country such as France, where the state is preeminent and present in all spheres of life shaping public identities, this role is visible and transparent.[9] The state in the United States is also important to specifying certain areas as lying outside the public sphere, such as religious belief and practice.

To outsiders, it is unremarkable to think of the United States as possessing a strong state. The global power and reach of the United States has been one of the most important aspects of international politics since the mid-twentieth century, and this feature has not diminished since the end of the Cold War. Indeed, in many ways, the collapse of the communist states of Eastern Europe has increased the significance of the

United States since globally we live in a unipolar world. However, to many Americans, this image of being a strong state has not yet percolated significantly into their perceptions of the organization, maintenance, and renewal of American nationhood since a forceful state is still antithetical to the rhetorical presumptions of strong individualism and strong group-based communities.

If outsiders see a stronger state than most Americans would recognize, then they also see a far more homogeneous and undifferentiated American nation than most Americans would recognize. Paradoxically, American leaders have been able historically, and at present, to marshal the image of a populace united around one-people rhetoric in international affairs. The whole language of Americanization and anti-Americanism has exaggerated this image internationally.[10] Yet the reality domestically, as we have seen throughout this book, is a nation dealing continually with the pressures arising from presumptions about group differences and the consequent conflicts among groups about membership in the nation.

There is a symbiotic relationship between America's self-presentation abroad and its domestic policies of group divisions. The international image of a monolithic and homogeneous American nationhood underpins the continued association of the United States with Americanization and globalization. This coupling fuels the biases of anti-Americanism. The stronger anti-Americanism is, the greater the tendency for domestic policy makers to fear group divisions in American politics and the stronger the urge to evoke the melting-pot liberalism so popular in the conventional narrative of American nationalism. This framework unavoidably clashes with the real demands of groups whose identities rest in race, ethnicity, and national background and who had no option other than to organize in terms of government-maintained group categories.

Internationally, being a nation of groups proves, on occasion, a virtue to be exploited in foreign affairs. The United States' presentation at the Brussels World Fair in 1958 did this in the Cold War setting. The "war on terrorism" has encouraged the promotion of a positive portrait of America's multiethnic character more forcefully to foreign audiences. For instance, President George W. Bush celebrated this aspect of American nationalism by mimicking the sort of language used in the late 1930s and early 1940s to celebrate America's ethnic diversity as a core value which could be mobilized to unite the nation during wartime. Like many of his predecessors, President Bush has invoked a quasi-Wilsonian role for the United States, often giving it a quasi-religious cast. Visiting China in February 2002, Bush used his live television broadcast as an opportunity to proselytize to the Chinese people the virtues of democracy and American values: "[L]ife in America shows that liberty, paired with law, is not to be feared." He continued: "[I]n a free society, diversity is not disorder. Debate is not strife. And dissent is not revolution. A free society trusts its citizens to seek greatness in themselves and their country."[11]

This sort of language, playing to an image of America's domestic group diversity, goes against the dominant rhetoric of nationhood, that of being one people, and has therefore to be employed cautiously. As a political force, the United States is undoubtedly strengthened by the ability of its leaders to mobilize a united populace around the one-people theme; however, beneath the surface of this one nation lie group divisions which have historically proved fissiparous and which have changed over time in response to new demands for political inclusion and unanticipated international pressures, but they have not dissipated.[12] Balancing these divisions within one-people rhetoric is a recurring test of being a forceful state.

There is, of course, a fundamental caveat to how the ideology of American nationhood has been built on a community of groups and the rhetoric of solidarity: such arrangements may not always endure. It is this warning about nationhood's nonteleological narrative which shines through the way in which, historically, the tensions between a group-calibrated nation and a strong state have been managed, refigured, and advanced by America's nation-builders. The story of American nationhood is a continuing one.

Notes

1. Commencement address at Howard University, "To Fulfill These Rights," June 4, 1965, by President Lyndon B. Johnson; emphasis added. President Johnson's candle was overshadowed, though not quenched, by the urban riots, mimicked in other cities, in Watts, Los Angeles, in August of that year and by the racialized drafting system that was recruiting Americans for military service in Vietnam. The LA riots left scores dead and an indelible image of urban mayhem and angry protest among those Americans too long excluded from the internal parameters of American nationhood: segregation of African Americans was not the only "huge wrong" requiring restitution. It was such grievances and feelings of exclusion that the agenda to acknowledge the group divisions of American society laid out by Lyndon Johnson, in his Howard University speech, had to address.

In December 1972, weeks before he died, Johnson spoke to a civil rights conference in Austin and accepted that the "black problem today" was not a local problem but one facing "this whole nation." Progress required overcoming this "unequal history," an experience applicable to other groups in American society. Quoted in Robert Dallek, *Flawed Giant: Lyndon Johnson and His Times 1961–1973* (New York: Oxford University Press, 1998), 621–622.

2. For the idea of nationhood, see Rogers Brubaker, *Citizenship and Nationhood in France and Germany* (Cambridge, Mass.: Harvard University Press, 1992); the most recent important development to this literature is Rogers M. Smith's concept of peoplehood, which he developed in his book *Stories of Peoplehood: The Politics and Morals of Political Membership* (Cambridge: Cambridge University Press, 2003). For the wider context, see Randall Hansen,

"Globalization, Embedded Realism and Path Dependence," *Comparative Political Studies* 35 (2002): 259–283, and Christian Joppke, ed., *Challenge to the Nation-State* (Oxford: Oxford University Press, 1998).

3. A representative definition is Anthony D. Smith's: "a named human community occupying a homeland, and having common myths and a shared history, a common public culture, a single economy and common rights and duties for all members." *Nationalism: Theory, Ideology and History* (Oxford: Blackwell, 2001), 13.

4. As scholars such as Benedict Anderson, Michael Hechter, and Anthony Marx, among others, have explained. See Benedict Anderson, *Imagined Communities* (London: Verso, 1983); Michael Hechter, *Containing Nationalism* (Oxford: Oxford University Press, 2000); and Anthony W. Marx, *Making Nation and Race* (New York: Cambridge University Press, 1998), "The Nation-State and Its Exclusions," *Political Science Quarterly* 117 (2002): 103–126, and *Faith in Nation* (New York: Oxford University Press, 2003). For overviews, see John Breuilly, "Historians and the Nation," in *History and Historians in the Twentieth Century*, ed. Peter Burke (Oxford: Oxford University Press for the British Academy, 2002), 55–87, and Peter Alter, *Nationalism* (London: Arnold, 1994). For an important recent contribution, see Anthony D. Smith, *Chosen Peoples: Sacred Sources of National Identity* (Oxford: Oxford University Press, 2003).

5. See Hechter, *Containing Nationalism*, 7, for a cogent definition of *nationalism* which presumes such consanguinity. Another useful definition is Jack Snyder's: "the doctrine that a people who see themselves as distinct in their culture, history, institutions, or principles should rule themselves in a political system that expresses and protects those distinctive characteristics. A nation is, therefore, a group of people who see themselves in these terms and who aspire to self-rule." *From Voting to Violence* (New York: Norton, 2000), 23.

6. This formulation was at the heart of President Abraham Lincoln's Gettysburg Address when he expounded that the union's preservation could only be justified by reference to the aspirations of the United States' founding documents. For an excellent account of how the idea of an American nation, distinct from the idea of America, was formulated during and immediately after the Civil War years, see Melinda Lawson, *Patriot Fires: Forging a New American Nationalism in the Civil War North* (Lawrence: University Press of Kansas, 2002).

7. This implication also explains why the commonly drawn dichotomy between ethnic and civic nationalisms fails to accommodate the American case. More generally, see James F. Hollifield, *Immigrants, Markets and States* (Cambridge, Mass.: Harvard University Press, 1992).

8. Because these identities are not always assumed voluntarily, this is not the same as pluralism.

9. Some scholars have developed arguments for multicultural citizenship, a different formulation from mine since it rests less on historical analysis of

groups' significance within individual polities. See Will Kymlicka, *Multicultural Citizenship* (Oxford: Oxford University Press, 1995); and Christian Joppke and Steven Lukes, eds., *Multicultural Questions* (Oxford: Oxford University Press, 1999).

10. See Bonnie Honig, *Democracy and the Foreigner* (Princeton, N.J.: Princeton University Press, 2001), on the role of the "foreigner" in political discourse.

11. Will Kymlicka, "Western Political Theory and Ethnic Relations in Eastern Europe," in *Can Liberal Pluralism be Exported?* ed. Will Kymlicka and Magda Opalski, 13–105 (Oxford: Oxford University Press, 2001).

12. For the conventional narrative, see Seymour Martin Lipset, *The First New Nation* (New York: Basic, 1963), and *American Exceptionalism: A Double-Edged Sword* (New York: Norton, 1996). And for an influential argument about the American nation's success in assimilating immigrants, see Lawrence H. Fuchs, *The American Kaleidoscope* (Middletown, Conn.: Wesleyan University Press, 1990).

13. Louis Hartz, *The Liberal Tradition in America* (New York: Harcourt, Brace and World, 1955). For the most important critique, see Rogers M. Smith, "Beyond Tocqueville, Myrdal and Hartz: The Multiple Traditions in America," *American Political Science Review* 87 (1993): 549–566.

14. Lipset, *The First New Nation*; John Harmon McElroy, *American Beliefs: What Keeps a Big Country and a Diverse People Together* (Chicago: Dee, 1999); and Jill Lepore, *A Is for American* (New York: Vintage, 2002). Even David Hollinger's recent important paper implicitly imputes a teleological success story to American nationalism: "The Historian's Use of the United States and Vice Versa," in *Rethinking American History in a Global Age*, ed. Thomas Bender, 381–395 (Berkeley: University of California Press, 2002).

15. It was this tradition of individualism which influential exponents of American political culture such as Gunnar Myrdal (in his idea of an *American creed*) and Louis Hartz (who employed the term *liberal tradition* to capture the United States' ideology) advanced. See Gunnar Myrdal, *An American Dilemma*, 2 vols. (New York: Harper and Row, 1944); and Hartz, *The Liberal Tradition in America*.

16. Ideas of postethnic or cosmopolitan identity express contemporary efforts to push group plurality or cultural diversity into American individualism. David Hollinger, *Postethnic America* (New York: Basic, 1995).

17. Hollinger, "The Historian's Use of the United States and Vice Versa," 293. Emphasis in original.

18. Hollinger, *Postethnic America*.

19. "Erasing America's Color Lines," *New York Times*, January 14, 2001.

20. Nathan Glazer and Daniel Patrick Moynihan, *Beyond the Melting Pot*, 2d ed. (Cambridge, Mass.: MIT Press, 1970).

21. See Russell Thornton, "Trends among American Indians in the United States," in *America Becoming: Racial Trends and Their Consequences*, ed. Neil J.

Smelser, William Julius Wilson, and Faith Mitchell (Washington, D.C.: National Academy Press, 2001), 135–169.

22. This is an implicit theme in works defending a liberal nationalism. See David Miller, *On Nationality* (Oxford: Oxford University Press, 1995); and Yael Tamir, *Liberal Nationalism* (Princeton, N.J.: Princeton University Press, 1993). And see Andreas Wimmer, *Nationalist Exclusion and Ethnic Conflict* (New York: Cambridge University Press, 2002). This expectation informs most accounts of the nationalist conflicts in settings as varied as the Basque region, Sri Lanka, Northern Ireland, Kashmir, Corsica, the Western Sahara, and Kosovo. An exception is Mark Mazower's *The Balkans* (London: Routledge, 2001). For a perspective which presumes that ethnic conflict will endure, known as the "minorities at risk" perspective, see Ted Robert Gurr, *Peoples versus States* (Washington, D.C.: U.S. Institute of Peace, 2000).

23. For American defenders of nationalist assimilation, the tension between group and individualistic sources of identity is often seen as a product of the 1960s, associated with the rise of multiculturalism and coinciding with what political scientist Robert Putnam has identified as a decline in social capital. Robert Putnam, *Bowling Alone* (New York: Simon & Schuster, 2000).

24. John A. Carver, Jr., assistant secretary of the Interior, in hearings before the Subcommittee on Constitutional Rights of the Committee of the Judiciary, U.S. Senate, 87th Cong., 1st sess., *Constitutional Rights of the American Indian*, August 29, 30, 31, and September 1, 1961 (Washington, D.C.: U.S. Government Printing Office), 12.

25. I take *democracy* to be understood in a standard Dahlian sense as a polity characterized by free and open elections, guaranteed political participation for all eligible citizens, and protection of civil rights. Robert A. Dahl, *Polyarchy* (New Haven, Conn.: Yale University Press, 1971).

26. Rogers M. Smith, *Civic Ideals* (New Haven, Conn.: Yale University Press, 1997).

27. John Gerring, *Party Ideologies in America 1828–1996* (New York: Cambridge University Press, 1998), argues that American political parties have been much more ideological than hitherto recognized by scholars.

28. As argued in Anders Stephanson, *Manifest Destiny: American Expansion and the Empire of Right* (New York: Hill and Wang, 1995).

29. See Kevin K. Gaines, *Uplifting the Race* (Chapel Hill: University of North Carolina Press, 1996).

30. The centrality of individualism as a value treasured by American public opinion is confirmed in numerous surveys yet it coexists with views whereby many Americans categorize fellow citizens by their race. Although individualism is a core American political value, Donald R. Kinder and Tali Mendelberg find that "individualism has essentially no role to play in explaining Americans' views on issues of race"; they add that "individualism, conceived of as a general principle, cannot explain white Americans' opinion on matters of race."

See "Individualism Reconsidered," in *Racialized Politics*, ed. David O. Sears, Jim Sidanius, and Lawrence Bobo, 66–76 (Chicago: University of Chicago Press, 2000), 48, 53; and Martin Gilens, *Why Americans Hate Welfare* (Chicago: University of Chicago Press, 1999); Tali Mendelberg, *The Race Card* (Princeton, N.J.: Princeton University Press, 2001); and Melissa S. Williams, *Voice, Trust and Memory* (Princeton, N.J.: Princeton University Press, 1998).

31. *Public Papers of the Presidents of the United States: Harry S. Truman, 1952–1953.* "Address at Memorial Hall In Buffalo," October 9, 1952, 771.

32. Aldon D. Morris, *The Origins of the Civil Rights Movement* (New York: Free Press, 1984); Doug McAdam, *Political Process and the Development of Black Insurgency* (Chicago: University of Chicago Press, 1982); and David L. Leal, "Political Participation by Latino Non-Citizens in the United States," *British Journal of Political Science* 32 (2002): 353–370.

33. Kymlicka, "Western Political Theory," among others, singles out this challenge as the most important aspect of nation-building.

34. David W. Blight, *Race and Reunion* (Cambridge, Mass.: Harvard University Press, 2001).

35. The North's largest memorial, the Gettysburg National Military Park, incorporates monuments to southern veterans. See Wallace Evans Davies, *Patriotism on Parade* (Cambridge, Mass.: Harvard University Press, 1955).

36. David Brion Davis, "The Enduring Legacy of the South's Civil War Victory," *New York Times*, August 26, 2001, sec. 4.

37. Kirk Savage, "The Politics of Memory: Black Emancipation and the Civil War Monument," in *Commemorations: The Politics of National Identity*, ed. John R. Gillis, 127–149 (Princeton, N.J.: Princeton University Press, 1994).

War memorials, monuments, and ceremonies have elicited attention as official expressions of collective recollection. See Carolyn Marvin and David W. Ingle, *Blood Sacrifice and the Nation: Totem Rituals and the American Flag* (Cambridge: Cambridge University Press, 1999); Barry Schwartz, "Social Change and Collective Memory: The Democratization of George Washington," *American Sociological Review* 56 (1991): 221–236, and "Memory as a Cultural System: Abraham Lincoln in World War II," *American Sociological Review* 61 (1996): 908–927; and Janet Siskind, "The Invention of Thanksgiving: A Ritual of American Nationality," *Critique of Anthropology* 12 (1992): 167–191.

38. Savage, "The Politics of Memory."

39. Opened in 1996.

40. McElroy, *American Beliefs*.

41. For instance, the U.S. Information Service distributed press releases in the 1940s and 1950s about the achievements or progress of individual African Americans in the hope this would offset the more general and common picture of discrimination and inequality. Such releases included "Working for World Peace: Dr. Bunche in History" and "Negro Hurdler Is Determined to Win Olympic Event." The media presentation of the awards for best actor and

best actress, won by African Americans, at the Oscar ceremony in 2002 seems only to confirm this tradition.

42. South Carolina's legislature voted in 2000 to remove the Confederate flag from the flagpole on the top of the state's capitol building. In Georgia, the governor and legislature reached an agreement—in secrecy—to fly the flag at a point away from the capitol building. These issues have not ended; see Terry M. Neal, "Confederate Flag Rising as Issue in South Carolina," *Washington Post*, February 5, 2002.

43. Quoted in Udo Hebel, "Historical Bonding with an Expiring Heritage: Revisiting the Plymouth Festivities of 1920–21," in *Celebrating Ethnicity and Nation*, ed. Jurgen Heideking, Genevieve Fabre, and Kai Dreisbach (Oxford: Berghahn, 2001), 264.

44. See Amy Kaplan, *The Anarchy of Empire in the Making of U.S. Culture* (Cambridge, Mass.: Harvard University Press, 2002), 35–36.

45. Quoted in Hebel, "Historical Bonding," 265.

46. And such selective memorializing is hardly unique to the United States as a cursory review of how some countries have censored memory of the Second World War attests. On Poland and France, see Jan T. Gross, *Neighbors* (Princeton, N.J.: Princeton University Press, 2001); and Henry Rousso, *The Vichy Syndrome* (Cambridge, Mass.: Harvard University Press, 1991), respectively.

47. *New York Times*, November 27, 28, 1970. And see Amy Adamczyk, "On Thanksgiving and Collective Memory: Constructing the American Tradition," *Journal of Historical Sociology* 15 (2002): 343–365, esp. 357–359.

48. A phenomenon discussed by John D. Skrentny in his book *The Minority Rights Revolution* (Cambridge, Mass.: Harvard University Press, 2002).

49. And see the International Convention on the Elimination of all Forms of Racial Discrimination, 1966.

50. Robert H. Haddow, *Pavilions of Plenty: Exhibiting American Culture Abroad in the 1950s* (Washington, D.C.: Smithsonian Institution Press, 1997), 172–173.

51. See Tony Smith, *Foreign Attachments: The Power of Ethnic Groups in the Making of American Foreign Policy* (Cambridge, Mass.: Harvard University Press, 2000); and Andrew J. Bacevich, *American Empire: The Realities and Consequences of U.S. Diplomacy* (Cambridge, Mass.: Harvard University Press, 2002).

52. Mary Dudziak, *Cold War Civil Rights* (Princeton, N.J.: Princeton University Press, 2000); and Philip A. Klinkner with Rogers M. Smith, *The Unsteady March* (Chicago: University of Chicago Press, 1999).

53. Cited in Edmund Morris, *Dutch: A Memoir of Ronald Reagan* (London: HarperCollins, 1999), 511. For an academic version, see McElroy, *American Beliefs*.

54. For a representative view of this populism, see Patrick J. Buchanan, *The*

Death of the West: How Dying Populations and Immigrant Invasions Imperil Our Country and Civilization (New York: Dunne, 2002). For an analysis, see Elliott R. Barkan, "Return of the Nativists? California Public Opinion and Immigration in the 1980s and 1990s," *Social Science History* 27 (2003): 229–283.

55. Some critics argue that democratic nationalism is merely a veneer beneath which discrimination of minorities persist. For instance, the requirement to learn English in schools and to acquire English as a condition of naturalization has been criticized as violating the claim to "ethnocultural neutrality," a charge leveled by the leading theorists of diversity, including Will Kymlicka, "Western Political Theory," 17. This criticism may be too harsh as it glides over both the historical transformation of American nationhood, examined in the ensuing chapters, and the dense variety of Americanness now observable in the United States. America has largely succeeded in precluding group divisions (with, for example, Spanish a second language de facto in many parts of the United States), particularly culturally based collectivities, from becoming the basis of distinctive territorial or nationalist claims.

PART I INTRODUCTION

1. Peter Alter, *Nationalism* (London: Arnold, 1994).

2. Toward Native Americans, the views of anatomy professor Samuel George Morgan, expressed in his book *Crania Americania* (Philadelphia, Pa.: Dobson, 1839), 82, regretting "the inaptitude of the Indian for civilisation" converged with nineteenth-century extinctionist inclinations. The painter Albert Bierstadt captured the last sentiment in the note to his 1859 painting, *Wolf River*, observing that "now is the time to paint them, for they are rapidly passing away and soon will be known only to history."

CHAPTER 2

1. In *Downes v. Bidwell* 182 U.S. 244 (1901).

2. William S. E. Coleman, *Voices of Wounded Knee* (Lincoln: University of Nebraska Press, 2000).

3. The assimilationist philosophy was established in the settlement reached in the General Allotment (Dawes) Act of 1887, which allocated small allotments to Indian families and dissolved tribal governments. See Brian W. Dippie, *The Vanishing American: White Attitudes and U.S. Indian Policy* (Middletown, Conn.: Wesleyan University Press, 1982), 177.

The Dawes Act dealt with "the allotment of lands in severalty to Indians on the various reservations and to extend the protection of the laws of the United States and the Territories over the Indians"; *Congressional Record, Senate,*

February 17, 1886, p. 1558, vol. 17, pt. 2, 49th Cong., 1st sess. The words are from the bill S.54.

4. See remarks by the commissioner of Indian affairs in the annual report of 1873, in Richard J. Perry, *Apache Reservation: Indigenous Peoples and the American State* (Austin: University of Texas Press, 1993), 144. More generally, see Frederick Hoxie, *A Final Promise: The Campaign to Assimilate the Indians 1880–1920* (Lincoln: University of Nebraska Press, 1989), and *Parading through History: The Making of the Crow Nation in America 1805–1935* (New York: Cambridge University Press, 1995); Francis Paul Prucha, *The Great Father: The United States Government and the American Indians*, vol. 2 (Lincoln: University of Nebraska Press, 1984).

5. The Carlisle School was opened in 1879. Much of its approach was borrowed from the Hampton Normal and Agricultural Institute in Hampton, Virginia, founded in 1868 for African-American students; it had a small number of Native American children among its student body.

6. Prucha, *The Great Father*, vol. 2, 694–700.

7. October 15, 1902, quoted in Renee Sansom Flood, *Lost Bird of Wounded Knee: Spirit of the Lakota* (New York: Da Capa, 1998), 218.

8. Francis Paul Prucha, *Americanizing the American Indian* (Cambridge, Mass.: Harvard University Press, 1973), 266.

9. In 1889. Thomas J. Morgan, "Supplemental Report on Indian Education," House of Representatives, Executive Document No. 1, 51st Cong., 1st sess., ser. 2725, pp. 93–97, reproduced in Nancy Shoemaker, ed., *American Indians* (Oxford: Blackwell, 2001).

10. Morgan, "Supplemental Report on Indian Education," 235–239.

11. David Wallace Adams, "Schooling the Hopi: Federal Indian Policy Writ Small, 1887–1917," in *American Vistas: 1877 to the Present*, ed. Leonard Dinnerstein and Kenneth T. Jackson (New York: Oxford University Press, 1995), 58; Prucha, *The Great Father*, vol. 2, 816.

12. Alexander Posey, *The Fus Fixico Letters*, ed. Daniel F. Littlefield, Jr., and Carol A. Petty Hunter (Lincoln: University of Nebraska Press, 1993).

13. Cited in Jace Weaver, *That the People Might Live: Native American Literatures and Native American Community* (New York: Oxford University Press, 1997), 92; Posey began writing in 1902.

14. Francis La Flesche, *The Middle Way: Indian Schoolboys of the Omaha Tribe* (Madison: University of Wisconsin Press, 1963), xvii.

15. Robert Gessner, *Massacre: A Survey of Today's American Indian* (New York: Harrison Smith, 1931).

16. Adams, "Schooling the Hopi," 124–135; Prucha, *The Great Father*, vol. 2, 841–862.

17. Ira Katznelson and Margaret Weir, *Schooling for All* (New York: Basic, 1985); David Tyack, *The One Best System: A History of American Urban Education* (Cambridge, Mass.: Harvard University Press, 1974); and M. J. Hirschman

and S. Steinmo, "Correcting the Record: Understanding the History of Federal Intervention and Failure in Securing U.S. Educational Reform," *Educational Policy* 17 (2003): 343–364.

18. Such sentiments echoed the Progressive reformer John Dewey's influential arguments. And see Marc Stears, *Progressives, Pluralists and the Problems of the State* (Oxford: Oxford University Press, 2002).

19. Nancy Foner, *From Ellis Island to JFK* (New York: Columbia University Press, 2000), 191.

20. Introduced in 1904. For comparison see Robert Mirak, *Torn between Two Lands: Armenians in America 1890 to World War I* (Cambridge, Mass.: Harvard University Press, 1983).

21. The bureau's Division of Citizenship Training was in charge.

22. Committee on Immigration and Naturalization, Education and Americanization, Hearings, House of Representatives, 66th Cong., 1st sess., October 16, 17, 23, and 27 (Washington, D.C.: U.S. Government Printing Office), 6.

23. Committee on Education and Labor, *Americanization Bill*, Hearings, Senate, 66th Cong., 1st sess., September 11 (Washington, D.C.: U.S. Government Printing Office, 1919), 6.

24. Committee on Education and Labor, *Americanization Bill*, 6.

25. Ibid.

26. Quoted in Stephen Meyer, "Adapting the Immigrant to the Line: Americanization in the Ford Factory, 1914–1921," *Journal of Social History* 14 (1980): 70.

27. In April 1914, Ford called upon Peter Roberts, author of the instructional manual *English for Coming Americans* (New York: Harper, 1909), to design an English-language curriculum at the plant.

28. Meyer, "Adapting the Immigrant," 77.

29. Cecila Elizabeth O'Leary, *To Die For* (Princeton, N.J.: Princeton University Press, 1999), 237–238.

30. Chester Himes, *The Quality of Hurt* (New York: Thunder's Mouth Press, 1971), 7.

31. U.S. National Advisory Committee on Education, *Federal Relations to Education: Report of the National Advisory Committee on Education*, pt. 1, *Committee Findings and Recommendations* (Washington, D.C.: U.S. Government Printing Office, 1931).

32. Authored by John W. Davis, Mordecai W. Johnson, and Robert Moton, presidents of three Black American institutions of higher education.

33. David G. Gutierrez, *Walls and Mirrors: Mexican Americans, Mexican Immigrants and the Politics of Ethnicity* (Berkeley: University of California Press, 1995), 13–38.

34. Juan Gomez-Quinones, *Roots of Chicano Politics 1600–1940* (Albuquerque: University of New Mexico Press, 1994), 221–247.

35. In 1915.

36. For the California program, see George J. Sanchez, *Becoming Mexican American* (New York: Oxford University Press, 1993), 87–107.

37. For other sources of Mexican-American ethnic identity, see Gomez-Quinones, *Roots of Chicano Politics.*

38. In February 1899. Quoted in Arturo Morales Carrion, *Puerto Rico: A Political and Cultural History* (New York: Norton, 1983), 146.

39. McKinley made his proclamation on December 21, 1898.

40. In April 1937. Quoted in Carrion, *Puerto Rico,* 237.

41. Moorfield Storey and Marcial P. Lichauco, *The Conquest of the Philippines by the United States 1898–1925* (New York: Putnam's, 1926), 206.

42. By May 1901, Taft conceded that "confidentially, Atkinson is not what the Commission hoped for. . . . He lacks, it seems to me, in force." Quoted in Glenn Anthony May, *Social Engineering in the Philippines* (Westport, Conn.: Greenwood, 1980), 87.

43. Quoted in May, *Social Engineering in the Philippines,* 89.

44. May, *Social Engineering in the Philippines.*

45. Quoted in ibid., 89.

46. Early twentieth-century American control of the Cuban education system was marked by a similar bias toward industrial rather than academic education.

47. But Fred Atkinson's second successor, David Barrows, director of the Filipino educational bureau between 1903 and 1909, moved the curriculum back toward a 3Rs content though he shortened the period spent in primary schools.

48. Bonifacio S. Salamanca, *The Filipino Reaction to American Rule 1901–1913* (Quezon City, Philippines: New Day, 1968), 70.

49. See Usha Mahajani, *Philippine Nationalism* (St. Lucia, Australia: University of Queensland Press, 1971), 253.

50. Quoted in Salamanca, *Filipino Reaction to American Rule,* 74.

51. Quoted in ibid.

52. Ibid., 78.

53. This is one of the points made by such writers as Arthur Schlesinger, Jr., *The Disuniting of America* (New York: Norton, 1992); J. Harvie Wilkinson III, *One Nation Indivisible: How Ethnic Separatism Threatens America* (Reading, Mass.: Addison-Wesley, 1997); and Peter Brimelow, *Alien Nation* (New York: Random House, 1995).

54. See for instance the study of the school at Chilocco based on interviews with more than fifty former students by the anthropologist K. Tsianina Lomawaima, *They Called It Prairie Light: The Story of Chilocco Indian School* (Lincoln: University of Nebraska Press, 1994).

55. National Resources Committee, *The Problems of a Changing Population* (Washington, D.C.: U.S. Government Printing Office, 1938), 238.

56. Moorfield Storey, *What Shall We Do with Our Dependencies* (Boston: Ellis, 1903), 21.

CHAPTER 3

1. Barry Alan Joyce, *The Shaping of American Ethnology* (Lincoln: University of Nebraska Press, 2001), 146–147.

2. Charles Wilkes, *Narrative of the United States Exploring Expedition during the Years 1838, 1839, 1840, 1841, 1842*, 5 vols. (Philadelphia: Lea and Blanchard, 1845).

3. For the wider context of antebellum America, see the excellent discussion in Bruce A. Harvey, *American Geographics: U.S. National Narratives and the Representation of the Non-European World, 1830–1865* (Stanford, Calif.: Stanford University Press, 2001).

4. The exhibition was put on display in 1848.

5. Harvey, in *American Geographics*, writes: "[G]eographical textbooks confirmed U.S. exceptionality in global terms and instructed children in the disciplinary skills deemed requisite to maintaining that elevated position. . . . They did not just reflect normative white culture—they produced that culture, every day, at the sites of middle-class instruction" (21).

6. In Susan Schulten, *The Geographical Imagination in America 1880–1950* (Chicago: University of Chicago Press, 2001), 34–35. Other atlases, produced by Cram, included comparable schemes.

7. By the 1850s geography textbooks commonly distinguished these "races" as Asiatic, Malay, European, African, and American, each equating with a different level of civilization. Joyce, *Shaping of American Ethnology*, 3–4.

8. Catherine A. Lutz and Jane L. Collins, *Reading National Geographic* (Chicago: University of Chicago Press, 1993). In *American Orientalism* (Chapel Hill: University of North Carolina Press, 2003), Douglas Little draws on this source in his analysis of U.S. policy toward the Middle East. For the wider context see Matthew F. Jacobson, *Barbarian Virtues: The United States Encounters Foreign Peoples at Home and Abroad 1876–1917* (New York: Hill and Wang, 2000).

9. See, for example, the account in Thomas G. Dyer, *Theodore Roosevelt and the Idea of Race* (Baton Rouge: Louisiana State University Press, 1980).

10. Louis Menand, *The Metaphysical Club: A Study of Ideas in America* (London: Flamingo, 2001).

11. Quoted in Robert W. Rydell, *All the World's a Fair* (Chicago: University of Chicago Press, 1984), 219, 220.

12. Quoted in ibid., 222.

13. This characterization also applies to the aspirations of fairs held by other countries, which projected those countries' images; see Burton Benedict, ed., *The Anthropology of World's Fairs* (London and Berkeley: Lowie Museum of Anthropology in association with Scolar Press, 1983).

14. Held in Philadelphia, Chicago, Atlanta, Nashville, Omaha, Buffalo, St. Louis, Portland, Seattle, San Francisco, and San Diego.

15. As masterfully dissected in Rydell, *All the World's a Fair*, and *World of Fairs: The Century-of-Progress Expositions* (Chicago: University of Chicago Press, 1993).

16. The list of participating scientists was distinguished (and included Ales Hrdlicka, Otis T. Mason, John Wesley Powell, W. J. McGee, Frederick Starr, and, indirectly, Franz Boas). For anthropologists, ethnologists, eugenicists, and geographers, the world fairs proved to be opportunities to collect and display educational exhibits demonstrating the racial and evolutionary logic of the world's physical history and white America's preeminence in any classification of material progress and racial success.

17. Pioneered by the American New Women photographers. See Laura Wexler, *Tender Violence: Domestic Visions in an Age of U.S. Imperialism* (Chapel Hill: University of North Carolina Press, 2000).

18. Ibid., 20.

19. For an excellent account see Joyce, *Shaping of American Ethnology.*

20. As ethnologist Otis Mason emphasized, among civilized communities could be found "a reverence for the government, called patriotism [which held] . . . the people of a nation together," whereas among Native American tribes, "the strongest civilized bond is that of kinship, which, after all, is a racial characteristic." Quoted in Rydell, *All the World's a Fair*, 59.

21. Emma Sickles aired her view that the exhibits at the Chicago Exposition misled Americans by presenting Native Americans as savage or in desperate need of Americanization. See Rydell, *All the World's a Fair*, 63.

22. The Johnston photographs of Washington were published in sixteen booklets entitled *The New Education Illustrated*. See Wexler, *Tender Violence*, 131–132.

23. Wexler, *Tender Violence*, 149–151.

24. Matthew F. Jacobson, *Whiteness of a Different Color* (Cambridge, Mass.: Harvard University Press, 1998); Noel Ignatiev, *How the Irish Became White* (New York: Routledge, 1995); and Thomas A. Guglielmo, *White on Arrival* (New York: Oxford University Press, 2003).

25. Quoted in Kirk Savage, "The Politics of Memory: Black Emancipation and the Civil War Monument," in *Commemorations: The Politics of National Identity*, ed. John R. Gillis (Princeton, N.J.: Princeton University Press, 1994), 134.

26. John Bodnar, *Remaking America: Public Memory, Commemoration, and Patriotism in the Twentieth Century* (Princeton, N.J.: Princeton University Press, 1992), 31.

27. Neil Smith, *American Empire: Roosevelt's Geographer and the Prelude to Globalization* (Berkeley: University of California Press, 2003).

28. Founded in 1866.

29. Stuart McConnell, *Glorious Contentment: The Grand Army of the Republic 1865–1900* (Chapel Hill: University of North Carolina Press, 1992), 8. On the

one-drop rule, see Scott L. Malcomson, *One Drop of Blood* (New York: Farrar, Straus, Giroux, 2000).

30. McConnell, *Glorious Contentment.*

31. Reed Ueda, "Ethnic Diversity and National Identity in Public School Texts," in *Learning from the Past*, ed. Diane Ravitch and Maris A. Vinovskis, 113–136 (Baltimore, Md.: Johns Hopkins University Press, 1995).

32. For absorbing analyses, see Cecilia Elizabeth O'Leary, *To Die For: The Paradox of American Patriotism* (Princeton, N.J.: Princeton University Press, 1999); and John Bodnar, ed., *Bonds of Affection: Americans Define Their Patriotism* (Princeton, N.J.: Princeton University Press, 1996).

33. O'Leary, *To Die For*, 200–201.

34. See Wallace E. Davies, "The Problem of Race Segregation in the Grand Army of the Republic," *Journal of Southern History* 13 (1947): 354–372; and McConnell, *Glorious Contentment*, 71, 213–218.

35. One example often noted by scholars was Woodrow Wilson's much reprinted and widely used *A History of the American People* (New York: Harper, 1902), which certainly displayed these characteristics.

36. Paul Robeson, *Here I Stand* (London: Cassell, 1988), 27.

37. Melissa Nobles, *Shades of Citizenship* (Stanford, Calif.: Stanford University Press, 2000); Anthony W. Marx, "Race-Making and the Nation-State," *World Politics* 48 (1996): 180–208.

38. Malcomson, *One Drop of Blood.*

39. It was only in 1983 that Louisiana repealed its one-drop classification statute.

40. A concern expressed by historian Thomas C. Holt, "Marking: Race, Race-Making and the Writing of History," *American Historical Review* 100 (1995): 1–20, esp. 4. And see Thomas Holt, *The Problem of Race in the Twenty-First Century* (Cambridge, Mass.: Harvard University Press, 2000).

41. As Ian F. Haney Lopez so effectively documents in *White by Law* (New York: New York University Press, 1996). On the experience of Armenian Americans establishing their "whiteness" see Robert Mirak, *Torn between Two Lands* (Cambridge, Mass.: Harvard University Press, 1983), 280–283.

42. Nobles, *Shades of Citizenship*, 36.

43. Ibid., 188.

44. Ibid., 57–58.

45. Ibid., 59.

46. Ibid., 188.

47. As reported in the Census of 1920.

48. Paula Marantz Cohen, *Silent Film and the Triumph of the American Myth* (New York: Oxford University Press, 2001).

49. "Message to Newly Naturalized Citizens," in National Archives, Record Group 12, Records of the Office of Education, Records of the Office of the Commissioner, Historical, 1870–1950, File 106: Americanization, Entry 6, Box 11.

50. On the earlier Cuban campaign see Gary Gerstle, *American Crucible* (Princeton, N.J.: Princeton University Press, 2001).

51. In November 1899; quoted in Willard B. Gatewood, Jr., *Black Americans and the White Man's Burden 1898–1903* (Urbana: University of Illinois Press, 1975), 282.

52. See Willard B. Gatewood, Jr., *"Smoked Yankees" and the Struggle for Empire: Letters from Negro Soldiers 1898–1902* (Fayetteville: University of Arkansas Press, 1987).

53. November 4, 1899, in ibid., 247.

54. James A. Le Roy, "Race Prejudice in the Philippines," *Atlantic Monthly* 90 (July 1902), 100–112.

55. Quoted in Gatewood, *Black Americans and the White Man's Burden,* 285.

56. July 11, 1891, in ibid., 14.

CHAPTER 4

1. In 1879. Quoted in Andrew Gyory, *Closing the Gate: Race, Politics and the Chinese Exclusion Act* (Chapel Hill: University of North Carolina Press, 1998), 3–4. For an overview of the United States' immigration policy, see Daniel J. Tichenor, *Dividing Lines: The Politics of Immigration Control in America* (Princeton, N.J.: Princeton University Press, 2002).

2. In *People v. Hall* 4 Cal. 399 (1854).

3. Stuart Creighton Miller, *The Unwelcome Stranger: The American Image of the Chinese 1785–1882* (Berkeley: University of California Press, 1969), 92–93.

4. Quoted in Paul Gordon Lauren, *Power and Prejudice: The Politics and Diplomacy of Racial Discrimination* (Boulder, Colo.: Westview, 1996), 41.

5. Leonard Dinnerstein, Roger L. Nichols, and David M. Reimers, *Natives and Strangers: A Multicultural History of America* (New York: Oxford University Press, 1996), 191.

6. Alexander Saxton, *The Indispensable Enemy: Labor and the Anti-Chinese Movement in California* (Berkeley: University of California Press, 1971).

7. Tomas Almaguer, *Racial Fault Lines: The Historical Origins of White Supremacy in California* (Berkeley: University of California Press, 1994).

8. Miller, *The Unwelcome Stranger.*

9. Joint Special Committee on Chinese, Senate Report No. 689, 44th Cong., 2d sess. (Washington, D.C.: U.S. Government Printing Office, 1877).

10. Quoted in Gyory, *Closing the Gate,* 93.

11. As recounted in Lucy E. Salyer, *Laws Harsh as Tigers: Chinese Immigrants and the Shaping of Modern Immigration Law* (Chapel Hill: University of North Carolina Press, 1995).

12. *Congressional Record,* 53d Cong., 1st sess., vol. 25, pt. 3, p. 3085, Novem-

ber 2, 1893; quoted in Rubin Francis Weston, *Racism in U.S. Imperialism* (Columbia: University of South Carolina Press, 1972), 25.

13. In *Chae Chan Ping v. United States* (Chinese Exclusion case) 130 U.S. 581 (1889).

14. *Plessy v. Ferguson* 163 U.S. 537 (1896).

15. Cited in Greg Robinson, *By Order of the President* (Cambridge, Mass.: Harvard University Press, 2001), 31.

16. Desmond King, *Making Americans: Immigration, Race and the Origins of the Diverse Democracy* (Cambridge, Mass.: Harvard University Press, 2000); and Denis Lacorne, *La Crise de L'Identitie Americaine: Du Melting-Pot au Multiculturalisme* (Paris: Fayard, 1997).

17. Henry Yu, *Thinking Orientals: Migration, Contact, and Exoticism in Modern America* (New York: Oxford University Press, 2001).

18. See David J. Hellwig, "Afro-American Reactions to the Japanese and the Anti-Japanese Movement, 1906–1924," *Phylon* 38 (1977): 93–104.

19. In 1912; quoted in Weston, *Racism in U.S. Imperialism*, 32.

20. Ho Yow, "Chinese Exclusion: A Benefit or a Harm?" *North American Review* 173 (September 1901): 329.

21. Laura Wexler, *Tender Violence: Domestic Visions in an Age of U.S. Imperialism* (Chapel Hill: University of North Carolina Press, 2000), 269.

22. The centerpiece of John W. Dower's *War without Mercy* (New York: Pantheon, 1986).

23. Secretary of Labor James Davis told the Union of American Hebrew Congregations: "It is not only evident to truly American peoples but even to these Orientals themselves that they will never become assimilated. They are not of us." Letter from Davis to Simon Wolf, Union of American Hebrew Congregations, March 5, 1923, in National Archives, RG 174, Records of the Department of Labor, General Records 1907–1942, Chief Clerk's Files, 163/127A–163/127D, Box 165, Folder: 163/127C, Americanization: Sundry Files 1922–23.

24. Yu, *Thinking Orientals*.

25. In 1891 to the American Colonization Society. Quoted in Edwin S. Redkey, *Black Exodus: Black Nationalist and Back-to-Africa Movements 1890–1910* (New Haven, Conn.: Yale University Press, 1969), 8.

26. Paul Gilroy, *Black Atlantic* (London: Verso, 1993).

27. Bruce A. Harvey, *American Geographics: U.S. National Narratives and the Representation of the Non-European World, 1830–1865* (Stanford, Calif.: Stanford University Press, 2001).

28. Some were Africans returning from a life of slavery, including African Muslims. See Allan D. Austin, *African Muslims in Antebellum America* (New York: Routledge, 1997).

29. Howard Temperley, "African-American Aspirations and the Settlement of Liberia," in *After Slavery*, ed. Howard Temperley (London: Cass, 2000);

Philip J. Staudenraus, *The African Colonization Movement 1816–1865* (New York: Columbia University Press, 1961); Tom W. Schick, *Behold the Promised Land: A History of Afro-American Settler Society in Nineteenth Century Liberia* (Baltimore, Md.: Johns Hopkins University Press, 1980); Marie Tyler McGraw, "Richmond Free Blacks and African Colonization 1816–1832," *Journal of American Studies* 21 (1987). The passage of the Fugitive Slave Act in 1850 did soften the views of some African Americans toward Liberian separatism given the act's implication that all freed blacks could be reclaimed by white persons.

30. Cited in Temperley, "African-American Aspirations," 90, from the records of the American Colonization Society.

31. In Richard Newman, Patrick Rael, and Phillip Lapsansky, eds., *Pamphlets of Protest* (London: Routledge, 2001), 290, 301, 302.

32. See the account in Daryl Michael Scott, *Contempt and Pity* (Chapel Hill: University of North Carolina Press, 1997).

33. Redkey, *Black Exodus*, 9–10.

34. See Thomas G. Dyer, *Theodore Roosevelt and the Idea of Race* (Baton Rouge: Louisiana State University Press, 1980); and Gary Gerstle, *American Crucible* (Princeton, N.J.: Princeton University Press, 2001).

35. Two accompanying resolutions addressed the practicalities of federally orchestrated emigration. Redkey, *Black Exodus*, 59–60.

36. Quoted in ibid., 66.

37. Such as the black-run Liberian Exodus Joint Stock Steaming Company. The United Transatlantic Society, founded by Benjamin Singleton, with branches in Tennessee and Kansas, supported African-American emigration to West Africa on the grounds that Black Americans could form autonomous communities there free from racism.

38. In 1890.

39. Michael C. Dawson, *Black Visions: The Roots of Contemporary African-American Political Ideologies* (Chicago: University of Chicago Press, 2001).

40. David Levering Lewis, *W. E. B. Du Bois: Biography of a Race* (New York: Holt, 1993), 132.

41. Though this visit to Europe ended with a spell in prison for Bechet, this time eleven months in a French jail after a shooting in Montmartre, and then deportation; recounted in Craig Lloyd, *Eugene Bullard: Black Expatriate in Jazz-Age Paris* (Athens: University of Georgia Press, 2000), 102–104.

42. Claude McKay, *A Long Way from Home: An Autobiography* (London: Pluto, 1985), 311.

43. Chester Himes, *The Quality of Hurt: The Autobiography of Chester Himes*, vol. 1 (New York: Thunder's Mouth, 1971), 3–4.

44. Susan Gubar, *Race Changes: White Skin, Black Face in American Culture* (New York: Oxford University Press, 1997), 14–16; Ruth Frankenberg, ed., *Displacing Whiteness: Essays in Social and Cultural Criticism* (Durham, N.C.: Duke University Press, 1997). Many did not choose this option, however.

45. Gayle Wald, *Crossing the Line: Racial Passing in Twentieth-Century U.S. Literature and Narrative Form* (Durham, N.C.: Duke University Press, 2000); and Hazel Carby, *Reconstructing Womanhood: The Emergence of the Afro-American Woman Novelist* (New York: Oxford University Press, 1987). On passing in literature, see Shawn Michelle Smith, *American Archives: Gender, Race and Class in Visual Culture* (Princeton, N.J.: Princeton University Press, 1999), 189; John Cullen Gruesser, ed., *The Unruly Voice: Rediscovering Pauline Elizabeth Hopkins* (Urbana: University of Illinois Press, 1996); and Pauline Hopkins, *Magazine Novels of Pauline Hopkins* (New York: Oxford University Press, 1988). And see Nella Larsen's neglected novel *Passing* (Harmondsworth, England: Penguin, 1997).

46. Charles W. Chesnutt, *The Quarry* (Princeton, N.J.: Princeton University Press, 1999).

47. For an account see M. M. Ngai, "The Architecture of Race in American Immigration Law: A Reexamination of the Immigration Act of 1924," *Journal of American History* 86 (1999): 67–92.

48. See the comments of Albert Johnson, chair of the House Immigration Committee, in Committee on Immigration and Naturalization, *Americanization of Adult Aliens*, Hearings, House of Representatives, 69th Cong., 2d sess., February 17, 1927 (Washington, D.C.: U.S. Government Printing Office, 1927), 17.

49. The Court interpreted the rule of "ineligibility to citizenship" to denote "all natives of Asia within designated limits of latitude and longitude, including the whole of India." *United States v. Thind* 261 U.S. 204 (1923), 215.

50. George J. Sanchez, *Becoming Mexican American* (New York: Oxford University Press, 1993), 209–211.

51. Matthew F. Jacobson, *Whiteness of a Different Color* (Cambridge, Mass.: Harvard University Press, 1998).

52. *Public Papers of the Presidents: Harry S. Truman*, June 25, 1952, 442.

53. Statement by Dean Rusk before the Subcommittee on Immigration and Nationality, House Judiciary Committee, 88th Congress, First Session, Hearings on "Immigration Reform," July 2, 1964 (Washington, D.C.: U.S. Government Printing Office, 1964), 4.

CHAPTER 5

1. Important essays by Robin D. G. Kelley are included in his collection *Race Rebels* (New York: Free Press, 1994). And see Richard Iton, *Solidarity Blues* (Chapel Hill: University of North Carolina Press, 2000); and Winston James, *Holding Aloft the Banner of Ethiopia* (London: Verso, 1998).

2. Quoted in Frederick C. Luebke, *Bonds of Loyalty: German-Americans and World War I* (De Kalb: Northern Illinois University Press, 1974), 141.

3. These began from the 1860s. See Benedicte Deschamps, "Italian Ameri-

cans and Columbus Day: A Quest for Consensus between National and Group Identities, 1840–1910," in *Celebrating Ethnicity and Nation*, ed. Jurgen Heideking, Genevieve Fabre, and Kai Dreisbach (Oxford: Berghahn, 2001). See also Thomas A. Guglielmo, *White on Arrival: Italians, Race, Color, and Power in Chicago 1890–1945* (New York: Oxford University Press, 2003); and Christopher M. Sterba, *Good Americans: Italian and Jewish Immigrants during the First World War* (New York: Oxford University Press, 2003).

4. Desmond King, *Making Americans: Immigration, Race and the Origins of the Diverse Democracy* (Cambridge, Mass.: Harvard University Press, 2000).

5. Heike Bungert, "Demonstrating the Values of 'Gemüthlichkeit' and 'Cultur': The Festivals of German Americans in Milwaukee 1870–1910," in Heideking, Fabre, and Dreisbach, *Celebrating Ethnicity and Nation*.

6. Luebke, *Bonds of Loyalty*, 116.

7. Quoted in ibid., 122.

8. Discussed in Cecilia Elizabeth O'Leary, *To Die For: The Paradox of American Patriotism* (Princeton, N.J.: Princeton University Press, 1999), 241.

9. Mark Ellis, "German-Americans in World War I," in *Enemy Images in American History*, ed. Ragnhild Fiebig-von Hase and Ursula Lehmkuhl (Oxford: Berghahn, 1997), 192.

10. Carl Wittke, *German-Americans and the World War* (Columbus: Ohio State Archaeological and Historical Society, 1936).

11. In April 1919. Quoted in Wittke, *German-Americans and the World War*, 181.

12. Gary Gerstle, *American Crucible* (Princeton, N.J.: Princeton University Press, 2001); and Ellis, "German-Americans in World War I."

13. Carol L. Schmid, *The Politics of Language* (New York: Oxford University Press, 2001).

14. Stephen Vaughn, *Holding Fast the Inner Lines: Democracy, Nationalism and the Committee on Public Information* (Chapel Hill: University of North Carolina Press, 1980), 49–51.

15. There were 234 papers in 1920, with a combined circulation of 240,000, compared with 554 in 1910. Ellis, "German-Americans in World War I," 199.

16. Wittke, *German-Americans and the World War*.

17. U.S. Congress, Senate, Committee on the Judiciary, *Hearings on the National German-American Alliance*, 65th Cong., 2d sess., on Senate Bill 3529. The subcommittee consisted of King, Senator Josiah Oliver Wolcott (Delaware), and Senator Thomas Sterling (South Dakota). Luebke, *Bonds of Loyalty*, 269–270.

18. Quoted in Kevin Kenny, *The American Irish: A History* (Harlow, England: Longman, 2000), 195, who rightly notes its significance.

19. Ibid., 196.

20. John Bodnar, *Remaking America: Public Memory, Commemoration and Patriotism in the Twentieth Century* (Princeton, N.J.: Princeton University Press, 1992), 69–70.

21. Ibid., 57–58.

22. John Bodnar, "Public Memory in an American City: Commemoration in Cleveland," in *Commemorations: The Politics of National Identity*, ed. John R. Gillis, 74–89 (Princeton, N.J.: Princeton University Press, 1994).

23. James R. Mock and Cedric Larson, *Words That Won the War: The Story of the Committee on Public Information 1917–1919* (Princeton, N.J.: Princeton University Press, 1939).

24. Quoted in Vaughn, *Holding Fast the Inner Lines*, 43.

25. Discussed in O'Leary, *To Die For*, 231.

26. It was founded under Executive Order 2594 in April 1917. For the best accounts see Mock and Larson, *Words That Won the War*; and the scholarly Vaughn, *Holding Fast the Inner Lines*.

27. Mock and Larson, *Words That Won the War*.

28. Later renamed the Division of Civic and Educational Publications.

29. Professor Guy Stanton Ford from the University of Minnesota.

30. Other pamphlets included *German War Practices, Conquest and Kultur: Aims of the Germans in Their Own Words, The German Whisper*, and *The President's Flag Day Address*.

31. Steven Casey, *Cautious Crusade* (New York: Oxford University Press, 2001), ch. 5.

32. Committee on Public Information, *War Cyclopedia* (Washington, D.C.: Government Printing Office, 1918), 15.

33. Support came from the National Education Association's Commission on the National Emergency in Education.

34. Quoted in Vaughn, *Holding Fast the Inner Lines*, 101.

35. Through the foreign section's three units, the Wireless-Cable Service, the Foreign Press Bureau, and the Foreign Film Division.

36. In Saul K. Padover, ed., *Wilson's Ideals* (Washington, D.C.: American Council on Public Affairs, 1942), 91, 90.

37. A point underscored by Frank Ninkovich, *The Wilsonian Century* (Chicago: University of Chicago Press, 1999), 50. See also Lloyd E. Ambrosius, *Wilsonianism* (New York: Palgrave, 2002); and Thomas J. Knock, *To End All Wars: Woodrow Wilson and the Quest for a New World Order* (New York: Oxford University Press, 1992).

38. Jonathan Rosenberg, "For Democracy, Not Hypocrisy: World War and Race Relations in the United States, 1914–1919," *International History Review* 21 (1999): 592–625.

39. Quoted in Paul Gordon Lauren, "Human Rights in History: Diplomacy and Racial Equality at the Paris Peace Conference," *Diplomatic History* 2 (1978): 268.

40. Marc Gallicchio, *The African American Encounter with Japan & China* (Chapel Hill: University of North Carolina Press, 2000); Akira Iriye, *The Globalizing of America 1913–1945* (Cambridge: Cambridge University Press, 1993).

41. Quoted in Lauren, "Human Rights in History," 264.

42. Noriko Kawamura, "Wilsonian Idealism and Japanese Claims at the Paris Peace Conference," *Pacific Historical Review* 66 (1997): 503–526.

43. Quoted in Lauren, "Human Rights in History," 271.

44. April 13, 1919; quoted in Paul Gordon Lauren, *Power and Prejudice: The Politics and Diplomacy of Racial Discrimination* (Boulder, Colo.: Westview, 1996), 100.

45. A point underlined by Gallicchio, *The African American Encounter*, 28.

46. Henry Yu, *Thinking Orientals: Migration, Contact, and Exoticism in Modern America* (New York: Oxford University Press, 2001).

47. In 1930. Quoted in Christopher Thorne, "Racial Aspects of the Far Eastern War of 1941–1945," *Proceedings of the British Academy* 66 (1980): 329–340.

48. In 1932. Quoted in Thorne, "Racial Aspects of the Far Eastern War," 340.

49. In 1919. Quoted in Gallicchio, *African American Encounter*, 40.

PART II INTRODUCTION

1. This is a growing subject of scholarship. See Carol Anderson, *Eyes Off the Prize* (New York: Cambridge University Press, 2003); Mary Dudziak, *Cold War Civil Rights* (Princeton, N.J.: Princeton University Press, 2000); Cary Fraser, "Crossing the Color Line in Little Rock: The Eisenhower Administration and the Dilemma of Race for U.S. Foreign Policy," *Diplomatic History* 24 (2000): 233–264; Philip A. Klinkner with Rogers M. Smith, *The Unsteady March* (Chicago: University of Chicago Press, 1999); Daniel Kryder, *Divided Arsenal* (New York: Cambridge University Press, 2000); Azza Salama Layton, *International Politics and Civil Rights Policies in the United States 1941–1960* (New York: Cambridge University Press, 2000); and Penny M. Von Eschen, *Race against Empire* (Ithaca, N.Y.: Cornell University Press, 1997).

2. *The Problems of a Changing Population*. Report of the Committee on Population Problems to the National Resources Committee (Washington, D.C.: National Resources Committee, May 1938).

3. "The Promise of Human Rights," *Foreign Affairs* (1948), reproduced in Allida M. Black, ed., *Courage in a Dangerous World: The Political Writings of Eleanor Roosevelt* (New York: Columbia University Press, 1999), 162.

CHAPTER 6

1. For an excellent account of how complicated assuming this new role was for many of America's leaders, see Randall B. Woods, "World War II, Congress and the Roots of Postwar American Foreign Policy," in *Vietnam and the American Political Tradition*, ed. Randall B. Woods, 42–57 (Cambridge: Cambridge University Press, 2003).

2. He wrote: "[A]gainst the background of Hitler's treatment of the Jews, the Negroes' plight in this country is . . . an embarrassment to the efforts of the war leaders." Reproduced in Albert Fried, ed., *Communism in America: A History in Documents* (New York: Columbia University Press, 1997), 317.

3. An incident which stirred much interest in Pan-Africanism at home and weakened the appeal of the CPUSA among African Americans for the Soviet Union's failure to support anti-Italy motions in the League of Nations. On the wider context, see James H. Meriwether, *Proudly We Can Be Africans: Black Americans and Africa 1935–1961* (Chapel Hill: University of North Carolina Press, 2002).

4. Reproduced in Fried, *Communism in America*, 329.

5. Doug McAdam, *Political Process and the Development of Black Insurgency 1930–1970* (Chicago: University of Chicago Press, 1999), 103–105.

6. December 13, 1941. Quoted in Beth Bailey and David Ferber, "The 'Double-V' Campaign in World War II Hawaii: African Americans, Racial Ideology, and Federal Power," *Journal of Social History* 26 (1993): 817–843, esp. 817.

7. For the general stance of black newspapers during World War I, see William G. Jordan, *Black Newspapers and America's War for Democracy 1914–1920* (Chapel Hill: University of North Carolina Press, 2001).

8. In June 1942. Quoted in Marc Gallicchio, *The African American Encounter with Japan & China* (Chapel Hill: University of North Carolina Press, 2000), 137.

9. Horace Clayton, "Fighting for White Folks?" *Nation*, September 26, 1942, cited in Gallicchio, *The African American Encounter*, 149.

10. Meriwether, *Proudly We Can Be Americans*. And see Cary Fraser, "Understanding American Policy towards the Decolonization of European Empires, 1945–64," *Diplomacy & Statecraft* 3 (1992): 105–125.

11. A problem addressed by Robert Weaver through his Negro Employment and Training Branch at the Office of Production Management.

12. Beth Tompkins Bates, *Pullman Porters and the Rise of Protest Politics in Black America 1925–1945* (Chapel Hill: University of North Carolina Press, 2001); Daniel Kryder, *Divided Arsenal: Race and the American State during World War II* (New York: Cambridge University Press, 2000).

13. Quoted in Kryder, *Divided Arsenal*, 56.

14. It became the March on Washington movement after the June 1941 meeting among Randolph, Walter White, and President Roosevelt resulted in the issue of Executive Order 8802.

15. Quoted in Bates, *Pullman Porters*, 170.

16. Quoted in ibid., 153.

17. It was ratified by Congress in March 1942. For the best account, see Greg Robinson, *By Order of the President* (Cambridge, Mass.: Harvard University Press, 2001).

18. Robinson, *By Order of the President*, 77–78.

19. Richard Drinnon, *Keeper of the Concentration Camp: Dillon S. Myer and American Racism* (Berkeley: University of California Press, 1987).

20. First in *Hirabayashi v. United States* (1943) 20 U.S. 81. The plaintiff, Gordon Kyoshi Hirabayashi, had failed to register for evacuation.

21. In April 1943 the commander of the West Coast, John De Witte, made this admission in his report on the evacuation; this document was destroyed or suppressed by the War Department anxious to win its case before the Court. Robinson, *By Order of the President*, 184–185.

22. *Korematsu v. United States* (1944), 323 U.S. 214.

23. A judgment which therefore echoed naturalization decisions and the *Plessy* case.

24. 323 U.S. 283.

25. These forces receive excellent discussion in Robinson, *By Order of the President*.

26. Within the administration, a division was clear between the president's military cabinet colleagues—who favored detention—and the Justice Department where Attorney General Francis Biddle counseled against this course. In fact, Biddle was excluded from the final approval issued by the president to Secretary of War Stimson and his assistant secretary, John McCloy, to proceed with a mass evacuation from military exclusion zones on the West Coast (though not from Hawaii). Evacuation subsequently became internment for an indefinite period while the conflict persisted. Robinson, *By Order of the President*, 107.

27. To borrow Henry Yu's term; see *Thinking Orientals: Migration, Contact, and Exoticism in Modern America* (New York: Oxford University Press, 2001).

28. For the best account see Michael Burleigh, *The Third Reich: A New History* (London: Macmillan, 2000).

29. Robert B. Westbrook, "In the Mirror of the Enemy: Japanese Political Culture and the Peculiarities of American Patriotism in World War II," in *Bonds of Affection: Americans Define Their Patriotism*, ed. John Bodnar, 211–230 (Princeton, N.J.: Princeton University Press, 1996).

30. At the time of their evacuation from the West Coast, Secretary of War Henry Stimson remarked, "[T]heir racial characteristics are such that we cannot understand or trust even the citizens Japanese." Quoted in John W. Dower, *War without Mercy* (New York: Pantheon, 1986), 80.

31. As reported from a meeting with a British official and quoted in Christopher Thorne, *Allies of a Kind: The United States, Britain and the War against Japan 1941–1945* (Oxford: Oxford University Press, 1978), 168. The Smithsonian professor Ales Hrdlicka, who organized the physical anthropology displays at several world fairs, was commissioned to investigate this hypothesis.

32. As superbly documented in Dower, *War without Mercy*.

33. Yu, *Thinking Orientals*.

34. The use of historical images—including references to the insularity of the pre-Meiji feudal era (1603–1867), the divinity of the emperor, and indestructible loyalty to the emperor—were more common in popular discussions of Japanese politics than the ahistorical cultural anthropology set forth by experts, which emphasized the enduring effects of child-rearing institutions on Japanese adulthood (a view especially associated with Geoffrey Gorer, who later applied it to analysis of the Soviet Union). In engaging in work for the Office of War Information, anthropologists such as Ruth Benedict and Margaret Mead were breaking with the stricture of their mentor, Franz Boas, who had insisted upon scholarly autonomy. Susan Hegeman, *Patterns for America* (Princeton, N.J.: Princeton University, 1999).

35. As recounted in Dower, *War without Mercy*, 118–146.

36. Julie Otsuka, *When the Emperor Was Divine* (New York: Knopf, 2002).

37. Yuri Kochiyama, quoted in Joann Foung Jean Lee, *Asian Americans* (New York: New Press, 1991), 13.

38. Quoted in Robinson, *By Order of the President*, 170, 171.

39. Robinson, *By Order of the President*, 173–174; and see Steven Casey, *Cautious Crusade* (New York: Oxford University Press, 2001).

40. Internment had a parallel in wartime France where between February 1939 and May 1946, 600,000 men, women, and children were placed in detention camps for significant periods of time. Denis Peschanski, *La France Des Camps: L'internement 1938–1946* (Paris: Gallimard, 2002).

41. Quoted in Robinson, *By Order of the President*, 112.

42. Richard M. Fried, *The Russians Are Coming! The Russians Are Coming!* (New York: Oxford University Press, 1998), 22–23.

43. Paul Kusada writing to Mrs. Afton Nance, quoted in David K. Yoo, *Growing Up Nisei: Race, Generation and Culture among Japanese Americans of California 1924–1949* (Urbana: University of Illinois Press, 2000), 109.

44. *Government Information Manual for the Motion Pictures*, June 1942, quoted in Peter Novick, *The Holocaust and Collective Memory* (London: Bloomsbury, 1999), 28.

45. Aspects of wartime treatment of ethnic or African Americans contradict both the optimism of the 1938 report on evolving attitudes in the American population and the images projected in Hollywood movies of a diverse nation pulling together to overcome its historical partiality toward some groups.

46. F. H. Matthews, "The Revolt against Americanism: Cultural Pluralism and Cultural Relativism as an Ideology of Liberation," *Canadian Review of American Studies* 1 (1970): 4–31.

47. *The Problems of a Changing Population*. Report of the Committee on Population Problems to the National Resources Committee (Washington, D.C.: National Resources Committee, May 1938), 234.

48. Ibid., 236.

49. Ibid., 236, 237.

50. An option taken up by 181 tribes representing 129,750 American Indians and rejected by 77 tribes on behalf of 86,365 American Indians; the IRA was the brainchild of John Collier, a pro–Native American commissioner.

51. Congressman John W. McCormack speaking at a public hearing of the Special Committee on Un-American Activities, House of Representatives, 73rd Congress, Second Session, June 5, 1934, Hearing No. 73–DC-4 (Washington, D.C.: U.S. Government Printing Office, 1934), 2.

52. Colin Powell's autobiographical journey offers an excellent account of the desegregation of the military as experienced directly; see *A Soldier's Way: An Autobiography* (London: Hutchinson, 1995).

53. Quoted in Kryder, *Divided Arsenal*, 32.

54. At a meeting in September 1940 with A Philip Randolph, Walter White, and T. Arnold Hill of the National Urban League, President Roosevelt reiterated the policy of segregation in the armed services. Bates, *Pullman Porters*, 152.

55. October 9, 1940; quoted in Neil A. Wynn, "The Impact of the Second World War on the American Negro," *Contemporary History* 6 (1973): 45.

56. It could administer the laws and therefore could not, in 1939, "act outside the law, nor contrary to the will of the majority of the citizens of the Nation." Quoted in Bailey and Ferber, "The 'Double-V' Campaign in World War II Hawaii," 817.

57. Gallicchio, *The African American Encounter*, 111.

58. Kryder, *Divided Arsenal*.

59. Casey, *Cautious Crusade*.

60. Quoted in Phillip McGuire, "Judge Hastie, World War II, and Army Racism," *Journal of Negro History* 62 (1977): 358.

61. Manuel G. Gonzales, *Mexicanos: A History of Mexicans in the United States* (Bloomington: Indiana University Press, 1999), 162.

62. Ibid., 163.

63. Ibid., 191. See also Carlos Munoz, Jr., *Youth, Identity, Power: The Chicano Movement* (London: Verso, 1989).

64. Mary A. Renda, *Taking Haiti: Military Occupation and the Culture of U.S. Imperialism, 1915–1940* (Chapel Hill: University of North Carolina Press, 2001); and Louis A. Peretz, Jr., *Cuba: Between Reform and Revolution* (New York: Oxford University Press, 1988).

65. Speaking in 1936. Quoted in Robert Dallek, *Franklin D. Roosevelt and American Foreign Policy 1932–1945* (New York: Oxford University Press, 1979), 137.

The twentieth-century foreign policy of the United States is a vast subject with a rich scholarly literature. See inter alia, Walter LaFeber, *The Cambridge History of American Foreign Relations*, vol. 11 (Cambridge: Cambridge University Press, 1993); Akira Iriye, *The Cambridge History of American Foreign Relations*, vol. 111: *The Globalizing of America 1913–1945* (Cambridge: Cambridge University Press, 1993); Frank Ninkovich, *The Wilsonian Century: U.S. Foreign Policy since 1900* (Chicago: University of Chicago Press, 1999), and *The United States and Imperialism* (Oxford: Blackwell, 2001); and John Lewis Gaddis, *The United States and the End of the Cold War* (New York: Oxford University Press, 1992).

66. Quoted in Dallek, *Franklin D. Roosevelt and American Foreign Policy*, 284.

67. The concerns were discussed in detail at meetings of the wartime War Cabinet's Reconstruction Problems Committee, chaired by Arthur Greenwood, deputy leader of the Labour party. See the material in the Arthur Greenwood Papers, Bodleian Library, Oxford University.

68. Quoted in David Stafford, *Roosevelt and Churchill: Men of Secrets* (London: Little, Brown, 1999), 207.

69. *Chicago Defender*, November 28, 1942, in Penny M. Von Eschen, *Race against Empire: Black Americans and Anticolonialism 1937–1957* (Ithaca, N.Y.: Cornell University Press, 1997), 26–27.

70. Dallek, *Franklin D. Roosevelt and American Foreign Policy*, 516.

71. Quoted in Robert L. Harris, "Racial Equality and the United Nations Charter," in *New Directions in Civil Rights Studies*, ed. Armstead L. Robinson and Patricia Sullivan (Charlottesville: University Press of Virginia, 1991), 129.

72. William Roger Louis, *Imperialism at Bay 1941–1945: The United States and the Decolonization of the British Empire* (Oxford: Oxford University Press, 1977), chs. 8, 11, 12, and 15.

73. Quoted in Stafford, *Roosevelt and Churchill*, 285.

74. Quoted in Kenneth R. Jankin, "From Colonial Liberation to Cold War Liberalism: Walter White, the NAACP and Foreign Affairs, 1941–1955," *Ethnic and Racial Studies* 21 (1998): 1078.

75. Quoted in Harris, "Racial Equality and the United Nations Charter," 136.

76. Quoted in Michael L. Krenn, *Black Diplomacy: African Americans and the State Department 1945–1969* (New York: Sharpe, 1999), 11.

77. Harris, "Racial Equality and the UN Charter"; Jankin, "From Colonial Liberation to Cold War Liberalism."

78. Jankin, "From Colonial Liberation to Cold War Liberalism."

79. Krenn, *Black Diplomacy*, 12.

80. Winston Churchill, "The Sinews of Peace," speech, March 5, 1946, delivered at Westminster College in Missouri. The speech is available at www.hpol.org/churchill.

81. Quoted in Krenn, *Black Diplomacy*, 13.

82. Quoted in Carol Anderson, "From Hope to Disillusion: African Americans, the United Nations, and the Struggle for Human Rights, 1944–1947," *Diplomatic History* 20 (1996): 543.

83. On relations between these two, see Jankin, "From Colonial Liberation to Cold War Liberalism."

84. Quoted in Harris, "Racial Equality and the UN Charter," 137.

85. The Colonial Conference, held on April 6, 1945, was attended by representatives from India, Puerto Rico, Jamaica, Indonesia, Burma, and the Gold Coast, among others.

86. The association nominated W. E. B. Du Bois to represent African-American interests at planning meetings for the United Nations. See Anderson, "From Hope to Disillusion"; and Jankin, "From Colonial Liberation to Cold War Liberalism."

87. Quoted in Harris, "Racial Equality and the United Nations Charter," 142.

88. This argument is made in particular by Kirsten Sellars in *The Rise and Rise of Human Rights* (Stroud, England: Sutton, 2002).

89. MacArthur served until April 1951.

90. In his impressive account of this period, *Embracing Defeat: Japan in the Wake of World War II* (New York: Norton, 1999), John W. Dower describes the Americans as "sentimental imperialists," 73, a term which I think misuses the concept of imperialism. For another fine study, see Ray A. Moore and Donald L. Robinson, *Partners for Democracy: Crafting the New Japanese State under MacArthur* (New York: Oxford University Press, 2002).

91. Dower, *Embracing Defeat*, 81.

92. These developments are explained in ibid., 217–224.

93. Ibid., 204–217, which uses the phrase "victors as viceroys."

94. *A New Educational Guidance* was circulated by the Ministry of Education in May 1946. In the section "Fundamental Problems in Constructing a New Japan," six chapters addressed, in turn, "1, self-reflection concerning Japan's present state; 2, eliminating militarism and ultranationalism; 3, promoting respect of human nature, personality, and individuality; 4, raising scientific standards and philosophical and religious refinement; 5, carrying out thorough-going democracy; and 6, constructing a peaceful nation of culture." Cf. Dower, *Embracing Defeat*, 248.

95. Yu, *Thinking Orientals*.

96. August 1944; cited in Casey, *Cautious Crusade*, 131.

97. April 11, 1942. Reported in Harold Ickes Diary, Microfilm Reel 5, Ickes Papers, Library of Congress.

98. Casey, *Cautious Crusade*, 134–135.

99. Burleigh, *The Third Reich*, 794–812.

100. "President Addresses the Nation. Address of the President to the Nation, the Cabinet Room." Washington, D.C.: White House, Office of the Press Secretary, September 7, 2003, p. 2.

CHAPTER 7

1. Quoted in Frank Ninkovich, *The Wilsonian Century: U.S. Foreign Policy since 1900* (Chicago: University of Chicago Press, 1999), 155.

2. NSC-68, April 1950, in Thomas H. Etzold and John Lewis Gaddis, eds., *Containment: Documents on American Policy and Strategy 1945–1950* (New York: Columbia University Press, 1978), 404. For discussions see Warner R. Schilling, Paul Y. Hammond, and Glenn H. Snyder, eds., *Strategy, Politics and Defense Budgets* (New York: Columbia University Press, 1962); and Paul Y. Hammond, *The Cold War Years: American Foreign Policy since 1945* (New York: Harcourt, Brace and World, 1969).

3. NSC-68 in Etzold and Gaddis, *Containment*, 432.

4. NSC-68 in ibid., 388.

5. NSC-68 quoted in ibid., 386, 387–388.

6. For survey confirmation of the importance of individualism as an American political value, see Donald R. Kinder and Tali Mendelberg, "Individualism Reconsidered: Principles and Prejudice in Contemporary American Opinion," in *Racialized Politics*, ed. David O. Sears, Jim Sidanius, and Lawrence Bobo, 66–74 (Chicago: University of Chicago Press, 2000).

7. Quoted in John Fousek, *To Lead the Free World: American Nationalism and the Cultural Roots of the Cold War* (Chapel Hill: University of North Carolina Press, 2000), 136.

8. Quoted in Azza Salama Layton, *International Politics and Civil Rights Policies in the United States 1941–1960* (Cambridge: Cambridge University Press, 2000), 82.

9. Quoted in *Congressional Record, Senate*, May 27, 1954, 7255.

10. Quoted in Richard M. Fried, *The Russians Are Coming! The Russians Are Coming!* (New York: Oxford University Press, 1998), 57.

11. Compare with South Africa, for instance, an undemocratic polity which maintained segregation through undemocratic means. This illiberal option was never open to the United States.

12. This tradition has continued with the United Nations passing declarations about the human rights of Individuals Who Are Not Nationals of the Country in Which They Live (1985), of Persons Belonging to National or Ethnic, Religious and Linguistic Minorities (1992), of Indigenous Peoples (1994), and of Individuals, Groups and Organs of Society to Promote and Protect Universally Recognized Human Rights and Fundamental Freedoms (1998).

13. Quoted in Carol Anderson, "From Hope to Disillusion: African Americans, the United Nations, and the Struggle for Human Rights, 1944–1947," *Diplomatic History* 20 (1996): 531–563.

14. Quoted in ibid., 342.

15. Ibid.

16. June 28, 1946. Quoted in Fousek, *To Lead the Free World*, 84.

17. Carol Anderson, *Eyes Off the Prize* (New York: Cambridge University Press, 2003).

18. Quoted in Dudziak, *Cold War Civil Rights*, 44.

19. W. E. B. Du Bois, ed., *An Appeal to the World: A Statement on the Denial*

of Human Rights to Minorities in the Case of Citizens of Negro Descent in the United States of America and an Appeal to the United Nations for Redress (New York: NAACP, 1947).

20. Layton, *International Politics and Civil Rights*, 56–57.

21. Recounted in Anderson, "From Hope to Disillusion," 561–562.

22. The depth of this change in stance by the NAACP is stressed by Gerald Horne, "Who Lost the Cold War? Africans and African Americans," *Diplomatic History* 20 (1996): 617–618; and see Penny Von Eschen, *The Empire Strikes Back* (Ithaca: Cornell University Press, 1997) and "Who's the Real Ambassador? Exploring Cold War Racial Ideology," in *Cold War Constructions: The Political Culture of United States Imperialism, 1945–1966*, ed. Christian G. Appy, 110–131 (Amherst: University of Massachusetts Press, 2000); and Anderson, *Eyes Off the Prize*.

23. See Anderson, *Eyes Off the Prize*.

24. In 1951, the Civil Rights Congress's document *We Charge Genocide*, delivered to the UN Committee on Human Rights, set out the mistreatment of African Americans and garnered international media coverage. It drew political attention to America's group divisions.

25. Carey Fraser, "Crossing the Color Line in Little Rock: The Eisenhower Administration and the Dilemma of Race for U.S. Foreign Policy," *Diplomatic History* 24 (2000): 261–262.

26. The United States was one of nine countries abstaining on the UN General Assembly's vote on the Declaration on the Granting of Independence to Colonial Countries and Peoples, 1960.

27. Gerald Horne, *From the Barrel of a Gun* (Chapel Hill: University of North Carolina Press, 2001).

28. In her book *Eyes Off the Prize*, Carol Anderson argues that the taint of communist support was so severe in this period that the NAACP retreated from pursuing human rights for African Americans, including economic and social rights, to a much narrower focus on civil rights.

29. For a critical discussion of Sampson see Horne, "Who Lost the Cold War?"

30. For the best accounts of the variants of black nationalism, see Michael C. Dawson, *Black Visions* (Chicago: University of Chicago Press, 2002); and Dean Robinson, *Black Nationalism in American Politics and Thought* (New York: Cambridge University Press, 2001).

31. Michael L. Krenn, *Black Diplomacy: African Americans and the State Department 1945–1969* (New York: Sharpe, 1999), 50; and Michael L. Krenn, "Limited by Tradition: Dean Rusk and the Desegregation of the Department of State 1961–1969," in *Architects of the American Century: Individuals and Institutions in Twentieth-Century U.S. Foreign Policymaking*, ed. David Schmitz and T. Christopher Jespersen, 121–143 (Chicago: Imprint, 2000), 123. These statistics were laid out in the *Pittsburgh Courier* and in other black newspapers, including the *Chicago Defender*, *Jet*, and New York's *Amsterdam News*.

32. Michael L. Krenn, "'Outstanding Negroes' and 'Appropriate Countries': Some Facts, Figures, and Thoughts on Black U.S. Ambassadors 1949–1988," *Diplomatic History* 14 (1990): 131–141. As early as 1947, efforts by President Truman's Committee on Civil Rights to engage the State Department about its record on African-American employment were rebuffed.

33. The speaker was Clifton Wharton, Sr. Quoted in Krenn, *Black Diplomacy*, 25.

34. Krenn, *Black Diplomacy*, 46–47.

35. Quoted in ibid., 82; and see Krenn, "Limited by Tradition."

36. In May 1956 the director of the Associated Negro Press, Claude Barnett, wrote chidingly of U.S. feebleness toward imperial interests to the assistant secretary of State: "Negroes in America . . . have not been unaware of the position taken by our United States representatives in supporting measures before the United Nations which favored the position of the colonial powers rather than the welfare of their black subjects." He added: "[F]requently the position taken seemed to clash with the traditional principles of our nation when the aspirations of subject people toward freedom and independence are considered. . . . Just what is the position of our State Department upon the problem of the colonial areas." Quoted in Krenn, *Black Diplomacy*, 70.

37. For overviews see Gerald Horne, "Race from Power: U.S. Foreign Policy and the General Crisis of 'White Supremacy,'" in *The Ambiguous Legacy*, ed. Michael J. Hogan, 302–336 (Cambridge: Cambridge University Press, 1999); and Fraser, "Understanding American Policy towards the Decolonization of European Empires."

38. Timothy P. Maga, "Battling the 'Ugly American' at Home: The Special Protocol Service and the New Frontier, 1961–63," *Diplomacy and Statecraft* 3 (1992): 130.

39. Established at Undersecretary of State Chester Bowles's suggestion and headed by Petro Sanjuan. See Maga, "Battling the 'Ugly American' at Home." And see Renee Romano, "No Diplomatic Immunity: African Diplomats, the State Department, and Civil Rights, 1961–1964," *Journal of American History* 86 (2000): 566–579.

40. Maga, "Battling the 'Ugly American' at Home," 135.

41. It was the responsibility of the House of Representatives' District of Columbia Committee.

42. Quoted in Romano, "No Diplomatic Immunity," 567.

43. See Martin Duberman, *Paul Robeson: A Biography* (New York: New Press, 1989), ch. 19; and Von Eschen, *The Empire Strikes Back*.

44. "Paul Robeson: The Lost Shepherd," *Crisis*, November 1951.

45. In 1951.

46. Mary L. Dudziak, "Josephine Baker, Racial Protest and the Cold War," *Journal of American History* 81 (1994): 563.

47. Fraser, "Crossing the Color Line in Little Rock," 238.

48. Memo, "Reaction to Racial Tension in Birmingham, Alabama," May 14, 1963, National Archives, Record Group 306, Office of Research, Research Memoranda 1963–82, Box 1, Folder: M-111-63.

49. Hazel Erskine, "The Polls: World Opinion of U.S. Racial Problems," *Public Opinion Quarterly* 32 (1968): 276.

50. Ibid.

51. Ibid.

52. International Communication Agency, Office of Research and Evaluation, "The European Elite Image of American Society," April 14, 1978, in National Archives, Record Group 306, Office of Research, Special Reports 1964–82, Box 18, Folder: S-4-78.

Among the educated urban French, racism was singled out as the United States' greatest problem, in urgent need of improvement. "The American Image among the Educated, Urban French," 1977, in National Archives, Record Group 306, Office of Research, Special Reports 1964–82, Box 18, Folder: S-43-77.

53. Fraser, "Crossing the Color Line," 235; and Penny M. Von Eschen, "Challenging Old Cold War Habits: African Americans, Race and Foreign Policy," *Diplomatic History* 20 (1996).

54. Quoted in Fraser, "Crossing the Color Line," 244. And see Horne, *From the Barrel of a Gun.*

55. Dudziak, *Cold War Civil Rights*, 172.

56. Brenda Gayle Plummer, *Rising Wind: Black Americans and U.S. Foreign Affairs 1935–1960* (Chapel Hill: University of North Carolina Press, 1996); Von Eschen, *The Empire Strikes Back.*

57. See Michael L. Krenn, "'Unfinished Business': Segregation and U.S. Diplomacy at the 1958 World Fair," *Diplomatic History* 20 (1996): 591–612; and Robert H. Haddow, *Pavilions of Plenty: Exhibiting American Culture Abroad in the 1950s* (Washington, D.C.: Smithsonian Institution Press, 1997).

58. Haddow, *Pavilions of Plenty*, 173.

59. Through the department's office of the U.S. commissioner general.

60. Under Commissioner General Howard Cullman.

61. Krenn, "Unfinished Business," 600.

62. For the images see Haddow, *Pavilions of Plenty*, 178.

63. Quoted in Krenn, "Unfinished Business," 603.

64. Quoted in ibid., 607.

65. Quoted in ibid., 610.

66. In February 1942.

67. Nancy E. Bernhard, "Clearer than Truth: Public Affairs Television and the State Department's Domestic Information Campaigns, 1947–1952," *Diplomatic History* 21 (1997): 548–549.

68. On the Office of Censorship, see Michael S. Sweeney, *Secrets of Victory:*

The Office of Censorship and the American Press and Radio in World War II (Chapel Hill: University of North Carolina Press, 2001).

69. Von Eschen, "Who's the Real Ambassador?" 127. See also Charles Hersch, "Poisoning Their Coffee: Louis Armstrong and Civil Rights," *Polity* 34 (2002): 371–392.

70. David Caute, *The Dancer Defects* (Oxford: Oxford University Press, 2003).

71. The Smith-Mundt (the U.S. Informational and Educational Exchange) Act, 1948, which was replaced by the Fulbright-Hays Act, 1961. For the broader context, see Frank Ninkovich, *The Diplomacy of Ideas: U.S. Foreign Policy and Cultural Relations, 1938–1950* (Cambridge, Mass.: Harvard University Press, 1981); and Caute, *The Dancer Defects.*

72. "Selection of Books in Information Libraries," May 1, 1953, in National Archives, Record Group 306, Office of the Administrator, 1952–55, Box 1, Folder: McCarthy.

73. See papers and correspondence in National Archives, Record Group 306, Office of the Administrator, 1952–55, Box 1, Folder: McCarthy. The file includes some robust exchanges between Senator McCarthy and USIA officers.

74. See Volker R. Berghahn, *America and the Intellectual Cold Wars in Europe* (Princeton, N.J.: Princeton University Press, 2001). In 1977 the USIA was merged with the State Department's Bureau of Educational and Cultural Affairs and renamed U.S. Information and Cultural Affairs (USICA).

75. See Frank Ninkovich, "The Currents of Cultural Diplomacy: Art and the State Department 1938–1947," *Diplomatic History* 1 (1977): 215–238, and *Diplomacy of Ideas.*

Congressional criticisms of both the cost and content of an exhibition of seventy-nine contemporary oil paintings, "Advancing American Art," organized by the State Department's Cultural Division in 1947, precluded a cultural, elite-focused approach. See Ninkovich, "Currents of Cultural Diplomacy"; and Emily S. Rosenberg, *Spreading the American Dream: American Economic and Cultural Expansion 1890–1945* (New York: Hill and Wang, 1982). And see Emily S. Rosenberg, "Consuming Women: Images of Americanization in the 'American Century,'" *Diplomatic History* 23 (1999): 479–497; and Francis Stonor Saunders, *Who Paid the Piper? The CIA and the Cultural Cold War* (London: Granta, 1999).

76. USIA, *The American Negro Today* (Washington, D.C.: USIA, 1956), 13. Another example is *Les Noirs dans la Vie Americaine* (Paris: Publication Bimensuelle des Services Americains d'Information, 1951).

77. Erskine, "The Polls."

78. "Statistical Profile of the Negro American," December 3, 1963, in National Archives, RG 306, Office of Research, Research Memoranda 1963–82, Box 1, Folder: M-409-63.

79. Points well made by Krenn, *Black Diplomacy*, 43.

80. Greg Robinson, *By Order of the President* (Cambridge, Mass.: Harvard University Press, 2001), 119–120.

81. President Johnson, January 13, 1965, "Message to the Congress Submitting Proposed Immigration Legislation," in *Public Papers of the Presidents of the United States: Lyndon Johnson, 1963–1969*, 10 vols. (Washington, D.C.: U.S. Government Printing Office, 1965–1970).

82. Statement by Secretary of Labor W. Willard Wirtz before the Subcommittee on Immigration and Nationality, House Judiciary Committee, 88th Congress, First Session, Hearings on "Immigration Reform," July 23, 1964 (Washington, D.C.: U.S. Government Printing Office, 1964), 6.

83. Statement by Secretary of State Dean Rusk before the Senate Judiciary Committee, Subcommittee on Immigration and Naturalization, July 31, 1963, 6.

84. The American Committee on Immigration Policies, *Our Immigration Laws* (Washington, D.C.: American Committee on Immigration Policies, 1964). It urged retention of national origins eligibility. Oddly, the committee linked immigration to the domestic migration of African Americans.

85. U.S. Congress, House Committee on the Judiciary, Subcommittee No. 1, Immigration, *Hearings on H.R. 7700 and 55, Identical Bills to Amend the Immigration and Nationality Act, and for Other Purposes*, 88th Cong., 2d sess., 3 vols. (Washington, D.C.: Government Printing Office, 1964), 735, 736.

86. Ibid., 798.

87. Statement by the president upon passage of the Immigration Bill by the House Judiciary Committee, August 3, 1965, in Legislative Background, Immigration Law–1965, Box 1, Folder: The Road to Final Passage, Lyndon B. Johnson Presidential Library.

88. Memoranda for Bill Moyers from Thomas R. Hughes, August 20, 1965, and from Jack Rosenthal, August 31, 1965; it was eventually recommended to Johnson in a memorandum prepared by Secretary of the Interior Stewart L. Udall, September 1965, in Legislative Background–Immigration Law–1965, Box 1, Folder: The Signing at Liberty Island, LBJL.

89. *Public Papers of the Presidents: Lyndon B. Johnson*, October 3, 1965. For the theoretical context, see Aristide R. Zolberg, "From Invitation to Interdiction: U.S. Foreign Policy and Immigration since 1945," in *Threatened Peoples, Threatened Borders*, ed. Michael Teitelbaum and Myron Weiner, 117–159 (New York: Norton, 1995).

90. Alison R. Bernstein, *American Indians and World War II* (Norman: University of Oklahoma Press, 1991), 35.

91. Such as marine Ira Hayes.

92. The Indian Claims Commission was established by Congress in 1946 (and remained in existence until 1978) to resolve disputes about government and bureaucratic fraud in respect to Native Americans' property and land rights. It

was associated in Congress particularly with the views of the chairman of the Committee on Indian Affairs, Senator Arthur V. Watkins of Utah. President Truman appointed Dillon S. Myer as commissioner of Indian affairs. Myer administered Japanese-American internment during World War II, and there were similarities in his approach to the two tasks.

93. In the 1960s.

94. Citing rights under the 1868 Treaty of Fort Laramie was a key strategy of Native American leaders from the 1960s. A copy was symbolically kept in the courtroom during the trial of leaders of the 1973 siege of Wounded Knee.

95. Frances Wise, quoted in James Wilson, *The Earth Shall Weep* (London: Picador, 1998), 395.

96. See Clyde Warrior's experience, for instance, in Wilson, *The Earth Shall Weep*, 388.

97. In 1972.

98. The U.S. Senate Committee on the Judiciary, under Chairman James Eastland, labeled AIM a revolutionary and violent organization, unrepresentative of Native Americans. See *Revolutionary Activities within the United States: The American Indian Movement.* Report of the Subcommittee to Investigate the Administration of the Internal Security Laws of the Committee on the Judiciary, U.S. Senate, 94th Cong., 2d sess., September 1976. (Washington, D.C.: U.S. Government Printing Office, 1976). The Wounded Knee trial has encountered fresh controversy over determining who killed the Native American activist Anna Mae Pictou Aquash; her frozen body was found in 1976.

99. Quoted in John William Sayer, *Ghost Dancing the Law: The Wounded Knee Trials* (Cambridge, Mass.: Harvard University Press, 1997), 93.

100. Quoted in Bernstein, *American Indians and World War II,* 170.

101. Letter to *New York Times,* March 12, 1950.

102. Philip A. Klinkner and Rogers M. Smith, *The Unsteady March* (Chicago: University of Chicago Press, 1999).

103. For the best account of a secular society, which the author distinguishes from the notion of civil religions, see Richard K. Fenn, *Beyond Idols: The Shape of a Secular Society* (New York: Oxford University Press, 2001).

104. NSC-68, "United States Objectives and Programs for National Security," April 14, 1950, in Etzold and Gaddis, *Containment,* 389. For an account of this memorandum's gestation, see Paul G. Pierpaoli, Jr., *Truman and Korea: The Political Culture of the Early Cold War* (Columbia: University of Missouri Press, 1999), 17–28.

105. Fousek, *To Lead the Free World,* ch. 3.

106. Quoted in Michael J. Hogan, ed., *The Ambiguous Legacy: U.S. Foreign Relations in the "American Century"* (New York: Cambridge University Press, 1999), 25.

CHAPTER 8

1. In 2003 such events were held at the University of Pennsylvania, Vanderbilt University, Washington University, St. Louis University, the University of Michigan, Michigan State University, and Stanford.

2. Residential segregation has not declined since the mid-twentieth century despite some shifting patterns of where groups live. For useful recent analyses see Lawrence Bobo and Camille Zubrinsky, "Attitudes on Residential Segregation: Perceived Status Difference, Mere In-Group Preference, or Racial Prejudice?" *Social Forces* 74 (1996): 883–909; and Michael O. Emerson, George Yancy, and Karen Chai, "Does Race Matter in Residential Segregation? Exploring the Preferences of White Americans," *American Sociological Review* 66 (2001): 922–935.

3. For a recent account of one aspect of the changing group politics of the United States, see Marcelo M. Suarez-Orozco and Mariela M. Paez, eds., *Latinos: Remaking America* (Berkeley: University of California Press, 2002).

4. For a valuable analysis of the extent to which diversity is now the mainstream of U.S. political culture, see Peter H. Schuck, *Diversity in America: Keeping Government at a Safe Distance* (Cambridge, Mass.: Harvard University Press, 2003).

5. Julian Murphet, *Literature and Race in Los Angeles* (Cambridge: Cambridge University Press, 2001).

6. For instance, Americans have become residentially more segregated in the 1990s than in the previous post-1964 decades. See "The Racial Divide Widens," *Boston Sunday Globe*, October 21, 2001, which details differential access to mortgages. See Gary Gerstle and John Mollenkopf, eds., *E Pluribus Unum? Contemporary and Historical Perspectives on Immigrant Political Incorporation* (New York: Sage Foundation, 2001); and Michael Jones-Correa, ed., *Governing American Cities: Inter-Ethnic Coalitions, Competition, and Conflict* (New York: Sage Foundation, 2001).

7. *Public Papers of the Presidents: Lyndon B. Johnson*, speaking in Lake County, Indiana, October 8, 1964.

8. See, for example, "The New Face of Race," *Newsweek*, September 18, 2000, pp. 38–65; or Darryl Fears and D'Vera Cohn, "Hispanic Population Booming in U.S. Census Finds Growth Outpacing Blacks," *Washington Post*, January 22, 2003.

9. Silvia Pedraza, "Beyond Black and White: Latinos and Social Science Research in Immigration, Race and Ethnicity in America," *Social Science History* 24 (2000): 697–726; Albert M. Camarillo and Frank Bonilla, "Hispanics in a Multicultural Society: A New American Dilemma?" in *America Becoming: Racial Trends and Their Consequences*, vol. 1, ed. Neil J. Smelser, William Julius Wilson, and Faith Mitchell (Washington, D.C.: National Academy Press, 2001); Carolos Munoz, Jr., *Youth, Identity, Power* (London: Verso, 1989); and J. Eric

Oliver and Janelle Wong, "Intergroup Prejudice in Multiethnic Settings," *American Journal of Political Science* 47 (2003): 567–582.

10. One assimilationist organization, the League of United Latin American Citizens, set up in 1929, made acquisition of English its principal plank.

11. Carol L. Schmid, *The Politics of Language* (New York: Oxford University Press, 2001), 27–30; and see Gareth Davies, "The Great Society after Johnson: The Case of Bilingual Education," *Journal of American History* 88 (2002): 1405–1429.

12. Raymond Tatalovich, *Nativism Reborn? The Official English Language Movement and the American States* (1995). For a critique and defense of traditional assimilation for Latinos, see Linda Chavez, *Out of the Barrio* (New York: Basic, 1991).

13. Don T. Nakanishi, "Political Trends and Electoral Issues of the Asian American Population," in *America Becoming: Racial Trends and Their Consequences*, vol. 1, ed. Neil J. Smelser, William Julius Wilson, and Faith Mitchell (Washington, D.C.: National Academy Press, 2001); and Gordon H. Chang, ed., *Asian Americans and Politics* (Stanford, Calif.: Stanford University Press, 2001).

14. Chang, *Asian Americans and Politics*.

15. Lisa Lowe, *Immigrant Acts: An Asian American Cultural Politics* (Durham, N.C.: Duke University Press, 1996); and Henry Yu, *Thinking Orientals: Migration, Contact, and Exoticism in Modern America* (New York: Oxford University Press, 2001). And see William Wei, *The Asian American Movement* (Philadelphia, Pa.: Temple University Press, 1993).

16. Quoted in Joann Foung Jean Lee, *Asian Americans* (New York: New Press, 1991), 107.

17. Lowe, *Immigrant Acts*; John Bodnar, "Public Memory in an American City: Commemoration in Cleveland," in *Commemorations: The Politics of National Identity*, ed. John R. Gillis, 76–89 (Princeton, N.J.: Princeton University Press, 1994).

18. See Neil T. Gotanda's essay in Chang, *Asian Americans and Politics*.

19. Min Zhou, "Contemporary Immigration and the Dynamics of Race and Ethnicity," in *America Becoming: Racial Trends and Their Consequences*, vol. 1, ed. Neil J. Smelser, William Julius Wilson, and Faith Mitchell (Washington, D.C.: National Academy Press, 2001).

20. For the broader context, see Thomas A. Tweed and Stephen Prothero, eds., *Asian Religions in America: A Documentary History* (New York: Oxford University Press, 1999).

21. Peggy Levitt, *The Transnational Villagers* (Berkeley: University of California Press, 2001), 11–14.

22. Quoted in ibid., 111.

23. Jose E. Cruz, *Identity and Power: Puerto Rican Politics and the Challenge of Ethnicity* (Philadelphia, Pa.: Temple University Press, 1998), xi.

24. For a moving account, see Harold P. Freeman, "Commentary on the Meaning of Race in Science and Society," *Cancer Epidemiology, Biomarkers and Prevention* 12 (2003): 232s–236s.

25. On changing memories of the Civil War, see William Blight, *Race and Reunion: The Civil War in American Memory* (Cambridge, Mass.: Harvard University Press, 2001).

26. For a recent discussion see Lawrie Balfour, "Unreconstructed Democracy: W. E. B. Du Bois and the Case for Reparations," *American Political Science Review* 97 (2003): 33–44.

27. Speaking in 1930. Quoted in historian Mark David Spence's account of how national parks were established in the United States: *Dispossessing the Wilderness: Indian Removal and the Making of the National Parks* (New York: Oxford University Press, 1999), 133.

28. This was agreed in March 2001, twenty-six years after a class action lawsuit, taken up by the U.S. Department of Justice, was brought against Mississippi by twenty-two Black Americans who argued that the state's retention of segregated universities resulted in more resources being spent on universities that were historically attended by white students than on those universities attended by blacks. The agreement requires Mississippi to spend $246 million on three universities whose student bodies are overwhelmingly black (Jackson State, Alcorn State, and Mississippi Valley State), $75 million on capital improvements for the three colleges, and the remaining sum on endowments and summer programs.

29. The Tulsa Race Riot Commission, appointed by the Oklahoma state legislature, produced a 200-page report in March 2001 in which it concluded that such reparations "will stand as symbols that fully acknowledge and finally discharge a collective responsibility." Some estimates of the death toll reach 300, and property was destroyed. The commission's report notes that "not one of these criminal acts was then or ever been prosecuted or punished by the government at any level, municipal, county, state or federal." It proposed five forms of compensation: cash payments to the 121 survivors; cash payments to authenticated descendants of survivors; a scholarship fund in memory of those who died; business incentives to revive the Greenwood area of Tulsa, which was devastated by the riot; and a memorial. For the best account, see Alfred L. Brophy, *Reconstructing the Dreamland: The Tulsa Riot of 1921* (New York: Oxford University Press, 2002).

30. The class action suit, led by the Mexican American Legal Defense and Education Fund, was served in July 2003.

31. For a recent account of the vagaries of this action, see Neely Tucker, "A Long Road of Broken Promises for Black Farmers: USDA Fights Claims after Landmark Deal," *Washington Post*, August 13, 2002.

32. The former mayor of York, Pennsylvania, faces charges of murdering a black woman in 1969, while the Ku Klux Klansman responsible for the Birming-

ham, Alabama, Baptist church bombing in 1963, which killed four African-American schoolgirls, has only recently been convicted.

33. Deloria and Wilkins conclude that since its passage in 1971 the settlement format has been employed to resolve "a wide variety of legal problems.... Thus disputes over water rights, land claims, railroad rights-of-way, restoration of federal recognition, and final settlement of boundary have all been the subject of these kinds of negotiations." Vine Deloria, Jr., and David E. Wilkins, *Tribes, Treaties and Constitutional Tribulations* (Austin: University of Texas Press, 1999), 160.

34. In 1976. Discussed in Mitchell T. Maki, Harry H. L. Kitano, and S. Megan Berthold, *Achieving the Impossible Dream: How Japanese Americans Obtained Redress* (Urbana: University of Illinois Press, 1999), 71–72.

35. James Bolner, "Toward a Theory of Racial Reparations," *Phylon* 29 (1968): 41–47; Carol M. Swain, "Affirmative Action: Legislative History, Judicial Interpretations, Public Consensus," in *America Becoming: Racial Trends and Their Consequences*, vol. 1, ed. Neil J. Smelser, William Julius Wilson, and Faith Mitchell (Washington, D.C.: National Academy Press, 2001).

36. Robert Dallek, *Flawed Giant: Lyndon Johnson and His Times 1961–1973* (New York: Oxford University Press, 1998), 621–622.

37. From 2003, such measures in federal government and federally funded programs will be guided by the findings of the 2000 Census. The case references are *Duke Power Co. v. Carolina Environmental Study Group Inc.* 438 U.S. 59 (1978); and *Regents of the University of California v. Bakke* 438 U.S. 265 (1978).

38. President Clinton's review committee on affirmative action identified "two general justifications" for affirmative action and linked them to the ideology of American nationalism: "remediation of discrimination, and promoting inclusion—both of which are consistent with the traditional American values of opportunity, merit and fairness." The policy was connected to that of diversity: "[I]n some areas (such as law enforcement), diversity is particularly important to the government's effectiveness at dealing with the broader community. Second, diversity of decisionmakers leads to better decisions, when the goal is a government that truly represents the interests of all the people." *Affirmative Action Review* (Washington, D.C.: White House Executive Office, 1995), 3, 14.

39. Some school districts, for instance, are devising "diversity indexes" to find ways of promoting integration without basing the strategy solely on race.

40. Hugh Davis Graham, *Collision Course: The Strange Convergence of Affirmative Action and Immigration Policy in America* (New York: Oxford University Press, 2002).

41. In his valuable account of different groups' achievement of rights, *The Minority Rights Revolution* (Cambridge, Mass.: Harvard University Press, 2002), John D. Skrentny runs the danger of reifying the dichotomy between those who belong in the American nation and those who do not by employing the term

minority; this usage overlooks the need to think about different groups as constitutive parts of the American nation, each with distinct traditions.

42. A point made by Thomas C. Holt, "Marking: Race, Race-Making and the Writing of History," *American Historical Review* 100 (1995): 1–20.

43. See Balfour, "Unreconstructed Democracy."

44. A committee representing 3,000 freed people who had settled on Edisto Island in South Carolina told Commissioner Howard Cullman just how cheated they felt: "General, . . . we were promised Homesteads by the government. If it does not carry out the promises its agents made to us . . . we are left in a more unpleasant condition than our former." Quoted in Eric Foner, *Reconstruction: America's Unfinished Revolution 1863–1877* (New York: Harper and Row, 1988), 160.

45. In 1887. His views were expressed in *Church News*, a publication of the African Methodist Episcopal church.

46. See Randall Robinson's *The Debt: What America Owes to Blacks* (New York: Penguin, 2000).

47. Including the NAACP, the National Urban League, and the Southern Christian Leadership Conference.

48. Eric Foner, "The Slaves of New York," *New York Times*, July 13, 2000.

49. Robinson, *The Debt*, 208, 246.

50. William Blight in *Race and Reunion* divides memories of the Civil War into three categories: a reconciliationist view, the "lost cause" southern view, and the emancipationist view. He shows how the first two dominated until the mid-twentieth century thereby precluding African Americans' rights. And see Melinda Lawson, *Patriot Fires: Forging a New American Nationalism in the Civil War North* (Lawrence: University Press of Kansas, 2002).

51. In a survey of 2,004 Americans conducted in July 2001, two-thirds of respondents predicted that race relations would always be a problem in the United States, a judgment shared by 45% of white interviewees. The poll also found a significant difference between white American and African-American perceptions about how fairly Black Americans are treated in American society. Gallup Organization poll reported in the *Financial Times*, July 11, 2001.

52. Some regained forfeited property under the Japanese-American Evacuation Claims Act, 1948.

53. Robert Sadamu Shimabukuro, *Born in Seattle: The Campaign for Japanese American Redress* (Seattle: University of Washington Press, 2001), 12–13.

54. Mas Fuka, quoted in Mitchell T. Maki, Harry H. L. Kitano, and S. Megan Berthold, *Achieving the Impossible Dream: How Japanese Americans Obtained Redress* (Urbana: University of Illinois Press, 1999), 114.

55. Maki, Kitano, and Berthold, *Achieving the Impossible Dream*; Shimabukuro, *Born in Seattle*.

56. Recounted in Maki, Kitano, and Berthold, *Achieving the Impossible Dream*, 82–83.

57. It was "the largest gathering of Japanese Americans since the camps." Shimabukuro, *Born in Seattle*, 49.

58. And, indeed, even commemoration: when the Washington state legislature allocated $26,000 for a sculpture to be built at Camp Harmony, the American Legion objected, demanding a Pearl Harbor memorial instead. Shimabukuro, *Born in Seattle*, 84–87.

59. Quoted in Maki, Kitano, and Berthold, *Achieving the Impossible Dream*, 70.

60. The Commission on Wartime Relocation and Internment of Civilians Act, 1980.

61. Issued in 1983.

62. Those entitled to recompense was estimated to number 60,000.

63. Maki, Kitano, and Berthold, *Achieving the Impossible Dream*, 145–146.

64. October 1990. The law has been amended several times to include groups whose eligibility was overlooked in 1988, such as Japanese Latin Americans forcefully transported to Japan and children of men serving in the 442d.

65. Henry Yu, *Thinking Orientals: Migration, Contact, and Exoticism in Modern America* (New York: Oxford University Press, 2001), 190.

66. Historian Peggy Pascoe notes that "these gaps between the (very narrow) modernist conception of race and the (very wide) range of racial identities and racial oppressions bedevil today's egalitarians." Peggy Pascoe, "Miscegenation Law, Court Cases, and Ideologies of 'Race' in Twentieth-Century America," *Journal of American History* 83 (1996): 68.

67. Its status was confirmed in January 1974 in Executive Order 11761.

68. Office of Management and Budget's Statistical Directive No. 15 (operative until 1997).

69. Melissa Nobles, *Shades of Citizenship* (Stanford, Calif.: Stanford University Press, 2000).

70. Commenced in 1994 and published in 1997.

71. The same framework, that is, the listing of races and the option to check off more than one, has been used in federal agency policy from 2003.

72. This view is periodically challenged by some scientists and social scientists.

73. Or, as sociologist Paul Gilroy remarks, "[R]aciology has saturated the discourses in which it circulates." *Between Camps: Nations, Cultures and the Allure of Race* (London: Penguin, 2000), 12. And see Claire Jean Kim, *Bitter Fruit: The Politics of Black-Korean Conflict in New York City* (New Haven, Conn.: Yale University Press, 2000).

74. Danzy Senna, *From Caucasia, With Love* (London: Bloomsbury, 2000), 408.

75. Joane Nagel, *American Indian Ethnic Renewal: Red Power and the Resurgence of Identity and Culture* (New York: Oxford University Press, 1996).

76. Which the United States ratified in October 1994.

77. "Initial Report of the USA to the UN Committee on the Elimination of Racial Discrimination" (Washington, D.C.: State Department, September 2000), 2.

78. National Park Service, *Revision of the National Park Service's Thematic Framework* (Washington, D.C.: National Park Service, 1994), 1.

79. Among numerous examples, see "The New Face of Race," *Newsweek*, September 18, 2000, 38–65; David Cole and John Lambeth, "The Fallacy of Racial Profiling," *New York Times*, May 13, 2001; "Racial Discord in a Maryland Town: Diversity—and Tension—on Rise at Damascus High School," *Washington Post*, June 24, 2002; "In Maine Town, Sudden Diversity and Controversy: Somali Influx Irks Mayor," *Washington Post*, October 14, 2002; and "Going by 'Joe,' Not 'Yussef,' but Still Feeling Like an Outcast," *New York Times*, September 11, 2002.

80. Levitt, *The Transnational Villagers*, 108.

81. "Secret Network Keeps Sororities White," *Guardian*, September 11, 2001.

82. As political sociologists Jeff Manza and Clem Brooks find in their book, *Social Cleavages and Political Change* (Oxford: Oxford University Press, 1999), esp. 156–162; and see the important work by Paul Frymer, *Uneasy Alliance: Race and Party Competition in America* (Princeton, N.J.: Princeton University Press, 1999); and Robert C. Lieberman, *Shifting the Color Line* (Cambridge, Mass.: Harvard University Press, 1998).

83. "Writing about Race," *New York Times Magazine*, July 16, 2000, 20. For a more cheering report about integration, see Lisa Frazier Page, "Acceptance amid the Diversity: At Andrews AFB, Multiracial Families, Friendships Thrive," *Washington Post*, July 16, 2002, which finds racial diversity welcomed at the air force base.

84. In their article, Logan and colleagues find a small but significant positive preference, unrelated to income, for living in ethnic communities, based on a study of fifteen groups of ethnic residents. John R. Logan, Richard D. Alba, and Wenquan Zhang, "Immigrant Enclaves and Ethnic Communities in New York and Los Angeles," *American Sociological Review* 67 (2002): 299–322.

85. See Michael Cox, G. John Ikenberry, and Takashi Inoguchi, eds., *American Democracy Promotion* (Oxford: Oxford University Press, 2000); Yossi Shain, *Marketing the American Creed Abroad: Diasporas in the United States and Their Homelands* (New York: Cambridge University Press, 1999); and Tony Smith, *Foreign Attachments: The Power of Ethnic Groups in the Making of American Foreign Policy* (Cambridge, Mass.: Harvard University Press, 2000). And see Andrew J. Bacevich, *American Empire: The Realities and Consequences of U.S. Diplomacy* (Cambridge, Mass.: Harvard University Press, 2002).

86. Douglas Little, *American Orientalism: The United States and the Middle East since 1945* (Chapel Hill: University of North Carolina Press, 2002).

87. Jeremy Bowen, *Six Days: How the 1967 War Shaped the Middle East* (New York: Simon & Schuster, 2003).

88. See speech by President George W. Bush at Whitehall Palace in London, November 19, 2003 (Washington, D.C.: White House Office of the Press Secretary, November 19, 2003).

89. For one recent discussion see Laura Blumenfeld, "Terrorism Jars Jewish, Arab Party Loyalties," *Washington Post*, December 7, 2003.

90. A representative example is "The New Face of Race," *Newsweek*, September 18, 2000, 38–65.

91. Carol M. Swain, *The New White Nationalism in America: Its Challenge to Integration* (New York: Cambridge University Press, 2002); see also Martin Gilens, *Why Americans Hate Welfare* (Chicago: University of Chicago Press, 1999); and Frymer, *Uneasy Alliance*. For a profile confirming Swain's concerns, see Nicholas D. Kristof, "Hate America Style," *New York Times*, August 30, 2002, reporting his interview with the Reverend Matt Hale of the World Church of the Creator.

92. Tali Mendelberg, *The Race Card: Campaign Strategy, Implicit Messages and the Norm of Equality* (Princeton, N.J.: Princeton University Press, 2001); for the political sociology context, see Manza and Brooks, *Social Cleavages and Political Change*.

93. Donald R. Kinder and Lynn M. Sanders, *Divided by Color* (Chicago: University of Chicago Press, 1996); Frymer, *Uneasy Alliance*; and Lawrence D. Bobo, "Racial Attitudes and Relations at the Close of the Twentieth Century," in *America Becoming: Racial Trends and Their Consequences*, ed. Neil J. Smelser, William Julius Wilson, and Faith Mitchell, 266–301 (Washington, D.C.: National Academy Press, 2001).

94. In his study of varieties of black nationalism, Michael C. Dawson comments, "[B]lack ideological visions continue to structure black public opinion and politics despite what public opinion theorists might predict." *Black Visions* (Chicago: University of Chicago Press, 2002), 316. Dawson also concludes that "black political thought as instantiated in today's black grassroots still stands in opposition to the current dominant understanding of the American Creed" (319).

95. This ideology is documented, from a 1993 survey of 1,206 respondents, in Darren W. Davis and Ronald E. Brown, "The Antipathy of Black Nationalism: Behavioral and Attitudinal Implications of an African American Ideology," *American Journal of Political Science* 46 (2002): 239–253.

96. Dinitia Smith, "Arab-American Writers, Uneasy in Two Worlds: Immigrant Authors Feel Added Burdens since 9/11," *New York Times*, February 19, 2003.

97. "Attacks and Harassment of Middle-Eastern Americans Rising," *New York Times*, September 14, 2001; "Feeling Like the Enemy Within," *Los Angeles Times*, September 20, 2001; "Travels and Travails: Japanese Americans Recall '40s Bias, Understand Arab Counterparts' Fear," *Washington Post*, September 20, 2001; and "Hate Crimes against Arabs Surge, FBI Finds," *Washington Post*, November 26, 2002, which reports an increase from 28 such crimes in the twelve months before 9/11 to 481 in the twelve months after. See also "U.S. Muslims See Their American Dreams Die," *Financial Times*, March 28, 2002. On the

conditions of those detained on immigration charges, see "Detainees Offer Glimpse of Life in N.Y. Facility," *Washington Post*, April 17, 2002.

98. For a view that African Americans hold less uncritical opinions of U.S. policy since September 11, see Bonnie Greer, "There Is Another America," *Observer*, December 16, 2001.

99. President Bush signed the order allowing military trials of noncitizens on November 13, 2001, using his powers as commander in chief, the September 18, 2001, congressional joint resolution, and provisions of the Uniform Code of Military Justice. On the same occasion, the Justice Department identified more than 5,000 people, mostly from Middle Eastern countries, to be detained and questioned.

100. A position which received judicial support in March 2003 when the three-judge panel of the U.S. Court of Appeals of the District of Columbia Circuit ruled that 650 suspected terrorists being held at the U.S. naval base in Guantanamo Bay have no legal rights in the United States and may not ask courts to review their detentions. It ruled that because Cuba has sovereignty over the base, U.S. courts lack jurisdiction. This judgment was rejected by the U.S. Supreme Court in June 2004 in *Rasul v. Bush* 321 F.3d 1134 (2004).

101. For a robust defense see William Taft, "Guantanamo Detention Is Legal and Essential," *Financial Times*, January 12, 2004. Taft wrote as a legal adviser to the U.S. secretary of State.

102. "Bush Visits Mosque to Forestall Hate Crimes," *Washington Post*, September 18, 2001; he spoke to Congress on September 20, 2001.

103. For investigations of the position of Muslims in U.S. society, see Yvonne Yazbeck Haddad and John L. Esposito, eds., *Muslims on the Americanization Path?* (New York: Oxford University Press, 2000); and Yvonne Yazbeck Haddad, ed., *Muslims in the West* (New York: Oxford University Press, 2002).

CONCLUSION

1. For an important recent explication of these concepts, see Roger Scruton, *The Need for Nations* (London: Civitas, 2004).

2. *Regents of the University of California v. Bakke* 438 U.S. 265 (1978).

3. For the broader theoretical context, see the debate initiated with Will Kymlicka's important book, *Multicultural Citizenship* (Oxford: Oxford University Press, 1995); and for the U.S. setting, see particularly Farley Reynolds, *The New American Reality: Who We Are, How We Got Here, Where We Are Going* (New York: Sage Foundation, 1996).

4. David Hollinger, "The Historian's Use of the United States and Vice Versa," in *Rethinking American History in a Global Age*, ed. Thomas Bender (Berkeley: University of California Press, 2002), 381–395, and *Postethnic America* (New York: Basic, 1995).

5. Gary Gerstle, *American Crucible* (Princeton, N.J.: Princeton University Press, 2001).

6. Rogers M. Smith, *Civic Ideals* (New Haven, Conn.: Yale University Press); and see Ira Katznelson, *Liberalism's Crooked Circle* (Princeton, N.J.: Princeton University Press, 1996).

7. "Going by 'Joe,' Not 'Yussef,' but Still Feeling Like an Outcast," *New York Times*, September 11, 2002.

8. Samuel Huntington, *Who Are We? The Challenge to America's National Identity* (New York: Simon & Schuster, 2004). For a less grim view see Nathan Glazer, *We Are All Multiculturalists Now* (Cambridge, Mass.: Harvard University Press, 1997).

9. Sudhir Hazareesingh, *From Subject to Citizen* (Princeton, N.J.: Princeton University Press, 1998), and *The Saint-Napoleon: Celebrations of Sovereignty in 19th Century France* (Cambridge, Mass.: Harvard University Press, 2004).

10. Among a substantial literature, see Richard Kuisel, *Seducing the French: The Dilemma of Americanization* (Berkeley: University of California Press, 1993); Richard Pells, *Not Like Us: How Europeans Have Loved, Hated and Transformed American Culture since World War II* (New York: Basic, 1997); John Lamberton Harper, *American Visions of Europe* (New York: Cambridge University Press, 1994); and Paul Hollander, *Anti-Americanism* (New York: Oxford University Press, 1992).

11. "President Bush Speaks at Tsinghua University," Beijing, People's Republic of China, February 22, 2002 (Washington, D.C.: White House, Office of the Press Secretary, February 22, 2002), p. 3.

12. In her book, Amy Chua makes divisions around ethnicity, when coupled with disproportionate wealth, the central faultline in developing countries and puts this down to a false linking of democracy and free markets: *World on Fire: How Exporting Free-Market Democracy Breeds Ethnic Hatred and Global Instability* (London: Heinemann, 2004). For the United States see Linda Faye Williams, *The Constraint of Race* (University Park: Pennsylvania State University Press, 2003).

Index

Bureau of Indian Affairs (BIA), 27, 131
Bureau of Public Instruction, 34
Bureau of the Census, 44
Bush, President George, 156
Bush, President George W., 105, 134,
    152, 165, 167, 168–169, 175–176
  Executive Order, 13th November
    2001, 148
Butler, Senator Matthew, 56
Byrd, James, Jr., 173

California Supreme Court, 50
Canary Islands, 117
Carter, President Jimmy, 156
Casement, Sir Roger, 57
Census, 139, 157–158, 163, 170, 172–173
  1850, 45
  1890, 45
  1910, 64
  1920, 60
  1990, 140, 150
  2000, 140, 150, 158, 169
Census Board, 45
Chesnutt, Charles, 58, 59
Chinese Americans, 22, 31, 49–51, 53–54,
    129, 138, 144, 156, 161, 169
and Exclusion Laws, 50–52: in
    California, 50; in Hawaii, 52; in
    Oregon, 50; in Washington, 50; in
    the Philippines, 52
Churchill, Winston, 96, 97, 99, 109
Civil Liberties Act (1988), 155
Civil Rights, 57, 84, 86–87, 90, 98, 100–
    101, 108, 111, 116, 121, 126, 134, 151,
    165, 171
  and Filipino nationalism, 47–48
  and Individualism, 136
  Internationalization of struggle, 113–
    114
Civil Rights Act (1964), 121, 127, 130,
    157
Civil Rights Congress, 120
Civil War, 11, 12, 147, 152
  Memory of, 42, 43, 154
Clan na Gael, 67
Claxton, U.S. Commissioner of
    Education Philander P., 70
Cleveland Cultural Gardens
    Federation, 68
Clinton, President Bill, 7, 152, 154, 168,
    173

Cloud, Henry Roe, 27
Cold War, 16, 17, 18, 105, 109–110, 116,
    119, 125, 134, 161, 175
  U.S. Strategy, 125
Collier, John, 132
Colonization, 54–56
Commission on Wartime Relocation
    and Internment of Civilians, 156
Committee on Public Information
    (CPI), 41, 66, 68–71
  Division of Civic and Educational
    Cooperation, 69–70
  Division of News, 69
Committee on un-American Activities,
    125
Congress, 32, 56, 59, 128, 136, 143, 155,
    156
  and American Indians, 131,150. *See
    also* American Indians
  Chinese Exclusion Law (1882), 50,
    86
  Immigration and Nationality
    (McCarren-Walter) Act (1952), 61
  Johnson Reed Act (1931), 59–61
Congress for Cultural Freedom in
    Western Europe, 125
Council on African Affairs, 98, 99, 111
Cox, James M., 66
Creel, George, 68–69, 70
Creel Committee. *See* Committee on
    Public Information.
Crist, Raymond, 28
Crummell, Alexander, 55
Cuban Americans, 17, 79, 161

Daniels, Jonathon, 115
Daughters of the American Revolution,
    128
Davis, Benjamin O., 94
Davis, Elmer, 124
Declaration of Independence, 6, 134
Declaration on Liberated Europe, 97
Decolonization, 85–86
Delaney, Martin, 55
Democratic Inclusion, 53, 80, 108, 112,
    123, 133, 137, 148–149, 150, 153, 156,
    166, 168, 174
Democratic Nationalism, 6, 8
Democratization, 116
  of Germany, 103–105
  of Japan, 101–103, 105